REGULATION, THE CONSTITUTION, AND THE ECONOMY

The Regulatory Road to Serfdom

James Rolph Edwards

D1153654

University Press of America, ® **Inc.**
Lanham • New York • Oxford

Copyright © 1998
University Press of America,® Inc.
4720 Boston Way
Lanham, Maryland 20706

12 Hid's Copse Rd.
Cumnor Hill, Oxford OX2 9JJ

Library of Congress Cataloging-in-Publication Data

Edwards, James Rolph.
Regulation, the constitution, and the economy : the regulatory road
to serfdom / James Rolph Edwards.
p.   cm.
Includes index.
1. Trade regulation—United States. 2. Economic liberties (U.S.
Constitution)   I. Title.
KF1600.E34 1998   343.73'08—dc21   98-39129 CIP

ISBN 0-7618-1261-X (cloth: alk. ppr.)
ISBN 0-7618-1262-8 (pbk: alk. ppr.)

Contents

Introduction

Chapters

Acknowledgements

Any scholar owes intellectual debts too numerous to mention. With regard to this work, however, the help of some persons should be acknowledged.

First, I would like to thank the Association of Private Enterprise Education for publishing part of the material for Chapter 8 as an article in the Fall 1998 issue of *The Journal of Private Enterprise*, and for awarding that paper a prize in their 1997/98 contest for essays in private enterprise, entrepreneurship, and society.

Second, I would like to thank the editors and publishers of *The Montana Professor,* Winter 1995 issue, in which part of the material in Chapter 10 of this book initially appeared.

Last, I would like to thank Peter Rabe, whose expertise in page layout, graphic design, and editing was invaluable in the preparation of the book for publication. Alas, Peter, there are only so many errors in the work of another that a human being can catch...

Introduction

The modern U.S. economy may be termed a regulatory welfare state. It is still largely capitalist and market oriented, but nothing is more characteristic of the American economy in the post-World War II period than the massive expansion of regulatory social and economic controls. The phrase 'regulatory welfare state' may more accurately characterize the American economy than those of other Western nations because regulation of private market activities here seems to have partly substituted for the more open nationalization of heavy industries that nations such as Britain, France, and others, long practiced to varying degrees. The huge denationalization wave that swept most such nations in the 1980s, following the example of the Thatcher government in Britain has, however, reduced that difference between those economies and ours.

Government regulation of private economic and other social activities appears to be as old as the first organized governments, though its extent has certainly waxed and waned over time, with important economic, political and legal effects. Indeed, for some time in U.S. history regulation was nearly abolished, or at least severely reduced. As it began to expand again in the late 19th century, and more so in the interwar period, primarily in the form of administrative rules and directives, it was regarded by segments of the judiciary as illegitimate, and a threat to the constitutional rule of law. A rehabilitation of that view is one of the prime purposes of this book.

One cannot measure or even identify fluctuations in the institutional practice of something such as regulatory law without definition, of course, and just precisely what is meant by 'regulation' is not easily explained. For one thing, it seems important to distinguish *administrative* regulation as a legal social control mechanism from statutory civil and criminal law. While a great deal of regulation is administrative in nature, however (that is, issued and enforced by bureaus, boards, commissions and other administrative agencies), defining regulation as entirely equivalent to such administrative directives may be too narrow. All laws have the intent of controlling or affecting human behavior, and many statutes have essentially the same form and goals as administrative regulations. Sometimes, in other words, Congress simply writes the regulations itself. More generally, however, it has economized on its own time, and insulated itself from the political consequences, by creating agencies to both write and enforce such rules. Consequently, most of the focus in this book will be on such administrative agencies and laws.

This book is at once a work in political science, economics, and to a lesser extent, economic history. I intend to delineate both the political and legal nature of regulation on the one hand, and its economic nature and consequences on the other, illustrating all such matters with historical references and empirical data where possible. This union of political and economic analysis hearkens back to the classical origins of economics, when it was known as political economy. In recent years the sundering of these disciplines has tended to heal, particularly as Neoclassical economists such as James Buchanan, Gordon Tulloch, Douglas North and others began applying their analytical tools to the understanding of the political policy process and the historical transformation of institutions.

It will be noticed that this book is incomplete. That cannot be helped. Regulation is now so voluminous and pervasive as to be beyond any treatment of finite magnitude. As anyone must, in such an effort, I made decisions on what to include and what not to include in an effort to economize on valuable space and time while attempting to provide an accurate overall picture. Transportation regulation is covered, but the regulation of savings and loans, natural gas, and certain other subjects I badly wanted to discuss, are not included. Hard decisions were made, and I still ended up with two more chapters than initially planned.

It will also be noticed that this is a rather angry book. So be it. Dispassionate analysis is a wonderful thing, but inadequate by itself when it discovers injustice. Pure mind games are ultimately unsatisfactory. The present investigation was motivated by a sense, shared by large portions of the U.S. population, that many things are wrong in America. Crime is massive, the family is rapidly disintegrating, as are morals and ethics generally. We feel much less free than Americans used to (with good reason) and per capita real output and income is growing more slowly than in earlier times, if at all. This should not be so if the massive expansion of income redistribution and regulation that has occurred over the same period was curing social and economic ills, as its proponents claim, unless some other powerful forces, yet to be explained, were offsetting their beneficial effects.

To the contrary, however, one senses that regulation and income redistribution are members of a set of related policy practices, all of which are expressions of the same mind set and ideology, which seems itself to be the central force behind the decay. That ideology, the interventionist or welfare liberal ideology, began to spread in America in the late 19th century, and gained widespread acceptance in the 20th. In recent years it is in disrepute and decline with the public at large, though it is still powerful in academy, government, the national press, the bureaucracy, and other centers of power. Even if it continues to decline, the institutional expressions of that ideology that have accumulated over the years, such as the welfare state, the regulatory bureaus and public education, have a force and momentum of their own which are not easily slowed, much less stopped.

But if they are moving us toward a precipice, as I believe they are, one must try, and thus the present book. It focuses narrowly and attempts to bring to the understanding of students of political science, economics and business the answers to a set of questions. What is the nature and what have been the historical and empirical effects of regulation? When people—usually, though not always, intellectuals, academics or politicians–demand regulation to deal with some alleged social ill, what exactly is it they are asking for? That is, what are its distinctive legal, institution and constitutional features? Is it really clear that massive regulation is necessary to a modern economy, and if so, how did we become a modern economy without it? Are alternative mechanisms of social control available, and if so, why is regulation preferred by so many of our intellectual and political leaders? Are their stated motives their actual motives, and what evidence does modern theory and research provide, that can answer such a question? Why is regulation prominently employed in some times and places, and less so in others?

Two factors will be discovered to be crucial in answering some of these questions. One, already mentioned, is the prevailing ideology. The other is the activity of self-interested individuals organized into political interest groups. Oddly, these two factors have, in recent years, come to be seen as conflicting explanations of government policies, particularly regulation. I regard this as an error. Ideology and interest group activity are complementary determinants of political behavior. *Ceteris paribus,* increased acceptance of an ideology denigrating the effectiveness and efficiency of private voluntary interactions under market incentives and favoring command and control policies for affecting the behavior of private citizens will increase regulatory activities and similar command and control methods. Likewise, greater or lesser degrees of special interest organization will affect such policies in reasonably obvious ways. The relationship between these factors will be explored later.

Last, one must say something about what should be done. One of the features of our present desperation is precisely a feeling of hopelessness; that events are beyond control, and that nothing can be done, at least in time. Yet in the very first chapter it will be shown that large scale changes in philosophy, understanding and policy have successfully reversed massively implemented bad policies in the past (even where they were supported by entrenched, organized interests), altering key institutions in ways that expanded freedom and prosperity. Our situation today is actually advantageous in one respect: we need not discover a new perspective, but only rediscover an older one that we once venerated. Indeed, *it is the same philosophy the adoption of which brought relief in that prior instance,* and it still has residual institutional expression in our law, politics and economy. I begin with some history, which will reveal much about the nature and political economy of regulation.

Chapter 1

Mercantile and Early American Regulation

It is vital to grasp that government regulation is *not* a modern phenomenon, but that it is also not a historical constant, at least at large magnitudes. Indeed, pervasive business regulation was a systematic characteristic of the late medieval economies preceding the rise of market economies, democratic governments and the industrial revolution. This systematic regulation, and its contingent practices, which together have come to be known as mercantilism, reluctantly gave way to the ideological, institutional and technological changes that gave rise to the modern Western nations. Nearly two thousand years of economic stagnation, poverty and tyranny collapsed, and reliable economic growth with rising real incomes for the *ordinary* person finally became the norm. Astonishingly, as Gertrude Himmelfarb recently demonstrated, even the morals of the general public greatly improved.[1]

Mercantile Rent Seeking

The mercantile states coalesced in the 14th and 15th centuries from the near anarchy that had previously characterized medieval Europe. Their primary feature was strong, centralized monarchic governments, such as those in France, Britain and Spain.[2] A crucial factor in this monarchic centralization appears to have been the support of the monarchs by merchant interests, in part searching for relief from the numerous, petty impediments to trade levied by every little fiefdom, town or principality.

The eventual removal of such local tolls and levies on the movement of goods allowed people to buy from whoever could produce and transport each good the cheapest and best, wherever that producer was located in the nation. Efficient producers of each product could expand their capital, employment and output, while inefficient producers would contract. The resulting reallocation of productive resources tended to integrate national economies, reduce costs, and allow more efficient internal division of labor. This was one of the *benefits* of the emergence of mercantile monarchies. Another was the associated "Age of Discovery," as the monarchs, who could support long distance expeditions in ways that small principalities could not, competed with one another for the discovery of new territories and improved international trade routes.

But the motives of the merchant interests and the monarchs in eliminating internal trade barriers and expanding international trade were not pure, to say the least. As barriers at the local level were largely removed, barriers to imports at the *national* level were instituted. This largely offset the benefits of improved internal resource allocation, and maintained medieval stagnation. The monarchs systematically granted and enforced monopolies and cartels over various lines of commerce, industry, and skilled trades (these latter often through the guilds) to favored individuals and producer groups. The cartels and monopolies would then, of course, act in the classic fashion to restrict production levels, raise prices, and extract economic rents (profits) from a luckless public too disorganized (and lacking an effective democratic mechanism) to have influence at court. Virtually the only important industries *not* so monopolized were those producing products of which the state itself was a heavy purchaser. The guilds operated in similar fashion to restrict entry to the trades, in order to keep the supply of those offering their particular services to the public scarce, and their incomes high.

The groups successful in attaining these grants of state protected monopoly were those who provided the highest bribes to the officials, supported the monarchy, and agreed to be taxed at the highest rates. The waste involved in such massive use of scarce resources in competitive efforts to obtain political income transfers, rather than employing them in production, is significant. In the graph below, line DD illustrates the market demand for a particular good or service. It is assumed to be linear for simplicity. Line S shows competitive long-run marginal and average unit cost of the good. Under competitive conditions, the market clearing price and quantities are Pc and Qc, or point A on the demand curve. If the industry is monopolized or cartelized, however, maximum profits will be obtained by restricting output to $Qm = 1/2 \ Qc$, raising the market clearing price to Pm, or point B on the demand curve.

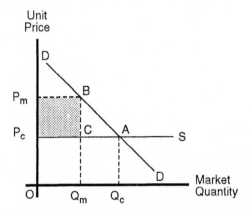

Graph 1.1: Social Costs of Successful Political Rent-Seeking

The monopolist makes profits equal to shaded area PmBCPc, which are redistributed to the firm (or cartel) from consumers of the product. Under the standard analysis of monopoly, the social losses are equal to the triangular area ABC (the 'Harburger triangle'). However, if the monopoly was gained through rent-seeking competition in the form of open bidding, bribery, lobbying, etc. to the monarch (or legislature) for a governmental franchise, the competitors collectively invest resources equal to the profit area (each investing a proportional share), and only the winning bidder obtains the profit itself. Thus the social losses equal the sum of the shaded rectangle and the Harburger triangle. Modern research indicates that this rent-seeking political exchange process supplies at least a partial explanation of the rise of the mercantile monarchies, since the rents potentially available to merchant and producer groups from the attainment by political favor of national monopolies and cartels were much larger than those attainable from simple local monopolies.[3]

It is important to grasp that, from a macroeconomic or social perspective, the systematic granting of monopolies and cartels over so many lines of production and trades was ultimately self-defeating. This is true for reasons in addition to the waste of scarce productive resources in the rent-seeking process itself. Consider that, in the aggregate, the real production of goods and services in a given time period *constitutes* aggregate real *income* in that time period, since it defines what is available to be consumed or traded for the production of those in other nations. When large numbers of producers are allowed by government enforced entry restrictions to reduce their output, aggregate income definitionally declines. Even those gaining from particular grants of monopoly end up having those gains eroded since they must purchase the outputs of other monopolies or cartelized tradesmen either as producer inputs or consumer goods. However, for some time this may have simply motivated people to engage in further rent-seeking, in a competitive effort to make relative gains.

Other crucial features of mercantile economies are correlative with its pervasive rent seeking character. mercantile states all instituted laws and practices aimed at restricting imports while expanding exports. The official ideologists of mercantilism argued that the resulting trade surpluses would cause the net international payments due to accrue as gold inflows, enriching the state. The brilliant David Hume eventually demonstrated the futility of protectionist policies aimed at accumulating gold. For one thing, on elementary principles of the quantity theory of money, such gold inflows would raise prices, reducing the value of each unit of money, and hence of the whole stock, negating the effect of the gold inflow on the *real* quantity of money. Moreover, gold flows through balances of international payments were self-eliminating as they acted, by adjusting national price levels, to equate the value of money everywhere.[4]

It is insightful, however, to look past the gold accumulation rationale and see the unity of protectionist policy with other elements of mercantilism. Simply notice that interests seeking state protection from competition through patents of monopoly or exclusive franchise will want, as part of the bargain, not only protection from potential domestic competitors, but also from international competitors, in the form of tariffs, quotas, or outright import bans. The monarchs and their political and intellectual supporters had to rationalize and justify these practices at the macroeconomic level, and an appeal to the common man's view that wealth consisted primarily in gold, was persuasive.

The same consistency explains the regulatory practice of mercantile states. It might at first seem inconsistent that the favored producer groups in each industry or trade had their production practices specified and regulated in detail by the state until one reflects on the nature of private cartels. Members of a cartel, who have colluded to reduce output and raise price, must worry about both external and internal competition. External entrepreneurs–attracted by the high rate of return that is the whole motive of the cartel restriction–are constantly attempting to either enter the business or supply a near substitute product. This adds to supply, reduces prices, and erodes the high rate of return.

But just as bad from the perspective of the cartel advocates, independent cartel members themselves are tempted to either undercut the high cartel price, or increase the quality of their own product. By doing so–as long as the others don't–they can increase their own profits and market share. These external and internal competitive pressures erode the cartel profits and often cause cartels to break down. In the case of a government granted cartel, to prevent this, the initial agreement must provide not only for state restrictions on external competitors, but also on internal practices. This was the function of the detailed mercantile government regulation and specification of industry work conditions and production methods.

As it eventually turned out, none of these methods were enough to preserve the mercantile system. State enforcement was strongest in the cities, and independent competitors began locating out in the suburbs and the countryside. Indeed, it was precisely in these rural areas, where business was competitive and unregulated, that the industrial revolution began. In addition, the self-defeating character of mercantilist restrictions, as even those with effective cartels were made worse off by the necessity of paying high prices for the cartelized production of others, may have become obvious to more and more people. Whether in cause or consequence, in the 17th and early 18th centuries the classical liberal political philosophy of natural rights, individualism, and constitutionally limited democratic government began to gain intellectual and ideological influence, particularly in Britain. In the associated political movement, the common law courts competed for power with the royal courts, and parliament struggled to reduce the political power of the Crown. Monarchy began to give way.

Only a few decades later, in the mid 18th century, *economic* liberalism appeared, shocking the world with its analytical power. First came the brilliant French Physiocrats, such as Turgot and Cantillon. Then came Adam Smith and the British classical economists. These thinkers discovered the basic principles of an economy based on private property and voluntary exchange in open, competitive markets. They demonstrated that under these institutional conditions there is an orderly and self-regulating economic process in which rational, self-interested individuals are guided by market price and profit signals to shift and allocate resources across occupations and industries in *socially* beneficial ways. Classical liberalism soon became a dominating political force in Britain, its American colonies, and other Western nations. The British Parliament privatized agricultural land, repealed the poor laws and freed the labor market. Feudal institutions were largely swept away, and mercantile monopolies, import restrictions and regulation were severely curtailed.

Smith and David Ricardo dealt crippling blows to the ideology of protection. Using the principles of absolute and comparative advantage they were able to demonstrate that an increase in world production, from which all nations could gain, would result from an international division of labor based on free trade.[5] This was a shock to people who had believed for centuries that the wealth of the world was a fixed sum, such that the only way for one nation to make gains in wealth or income was through conquest from other nations. This belief had been reinforced by centuries of economic stagnation, and had generated centuries of bitter warfare. It was no accident that Smith called his great book *The Wealth of Nations*, or that as the policies of mercantilism lost favor and those of the Classical liberals replaced them, the wealth of the nations grew. It was also no accident that the 100 years from the end of the Napoleonic wars in 1815 to the beginning of World War I in 1914, the longest period of comparative international peace in the known history of the world, corresponded with the classic period of limited government and free trade.[6]

The Constitution and
Regulation in Early America

Adam Smith's *The Wealth of Nations* was published in 1776, the same year as the Declaration of Independence, so it is fair to say that it was the *political* philosophy of classical liberalism, more than economic liberalism, that motivated the founders of the American Republic.[7] Nevertheless, the founding fathers not only had historical knowledge but direct experience with the evils of mercantile policies, and did their best to end them. Fortunately, most feudal institutions, such as land tenure, did not take root in early America. The temptation to colonial (and later, state) government leaders to engage in mercantile practices was hard to resist, however, and many had begun levying restrictions on imports from other colonies by the time of the constitutional convention. Concerned with preventing such interstate trade barriers and creating an integrated economy, the founders added a clause to the Constitution granting Congress–not the states–the authority to regulate interstate commerce. Indeed, not only many of its specific provisions, but much of the basic structure of the constitution, as a set of prescriptive and proscriptive limits on governmental power, was arguably intended to prevent rent seeking mercantile practices, by denying government the authority to grant favors to special interest groups.

The effect of protecting private property, freeing the market, and reducing political rent-seeking was to create an efficient set of incentives motivating the American people to employ resources productively. The natural self-reliance, individualism and creativity of the populace was released to generate an immense wave of inventiveness and innovative entrepreneurial activity. New products, methods of production, improvements in transportation and communication emerged at a pace never before seen in world history. Add to this the abundant resources available to be discovered and developed profitably by private entrepreneurs as the populace expanded westward, and the result was rapid and sustained growth in real output and incomes.[8]

Early supreme court decisions helped. For example, early in the 19th century the state of New York granted famed inventor Robert Fulton a monopoly over steamboat passenger transportation in New York. A competitor, Thomas Gibbons, hired young Cornelius ('Commodore') Vanderbilt in 1817 to break the monopoly. Vanderbilt did so, running passengers between New Jersey and New York at low rates the Fulton monopoly could not match. The U.S. Supreme Court, in the case of *Gibbons versus Ogden* (1824) declared New York's monopoly grant invalid, pointing out that only the federal government could regulate interstate commerce.[9] This and similar decisions, along with a narrow interpretation by Congress of its own regulatory power under the commerce clause, kept regulatory and monopoly practices small at both the state and federal levels for over half a century.

Admittedly, even some early Supreme Court decisions cut the other way. In *McCulloch vs. Maryland* (1819) the Marshall court upheld creation of the Second Bank of the United States, with special powers not granted to other banks. The government wanted the bank as a centralized institution in which to deposit tax revenues and from which to disburse expenditures, and perhaps–indeed probably–for other reasons. It is historically undeniable that central banks were, originally, quintessential mercantile rent seeking institutions. The prototype of all such banks was the Bank of England, created by Royal charter in 1692 at the behest of William Patterson, a known financial huckster, and his associates. Patterson's group obtained monopoly authority over the issuance of convertible banknotes, which eventually led to control over the British money supply. The bank was also to hold government deposits, and was granted other special advantages over private banks. The monarchy, for its part, obtained agreement that the bank would make loans to the crown, which was finding it difficult to finance wars since it had reneged on several previous debts.[10] Every central bank since has had, as a central function, the loaning of money to its government creator, and the creation of money itself, both processes which, among other things, allow governments to escape the financial constraints of open and honest taxation.

McCulloch vs. Maryland involved two issues. The case arose because the State of Maryland placed a tax on the assets of the bank of the U.S. in its borders, so one issue was whether states could tax federal government property. The Court properly denied their ability to do so, since the power to tax federal institutions was the power–by setting the tax sufficiently high–to destroy them. The more fundamental issue, however, concerned the right of Congress to establish a central bank when *no* such authority was expressly granted in the Constitution. Marshall justified the action of Congress, however, on the basis of the "necessary and proper" clause (Article I, Section 8), which says that Congress may make all laws that are "necessary and proper" for carrying out its specifically mandated functions.

As a constitutional test Marshall's decision was certainly correct, though as applied to this particular case, it was wrong. It was in *no* sense necessary for the federal government to charter a bank to manage its revenues. Both prior and subsequent history demonstrated that the government could perform its monetary and budgetary functions without such a bank. The damage done by Marshall's error here was severe–Second Bank monetary mismanagement generated a financial panic that injured many people in 1819–but historically limited. Strong political interests opposed central banking in the early U.S. precisely because of its unsavory character and history. President Andrew Jackson knew that, among other dangers, the bank had the effect, by its concentration of federal deposits that had previously been spread among many banks, of conferring heavy benefits to a favored few. Consequently he withdrew federal deposits from the bank and let its charter expire in 1836. So despite some Court decisions such as *McColluch vs. Maryland*, the basic thrust of constitutional interpretation in both the executive and judicial branches during the pre-Civil War period was to *limit* state and federal regulation.

This is true despite the fact that certain forms of regulation were chronic and prominent in the period. Before 1837 states had a right to grant or withhold corporate charters, and though state laws have since allowed anyone to incorporate, states have carefully maintained the right to grant or withhold business licenses since then. Largely due to this authority, state governments chronically regulated and interfered with banking. As a direct consequence, and due to the particular forms this regulation took, the U.S. has always had a poor banking system, and has suffered significant monetary instability.[11] The states also frequently engaged in subsidization of infrastructure development.

Another industry that was heavily regulated and manipulated by the states and municipalities at an early date, before federal regulation became prominent, was the railroad industry. These interventions took various forms, but prominent methods were the use of land grants and subsidies to encourage building where it would not otherwise occur, and the requirement of a franchise for permission to build. The character of many such regulatory interventions may be illustrated by another event in Cornelius Vanderbilt's life. After the Civil War began Vanderbilt sold his steamships and in 1863 he bought control of the New York & Harlem railroad. It had been the first railroad in New York City. The road was in financial difficulty, but could be made profitable by extending its track down Broadway to the Battery. In order to do this, Vanderbilt needed a franchise from the city council. The city council, however, would not issue a franchise without being bribed, so he paid their extortion. What he didn't know, but the Aldermen did, was that such a franchise was illegal, and would be nullified by the state legislature when they heard of it.

When the franchise was issued, the price of Vanderbilt's railroad stock went to seventy-five dollars a share. The Aldermen and a clique of speculators then wrote 'short sale' contracts for future sales of New York & Harlem stock at that price, even though they owned little or none. As soon as the legislature objected to Vanderbilt's franchise, as they expected, the Aldermen revoked it. The price of his stock began to fall and the Aldermen and their cohorts stood to make a large profit by purchasing low and delivering high. Vanderbilt spoiled the plot, however, by entering the market and buying large amounts of his own stock to keep its price from falling below the delivery price contracted by the short-sellers. In fact, he bought so much that its price increased. As a result, come delivery time the Aldermen had to purchase New York & Harlem shares at a high price from Vanderbilt himself to sell them right back to him at a low price (since he had also bought the short-sale contracts), and were financially ruined.

Amazingly, powerful members of the New York legislature tried the same thing on Vanderbilt only one year later when he bought the Hudson River Railroad and needed legislative authorization to consolidate it with the New York & Harlem. Again, the crooked politicians promised, in return for bribes, to introduce and support authorization for Vanderbilt to do something the legislature should never have had the regulatory power to forbid in the first place. Then, when the price of his railroad stock rose, they sold it short. Vanderbilt had to scratch for resources, even borrowing a million dollars from an old friend, but his massive purchases of his own stock, after the promised permission was denied by the legislature, ruined many of its prominent members.[12]

The Supreme Court and Post-Civil War Regulation

It is important to note clearly both the similarities and differences between U.S. and mercantile state practices, since both are instructive. First, remember that the mercantile nations eliminated or severely reduced *internal* trade barriers (just as the U.S. did) then replaced them with barriers on international trade. Now remember that, from its inception, the U.S. was a high-tariff nation. At a certain level, therefore, the U.S. seems to have followed the classic mercantile pattern. Still, the U.S. was democratic, not monarchic, with severe Constitutional limits on even democratic governmental power to interfere with individual rights and private property. Hence its national trade policy was *not* an expression of any systematic, rent-seeking mercantile policy of internal monopoly and governmental regulation, or at least not so before the 20th century.

This is not to say that politics and special interests had no effect on national tariff policy. The tariff had important interregional effects, benefiting industry in the North, which was a net exporter, and harming the South, which imported many manufactured products that were the primary focus of protection. And it must be remembered that, though Northern hostility to slavery was the most immediate issue causing the Southern secession, Northern high tariff policy was an equal, long simmering source of Southern resentment. Indeed, relatively few southerners owned slaves, and much evidence indicates that both the political elites and ordinary citizens in the South were just as committed to human liberty and limited government as were Northern citizens.[13]

It is common to interpret the Civil War, by freeing the slaves, as representing the culminating institutional expression of the classical liberal ideology; the final removal of institutionalized self-contradiction. And certainly the massive entrepreneurial activity, industrialization and economic growth in the remainder of the 19th century, which vaulted the U.S. to the position of being simultaneously the greatest agricultural and industrial nation on earth, represents a culminating expression of the ideology of freedom in practice. Nevertheless, the horror of the Civil War, and the systematic, coercive violations of Constitutional rights entailed in its prosecution, seem to have shocked many American's attitudes in an interventionist direction. In addition, through an organized political campaign, public (i.e. government controlled and subsidized) education largely displaced and replaced private education in the middle decades of the century, and began inculcating the young with increasingly statist perspectives. For these and other reasons, the classical liberal ideology that gave rise to the Constitution and consequent American prosperity, began everywhere to lose influence in the minds of the intellectual classes, the political elites, and the common man.[14]

Many events, such as the appearance in this period of the progressive movement that eventually became modern, interventionist, welfare liberalism (stealing the very name of the limited government philosophy, while distorting its meaning), indicate the loss of libertarian belief. An important related indication for the present discussion, however, is a series of Post Civil War Supreme Court decisions expanding federal and state regulatory power. The first of these, the case of *Munn vs. Illinois* (1877) arose when rural, agricultural interests pressured midwestern state governments to pass laws regulating the prices charged by railroads, grain elevators, and other businessmen with which farmers dealt.

These laws clearly violated long established and constitutionally protected freedoms of contract and private property. They were also obvious outcomes of political rent seeking by organized and powerful special interests who wished to benefit themselves by getting government to force lower rates on other businesses whose services they purchased. Prior Supreme Courts would have invalidated these laws, but the extant court decided that "property used in a 'public' fashion, affecting the public at large, grants the public the right to control it for the public good." Read literally through its terminological confusion, this amounts to saying that the act of employing private assets in business automatically transforms them into public property, to be politically regulated at will. A clearer expression of socialist principle would be difficult to find, and it is shocking to see it appear so nakedly, expressed by so powerful an institution, at so early a date. Nevertheless, it has been the basis for economic regulation in the U.S. ever since.

The Court eventually realized that it had gone too far. In the case of *Chicago, Milwaukee and St. Paul Railroad vs. Minnesota* (1890) the Court tried to place some limits on regulatory authority. In this decision it said that the states could regulate business as much as they liked, as long as such regulation was 'reasonable'. Thus began the "substantive due process" period, in which the courts judged the reasonableness of state and federal regulatory activities. Staunch advocates of expanding regulation have reviled this Supreme Court practice because, occasionally, the court would find some state or federal regulatory act unreasonable, and declare it unconstitutional. In contrast, conservative critics of regulation, such as Bernard Siegan, have praised substantive due process, and advocated its return.[15]

In reality, both are wrong. The failure of the Court was in not supplying a *more* stringent test of regulatory acceptability, based on clearer constitutional principle, such as, for example, the takings clause of the 5th amendment. Failure to do so left court interpretations of 'reasonableness' of particular state and federal regulatory acts a matter of essentially personal or ideological interpretation. The inevitable followed. As late as the early 1930s many New Deal acts such as Roosevelt's National Industrial Recovery Act, which attempted the explicit, total cartelization of American industry, and the Agricultural Adjustment Act, which regulated agricultural prices and production, were declared unconstitutional. But interventionist liberalism increasingly became the dominant ideology, and for the next sixty years the court virtually *never* found a state or federal regulatory act, no matter how intrusive, outrageous or dictatorial, to be unreasonable.[16]

A third crucial 19th century precedent expanding regulatory authority was set in the case of *McCray vs. U.S.* (1904). The case arose because artificially colored margarine was invented. It was a low cost substitute for butter and its makers began to compete successfully for customers. In a blatant act of political rent seeking, butter producers prevailed on the state to place a special, clearly discriminatory tax on margarine. In a ruling obviously benefiting the *special* interests at the expense of the consuming public, the court upheld the tax. In so doing it established the right of states to tax for regulatory purposes. It is worth noting that the federal government had already begun using taxation in this manner, when it placed a tax on the notes of state chartered banks in 1865 and drove the notes out of circulation, in order to leave federally chartered bank notes the dominant currency.

The basic authority for federal regulation, as already mentioned, comes from the Commerce Clause, which grants power to Congress to regulate interstate commerce. The clause is limiting, however, because it implies that production and exchange occurring entirely within a state is beyond federal regulatory authority. Indeed, even today, Congress sometimes takes this limit seriously. Much of the expansion of federal regulatory power over time, however, has come in the form of decisions interpreting the Commerce Clause more broadly. This trend began with *Swift vs. U.S.* (1905), in which the court said that economic activities that *might eventually* become part of interstate commerce were subject to federal regulation. Clearly, once such hypothetical possibilities are accepted as justifying federal regulatory control over private economic activities, the Commerce Clause as a constitutional impediment to such control, no longer exists.

For purposes of the discussion in subsequent chapters of this book, however, perhaps the most important of these early Supreme Court decisions expanding regulatory power was that of *U.S. vs. Grimaud* (1911). The primary decision here was that *administrative rulings* (regulations) *have the force of law*. One cannot overemphasize the vital character of this decision for what was to come. If Congress, State legislatures and the courts had decided that administrative regulation was to expand as a legal mechanism of social and economic control in competition with statutory law and common law, this decision had to be made. Regulatory rulings are either the equivalent of laws or they are mere suggestions, and of no force.

Such a decision would have shocked any member of the Court prior to the Civil War. Indeed, none of the reasoning upon which these decisions were based would have passed Constitutional muster in the pre-Civil War Courts, whose justices took concepts of individual rights, private property, and the rule of law, not of men, seriously. The philosophy of the political and legal elites had clearly changed. Precedents were established for a massive expansion of regulatory control over private business and occupational activities, which soon followed. At every step it was argued that the traditional legal mechanisms and competitive market institutions that had worked so well in that past in disciplining self-interest were inadequate in the new economic environment, and that regulation was necessary to protect the public. It would seem rather odd, though, if the mechanism of social control necessary for dealing with a dynamic industrial society that had risen in a framework of Constitutional law and limited government was a form of law characteristic of late medieval dictatorships.

Notes

1   Gertrude Himmelfarb, "A De-Moralized Society: The British/American Experience," *The American Educator* (Winter 1994-95): 14-43. Himmelfarb regards this moral improvement, which occurred both in Britain and the U.S., as occurring *despite* the Classical Liberal Individualist ideology, as a result of the spread of Victorian values. In my opinion, *only* in a society of free institutions based on such an ideology, which presumes both the cognitive efficacy and personal responsibility of the individual, will strong moral values come to dominate.

2   See Robert B. Ekelund and Robert D. Tollison, *Mercantilism as a Rent-Seeking Society* (College Station: Texas A&M Press, 1981). Specifically on French Mercantilism, see, by the same authors, "A Rent Seeking

Theory of French Mercantilism," in James M. Buchanan and Robert D. Tollison, *The Theory of Public Choice-II* (The University of Michigan Press, 1984).

3 North and Thomas argue that the European nation states emerged because, as markets and trade expanded, protection was needed over distances that could not be supplied by feudal baronies, local principalities and small kingdoms. This is insightful, and certainly the process of political consolidation did begin in the 13th century when population and markets were expanding. But in the 14th and 15th centuries when the modern nation states actually appeared, by North and Thomas' own account both population and trade were *contracting* due to the Malthusian checks of famine and pestilence, generating all sorts of protectionist practices and institutions. See Douglas North and Robert Paul Thomas, *The Rise of the Western World* (Cambridge University Press, 1973): Chapters 7 and 8.

4 David Hume, "Of the Balance of Trade," reprinted in Eugene Rotwein, ed., *Writings on Economics* (Books for Libraries Press, 1955).

5 Any modern principles level economics text teaches these principles clearly. See James D. Gwartney and Richard L. Stroup, *Economics: Private and Public Choice* (7th edition: The Dryden Press, 1995): 859-865.

6 See Karl Polanyi, *The Great Transformation* (Octagon Books, 1975).

7 Recent research shows, however, that by the 1790s economic Liberalism had become a dynamic force in the minds of the Republican revolutionaries who opposed aristocratic Federalism and elected Thomas Jefferson President in 1800. See Joyce Appleby, *Capitalism and a New Social Order: The Republican Vision of the 1790s* (New York University Press, 1984).

8 See Douglas C. North, Terry L. Anderson, and Peter J. Hill, *Growth and Welfare in the American Past: A New Economic History* (3rd edition: Prentice-Hall, 1983): 12-40.

9 See Burton Folsom, *The Myth of the Robber Barons* (Young America's Foundation, 1991): pp. 2-3.

10 Elgin Groseclose, *Money and Man: A Survey of Monetary Experience* (4th revised edition, University of Oklahoma Press, 1976): 175-176.

11 George Selgin, "Legal Restrictions, Financial Weakening, and the Lender of Last Resort," *The Cato Journal* 9 (Fall 1989): 429-459. However, financial panics were really fairly infrequent, and there is little evidence that their effect on the economy was great. See Gerald P. Dwyer, Jr., and

R. Alton Gilbert, "Bank Runs and Private Remedies," Federal Reserve Bank of St. Louis *Review* 71 (May/June 1989): 43-61.

12 See Alvin F. Harlow, *The Road of the Century* (Creative Age Press, 1947): 166-173, and David Marshall, *Grand Central* (McGraw-Hill, 1946): 60-64.

13 See, for one indication, Randall G. Holcombe, "The Distributive Model of Government: Evidence from the Confederate States Constitution," *Southern Economic Journal* 58 (January 1992): 762-769. In addition, studies of the diaries of the Southern soldiers do *not* reveal that they believed they were fighting primarily to maintain slavery.

14 Chapter 10 below expands on this history and the ideological struggle of the late 19th century.

15 Bernard Siegan, *Economic Liberties and the Constitution* (University of Chicago Press, 1980).

16 In 1995 the Court once again asserted its power of judicial review over such legislation. It declared a federal law prohibiting possession of a gun within 100 yards of a school to be unconstitutional.

Chapter 2

Constitutional Democracy and Regulation

The American economy, once largely free, is increasingly regulated. To understand regulation and regulatory law, or as it is often termed, administrative law, it must be contrasted with other forms of law. Since the most fundamental law in the U.S. is the Constitution it is appropriate to begin there, and even before, with the philosophy that guided its construction and the creation of American political and legal institutions. That philosophy–classical liberalism–is best traced to John Locke.[1]

Predation, Rights, and Government

Like Thomas Hobbes before him, Locke began his analysis with men in an imagined 'state of nature' absent government. Lock assumed that individuals have natural rights, in the form of property rights, including, among others, the rights of self-ownership (what we would now term self-determination), free association, self-defense, and private property in externals. Locke agreed with Hobbes that most people find the state of nature unsatisfactory, because the predatory activities of some of their number do not allow the maintenance of their natural rights and freedoms. Hobbes, however, had argued that the horrors of anarchy required establishment of an unlimited monarchy, or leviathan. Locke saw a better solution. The autonomous individuals composing (or potentially composing) society could establish government by a social contract between and among themselves, elect its prime decision makers, and vest them with a monopoly over the use of force. This process necessarily involves granting government the necessary resources to guarantee it the monopoly (or at least superiority) over the use of force, hence an agreement to be taxed as necessary to provide that power is a key element of the social contract. Since the governmental authorities are simply agents of the general citizenry, with delegated powers, *they may only use this force in ways that citizens could employ force by natural right in the state of nature.* No one can delegate rights, powers or authority to others that they themselves do not have.

The problem then, is to so structure governmental institutions as to insure that its delegated power will be employed to maintain–not destroy–individual rights. It is a severe problem, since the government itself will be composed, at any given time, of a subset of the population. For the same reasons that many people cannot be trusted in the state of nature, they cannot be trusted with excessive power in government. Indeed, by concentrating power in government it becomes attractive to precisely those people who would use force or fraud to dominate and redistribute wealth from others to themselves in the state of nature, to strive to gain control of government to employ its power for the same purpose.

The ideal is to so constitute government and structure the incentives faced by those composing it that such misuse of power is prevented, and they act instead to *minimize* the use of force in human affairs. That is, government is to apply its power in enforcing contracts (including the social contract) and punishing violent crimes, theft and fraud, forcing people to interact with one another on an honest, mutually voluntary, and hence mutually beneficial basis. It is to otherwise employ force only as necessary to obtain the resources required for it to effectively secure rights. Beyond that it is to leave people free to choose and act for themselves, rising or falling on the basis of, and bearing personal responsibility for, their own decisions. The presumption is that the establishment of these conditions of security, peace, freedom and justice, will not only be satisfying to society's members in itself, but will result in an increased aggregate output and income, an assumption that has been overwhelmingly, historically justified. *In the provision of such necessary 'public' goods, therefore, government is literally productive.*

Locke's conception was not entirely perfect. Since then we have learned a little more about the nature of public goods. Basically, public goods are those which, in addition to being socially necessary (or at least desirable), are non-excludable and non-depletable. That is, once someone provides a public good, others cannot be excluded from benefiting, hence they cannot be required to pay by a private provider. Also, additional users do not deplete the existing supply. Private firms will not provide a public good, or will not provide enough of it, since many people, who cannot be excluded from its benefits and do not deplete the existing supply, will not pay. Instead they will 'free ride' on the contributions of others, and revenues will be inadequate to provide the optimal amount. Private goods, in contrast, are both excludable and depletable, so they can be provided by competing private firms to willing customers in a free market. Entry of new firms will occur to eliminate economic profits in a given industry, and exit will act to eliminate economic losses, until the optimal amount of a private good is supplied.

In addition to being non-excludable and non-depletable, public goods are usually 'system goods' in which separate units are elements in a single system, hence the provider is a natural monopoly. National defense is a perfect example of a public good. Once it is provided everyone, whether payer or non-payer, benefits, and population growth does not deplete the existing supply. The very notion of a competitive industry in which separate firms each provide 'national defense' only to their own voluntary customers—excluding non-payers—is absurd. Since defense must be organized and coordinated, separate units must be elements in a single system, with a single monopoly provider. Competing private provision is excluded by definition. This is why the legal system and law enforcement are also public goods. There must be a single system of laws, and separate police agencies must have defined, separate legal jurisdictions in the overall system of law enforcement.

Since everyone benefits virtually simultaneously and continuously from the provision of public goods such as systems of law, law and contract enforcement, and national defense, but such goods cannot be provided through the market, they must generally be publicly provided and financed by taxation. It is crucial to note that the tax provision of true public goods is *not* redistributive. The point of tax provision is only to make individuals pay their fair share for a good from which *they* (and everyone else) are benefiting. Indeed, the tax provision prevents a redistribution that would occur if the good were provided by voluntary payments from a subset of the population. The number of true public goods may be larger than Locke thought, but it is much smaller than modern interventionist liberals believe.[2]

Nevertheless, in the classical liberal philosophy of Locke and his successors was born an enormous number of the basic political principles of Western society: that individual's natural rights *precede* government, and are the source if its power rather than being derived from it; the social contract or constitution as the proper origin of government; that social aggregates are simply composed of individuals; the rule of law, not of men; popular sovereignty and democracy; suspicion that self-interest dominates in human nature so that both government itself and constitutional limits on even democratic governmental authority are required; the sanctity and productivity of private property; the negative state that secures rights and otherwise leaves people free, et al. One of the prime criticisms of Locke in his day was that, historically, governments had not originated in the way that he described. It is a testament to the power of ideas, however, that less than a century after his death, the founding fathers of the American republic deliberately employed a strikingly Lockean political process to establish a government on precisely the lines he advocated.

Classical Liberalism and the Constitution

That Lockean classical liberal political theory, modified to degrees by experience and by complementary indigenous perspectives, guided the founders of the American republic, is indisputable. Consider the famous sentence from the Declaration of Independence:

> WE hold these truths to be self-evident, that all Men are created equal, that they are endowed by their Creator with certain unalienable Rights, that among these are Life, Liberty, and the Pursuit of Happiness –that to secure these Rights, Governments are instituted among Men, deriving their just Powers from the Consent of the Governed, ...

This sentence expresses the key principles of classical liberal political theory, principles that they struggled to put into practice at the Constitutional convention. Consider the preamble:

> We the People of the United States, in Order to form a more perfect Union, establish Justice, insure domestic Tranquility, provide for

the common defense, promote the general Welfare, and secure the Blessings of Liberty to ourselves and our Posterity, do ordain and establish this Constitution for the United States of America.

Virtually every element of the structure of government mandated in the Constitution was designed to restrain the illegitimate use of governmental power and focus on the provision of those public goods necessary for the maintenance of rights. Representative democracy expressed through competitive elections for the Presidency and Congressional seats is one such element. Terms of office and competitive elections allow the removal from office of those who harm the public through abuse of power. It is no small insight that the idea of representative democracy probably stemmed from observation of market competition. The ability of consumers to substitute freely between competing, independent providers of a product disciplines the behavior of those firms, since those that treat customers badly quickly lose them to firms that treat them well. Representative democracy is an attempt to apply the same principle to a political system, for the same reasons.[3]

To the founders, representative democracy was not a sufficient check by itself on possible bad behavior and destruction of individual rights by government, however. Following the advice of Montesquieu, they divided the three fundamental powers of government, legislative, executive (or administrative), and judicial, into three separate governmental branches, with checks and balances between them. The President does not legislate; he commands the forces of national defense and the bureaucracy that administers and enforces the laws. Congress legislates, with assent of the President, who may veto their enactments. The President may not absolutely forbid legislation, however, since the veto can be overridden by Congressional supermajority vote. The Supreme Court and lesser federal courts interpret the laws, and the Supreme court may even judge their constitutionality, invalidating those that fail its tests. But the President, with Congressional assent, appoints members of the judiciary, and Congress can limit the jurisdiction of the courts. The clear intent of all of this was to divide power, preventing the concentration of legislative, executive and judicial functions in the same persons, to limit the abuse of power at the hands of even democratically elected officials.

Even these constraints were not enough. Article I Section 8, which establishes the extent (and thereby the *limits*) of the legislative power of

Congress, provides both a specific list and a general statement of authority. The general statement is known as the 'general welfare' clause. It provides that Congress can levy taxes to pay debts and provide for the common defense and general welfare of the United States. The phrase "general welfare," which was also contained in the preamble to the Constitution, quoted above, is crucial. Far from constituting a blanket grant of power for unlimited and arbitrary income redistribution, as is now claimed, it was intended to *limit* congressional legislation and supporting taxation to the provision of true public goods, from which *all* members of the public benefit simultaneously and continuously. As pointed out above, national defense is a perfect example, and the intention in the general welfare clause was to admit the existence of some others, which were not specified, but could be recognized by meeting that test. For about the first 150 years of our national history the general welfare clause was interpreted, properly, to *forbid* federal income transfers, since they benefit some only by hurting others, and hence do not demonstrably increase the *general* welfare.

Last, with a degree of redundancy that NASA would appreciate, the Founders added a bill of rights as a final source of protection against abuse of governmental power. These ten amendments protect such things as the freedoms of religion, speech and press, the rights of personal privacy and security in people's homes, weapons ownership, due process of law for those accused of crimes, and jury trial. The protection was provided by specifically forbidding legislation denying such rights and freedoms. And in recognition that not all rights could be enumerated in the Constitution, the ninth amendment specifically states that the failure to do so is not to be construed as denying that people have such rights.

Regulation and The Separation of Powers

Against the standard of the Constitution, certain characteristic features of regulatory law as it has developed in the 20th century stand out in high relief. The Supreme Court established in *U.S. vs. Grimaud* (1911) that *administrative rulings* (regulations) *have the force of law.* Even before then such 'laws' were being made by appointed officials of executive branch agencies, who were not elected legislators. In addition, the agencies both enforced their own rules and exercised judicial functions, thus combining all three powers in the same agencies. These conditions required a great deal of justification. This is made plain on the very first substantive page of an early comprehensive treatise on administrative law.[4]

> "Administrative law," as the term is generally used today and for the purposes of this article, is concerned with the legal problems arising out of the existence of agencies which to a noteworthy degree combine in a single entity legislative, executive, and judicial powers which, in the American system of law, were traditionally kept separate.

That administrative agencies, in the process of formulating and enforcing rules and regulations, were both legislating and enforcing their own laws, was not a fact that could entirely be denied. That the Constitution mandated the separation of such powers (and that most state constitutions had the same requirement) was also known to all concerned. When those subjected to the regulations noticed this it resulted in many challenges in the courts. How were the agencies, their supporters, and the judiciary, who were increasingly infected by the same interventionist, technocratic ideology, and determined not to be stopped by what they regarded as an antiquated 18th century document, to rationalize this circumvention of Constitutional restriction?

Certainly, lip service to the plain intent of the Constitution was necessary. Accordingly, the general rule stated by the courts was that no legislature may delegate to administrative agencies its legislative power except where authorized by the Constitution under which that legislature gained its own authority.[5] The U.S. Constitution, of course, says nothing that prohibits states from writing constitutional provisions allowing their legislatures to delegate legislative power to state administrative agencies. However, it grants no specific authority to Congress to delegate such powers to federal agencies, so the requirement of separation of powers was inherently more restrictive at the federal level.

The next step, however, was for the courts to assert that the rule only prohibits delegation of powers that are *inherently* or *strictly* legislative. With this decision, that there are at least some significant (legislative) powers that are not 'strictly' legislative, hence can be delegated by Congress or state legislatures to executive branch agencies, boards and commissions, the chiseling at the margins that defines the process of Constitutional decay began. The inherently legislative power, that cannot be delegated, the courts decided, is the power to set *policy* by law, that is, to make the law itself. But how the purposes of the law are to be achieved can be delegated. In other words, as long as Congress or state legislatures write laws stating policy objectives and creating executive branch agencies to enforce and administer those policies, they can grant those agencies discretion to write specific rules and regulations aimed at carrying out the law (and change them at will), without unconstitutionally delegating their legislative power. Such regulations may carry civil or even criminal penalties.

Some early court decisions appeared to place strict limits on the rule making discretion of regulatory agencies, stating that the discretion must be guided by the statute authorizing it, or be circumscribed by statutory limits. Arbitrary and uncontrolled discretion is precluded. Also, the legislature, not the agency, was to specify any criminal penalties for violations of the rules. And the basic policy objective itself had to be constitutional. Since the World War II case of *Yakus vs. United States* (1944), however, not only has the scope of governmental action that the courts consider constitutional been enormously widened, but it has been accepted that broad and general legislative standards, guidelines, and limits for agency regulation suffice. Indeed, in cases where the powers exercised are strictly administrative, or where standards are found in other laws or in executive orders, courts have found the complete *absence* of such standards in the initial enabling legislation acceptable. The only flicker of light in this long dark tunnel came in the 1970 case of *Industrial Union Department, AFL-CIO vs. American Petroleum Institute* (commonly known as the *Benzine* case). In a minority opinion since unheeded, Justice Rehnquist asserted that such broad and vague delegations of legislative power should be considered unconstitutional.

The Ideology of the Courts

Many of the court decisions passing on the validity of administrative law contain extralegal–one might even say ideological–arguments designed to explain the perceived necessity for granting administrative agencies legislative and judicial powers. It is frequently argued, for example, that regulation has advantages over courts in dealing with the social problems at which regulation is aimed. For one thing, courts cannot initiate or control the range of investigations, while regulatory agencies can. Again, resort of private parties to the courts is sporadic and intermittent, while agencies can engage in continuous supervision of the regulated populations. They can also dispense with many of the formalities and delays ordinarily involved in court proceedings. In addition, agencies can maintain staffs of specialized experts in the areas being regulated, which are not readily available to the courts.

This claimed superiority of the regulatory mechanism, while widely asserted, is never proved. It has *not* been shown, for example, that the substitution of regulation for tort law in matters of pollution in the 20th century has resulted in superior control. Regarding the sporadic nature of the civil and criminal law in comparison to administrative legal procedure, there are very good reasons–having to do with liberty and the maintenance of rights–that the judicial mechanism comes into play only after a complaint of harm and formal charge is made. Likewise, the formalities and details of court procedures developed over time to preserve rights and establish justice. The argument that continuous supervision of target populations is necessary to deal with social problems is not only dubious, it begs the whole question of whether such supervision is compatible with a free society. Clearly, not only is Big Brother watching, but the advocates of regulation very much *want* him to watch, and watch continuously.

Another argument employed by some courts in justifying delegation of legislative powers to regulatory agencies is a version of what may be termed the contracting cost argument. It is well known among economists that private contracts are nearly always incomplete, because the cost of conceiving and specifying every possible contingency that might arise over the duration of the contract is prohibitive. Of course, problems often arise over precisely such contingencies, and resort may then be had to the courts for adjudication of a dispute between the parties. Much the same is argued to apply to enabling legislation creating an administrative agency. The costs of legislative completeness are prohibitive, so legislative power to deal with unforeseen details and contingencies as they arise must be delegated to such agencies. This provides 'flexibility' in dealing with changing situations over time, which is considered, by many judicial advocates of regulation, to be essential and beneficial.

Second thoughts are in order, however. Certainly it is true that legislators cannot anticipate, in any reasonable amount of time, every possible future condition or contingency relating to economic or social behavior they wish to control with a law. But the legislative process is ongoing. When the effects of a law in practice are not as initially intended, or changes in conditions and new contingencies are observed, adjustments in the law can be made. What this particular argument for administrative regulation really reduces to is a claim that more laws and more frequent adjustments in laws are needed than Congress and State legislatures can accomplish given their time and numbers, hence they must create additional 'mini-legislatures' in administrative agencies to accomplish the additional necessary legislation.

Whether that is true or not, however, is precisely one of the main things at issue, and is not to be established by this sort of dogmatic assertion. Empirical economic literature has much more to say about whether regulation has, in the past, really been necessary and beneficial on net or not, hence whether and to what degree it is necessary in the present and is likely to be so in the future. That matter will be discussed in later chapters. What can be said here is that, while public well being is benefited by the legislative provision of necessary public goods, it is certainly *not* obvious, *a priori,* that it is a positive *linear* function of the volume and/or frequency of adjustment of laws.

Rather the opposite seems more true. Much of the benefit of a system of law is lost if the laws are not relatively few and stable, so that the rules can be known and people's lives adjusted to them. The vaunted advantage of regulation in providing many more rules and more frequent adjustment in such rules is precisely one of its greatest sources of harm, since it generates immense confusion, uncertainty, instability and risk. Indeed, it seems to many of us almost certain that the list of true public goods is rather small, and beyond that the aggregate marginal productivity (both in physical output and subjective utility terms) of additional legislation becomes negative rather fast.

One more closely related theoretical argument for regulation prominently employed by the courts needs mention. The claim is made that the complexity of a modern, industrial/technological economy and society itself requires detailed and extensive legal intervention in order to coordinate and control its diverse elements and operations in any rational fashion. As it applies to justification of extensive regulation, this argument is actually borrowed from socialist theorists who long employed it to justify more open and comprehensive nationalization and centralized planning.

This argument has been historically disproved by the fall of communism and central planning systems everywhere in recent years. Not only were such nations tyrannical and murderous, but none even achieved the promised economic and social efficiency. This accords with a purely theoretical response to the interventionist argument: the very complexity of modern society may be precisely what makes either comprehensive central planning or detailed government regulation unfeasible. What such complexity actually requires is the *dispersed* decision making, personal adjustments and coordination that characterizes, and occurs through, the voluntary actions and interactions of free individuals in decentralized markets.[6]

Even if it were true, as seems highly dubious, that in order for our complex, modern society to operate efficiently Congress must delegate extensive legislative authority to executive agencies so that they may supply necessary regulation, there would be dangers. The courts have sometimes recognized this. Consider, for example, what a Minnesota court said in the case of *Juster Brothers vs. Christgau*.[7]

> The tendency to sacrifice established principles of government in order to secure centralized control and efficiency in administration may easily be carried so far as to endanger the very foundations upon which our system of government rests.

Indeed, in a dissenting opinion in another case, *Securities and Exchange Commission vs. Chenery Corporation* (1947), Judge Jackson argued that administrative law embraces elements considered hostile to the common or traditional law and subversive of the rule of law. For some time, as regulatory law expanded at the expense of common law, this view was echoed in other court decisions, and was only gradually suppressed.

The Decline of Democracy

The simple truth is that regulators both pass and enforce laws, in violation of the Constitutional separation of powers, and that they do so though they are appointed, not elected, in violation of the most basic principles of representative democracy. The sheer volume of such undemocratic legislation is astonishing. In the 1990s new regulations printed in the Federal Register have regularly exceeded 60,000 pages per year.[8] That does not entirely constitute an addition to the total, since some regulations simply alter prior regulations, but the same is true of statutory law, probably in about the same proportions. 60,000 pages of regulations equals a large fraction of the annual statutory output of Congress. The relative magnitude of the two may be argued to roughly indicate the degree to which America is no longer a democratic nation, much less a Constitutionally limited republic.

That regulators legislate, in most cases, only within parameters set by Congressional enabling legislation may be true, but as even the courts have recognized, the law would have no meaning without those administratively determined specifics. Consider this statement from the case of *Commission vs. Anheuser-Bush.* [9]

> The administrative agency may be given the power to "fill in the details," but the details are of the essence; they give meaning and content to vague contours.

One anticipates the response that that regulatory legislation involves no loss of democratic control since it depends for its authorization on, and has limitations set by, enabling legislation, and is also subjected to ongoing Congressional supervision through oversight committees. Indeed, two economists, Barry Weingast and Mark Moran, studying the Federal Trade Commission, found evidence that the FTC catered strongly in its policy actions to the preferences of the members of the relevant Congressional oversight committees. Among other things, they concluded that the grant of legislative authority to the FTC involved no loss of democratic control.[10]

Other empirical data contradicts this claim, however. While the members of most of the state public utility commissions that fix prices and specify allowable rates for return for their franchised electricity and natural gas monopolies are appointed, some states elect the members of such commissions. Using data for 1967 and 1980 Mark Crain and Robert McCormick found that, on average, prices and rates of return were lower, both for electricity and natural gas, in those states that elected their commissions.[11] Clearly, franchising legislative power to appointed boards and commissions *does* insulate them to some degree from democratic control by the *public*.

It is not obvious from a congruence of Congressional preferences and agency policies that there is much correlation between the preferences of the *public* and those of the agency administrators. Nor is it even obvious from such a congruence that the former uniquely determined the latter. One of the most important observations about the growth of bureaucracy and regulatory agencies, is that the members of those organizations have themselves become highly organized, powerful and effective legislative lobbyists. They vote in larger proportions than the general public, contribute large amounts of money to the Campaign funds of sympathetic Congressional candidates, engage in organized testimony on all legislation affecting their agencies, and have expertise on regulatory issues far superior to the members of the oversight committees.

For all these and other reasons, the preferences of the regulators generally carry far more weight with legislators on issues relating to agency policies than do those of the disorganized and rationally ignorant general public.[12] I have never seen, for example, a piece of legislation dealing with monetary or banking policy that was opposed by the Federal Reserve make it through the House or Senate Banking committees. Indeed, legislation affecting the powers and budgets of agencies, such as the misnamed Depository Institutions Deregulation and Monetary Control Act of 1980 (which was actually designed to increase the power of the Federal Reserve) is often largely or partly initiated and written by personnel in the agencies themselves, then submitted through sympathetic members of Congress. The preferences of agency administrators are, of course, clear: virtually any legislation that increases their budgets and power to regulate people's lives is in their interest.

Where then is the linear democratic control that allegedly runs from the public to legislators to regulatory agencies? Can one honestly deny that when majorities of Congress, with Presidential consent, franchised their legislative authority to unelected executive branch officials they not only engaged in tacit collusion to circumvent the Constitutional separation of powers, but deliberately generated an essentially undemocratic, if not *anti-democratic* mechanism of social and economic control? Who can really deny that regulatory law is a command and control legal mechanism that is essentially incompatible with a democratic system, and that its substitution over time for other social control mechanisms has seriously expanded the rule of men and diminished the rule of law?

Notes

1 John Locke, *Of Civil Government, Second Treatise* (1689) (Henry Regnery, 1955). The term 'classical liberalism' is employed here to distinguish the original, libertarian-individualist philosophy of Locke, Hume, the Mills, and the American Founders from the modern left-wing interventionist ideology that is nowadays popularly associated with the term 'liberal'. Long in hiatus, classical liberalism is now rapidly being revived, as discussed in the final chapter of this book.

2 The concept is certainly capable of much abuse. Many goods that can in

fact be supplied efficiently by private firms *if the property rights over the necessary resources are established and protected by law* are falsely claimed to be public goods requiring government ownership, provision, regulation, or subsidization.

3 Political competition, though it has benefits, is less effective than business competition because it is intermittent, while consumer substitution in the market is continuous, thus providing continuous discipline. The intermittent competition may be more appropriate in the political sphere, however, since it insulates politicians from immediate popular passions and prejudices, allowing a necessary calm consideration and analysis into the legislative process, as the founders intended.

4 *American Jurisprudence, Second Edition: Administrative Law* (The Lawyers Co-operative Publishing Company, 1962): 806. Hereafter cited as Am. Jur. 2d.

5 *Am. Jur. 2d*: 897-898.

6 See F. A. Hayek, "Economics and Knowledge," and also his "The Use of Knowledge in Society," both in F. A. Hayek, *Individualism and Economic Order* (University of Chicago Press, 1948).

7 214 Minn 108

8 Cesar Conda, "The Regulatory Tide: High and Rising," *Issue Brief* (Institute for Policy Information: September 1994).

9 181 VA 678.

10 Barry R. Weingast and Mark J. Moran, "Bureaucratic Discretion or Congressional Control? Regulatory Policymaking by the Federal Trade Commission," *Journal of Political Economy* 91 (October 1983): 765-800.

11 See W. M. Crain and R. E. McCormick, "Regulators as an Interest Group," in James M. Buchanan and Robert D. Tollison, *The Theory of Public Choice* (University of Michigan Press, 1984): 323-337.

12 The phrase "rational ignorance" refers to the small incentive most members of the general public have to inform themselves about legislative policies that have dispersed costs, such that they each hurt a particular person only a little, even though the cumulative impact of many such programs may be to harm each such person a great deal.

Chapter 3

Command, Control, and Confiscation

Regulation is a distinct mechanism of social control, which differs significantly from more traditional mechanisms. The previous chapter identified two of its distinctive features: its anti-democratic character as a form of law, and its combination of legislative, executive and judicial functions in the same agencies, in violation of the constitutional separation of powers. Certain other important and defining features of regulation require identification and evaluation by constitutional and other legal standards. First, regulation involves a command and control enforcement mechanism with particular features. Second, agency methods of adjudication of accused violators of regulatory rules contrast with judicial methods. And third, regulation normally takes private property, at least partly. All of these characteristics of the regulatory mechanism have important implications for a free society.

Regulatory Command and Control

Courts concerned either with maintaining the constitutional separation of powers or with rationalizing and justifying the lack of such separation in regulatory agencies, have wrestled intellectually with the distinctions between legislative and judicial functions. Analytically, they have epitomized the former as being prospective and general, in that it sets general rules for future action. The judicial function, in contrast, is retrospective and particular, dealing as it does with specific alleged past violations. As a form of legislation (apart from tax laws), regulation is distinct in applying force against persons to forbid or mandate specific actions *without showing either that those persons have (or would have) harmed anyone by the forbidden actions, or benefited anyone by the mandated actions.* This is the command element of regulation.

A second distinct feature of regulation is its focus on the *present,* and concerns what occurs in between the promulgation of rules and adjudication of alleged violations. This consists, ideally (in the minds of its advocates) in continuous monitoring and supervision of the regulated population. Quintessential examples might be EPA devices emplaced to continuously monitor air quality in urban locations, or emissions from plants in regulated industries. This, in combination with the adjudication methods to be discussed in the next section, is the control element of regulation. Inadequate resources prevent such continuous monitoring in many cases (resulting in random inspection as a best approximation), as the agencies repeatedly complain when they ask for increased budgets. This, however, does not deny continuous supervision as the essential ideal of regulation. The very complaint confirms it. Indeed, much of what we mean by the phrase "to regulate," is not just to specify rules, but to continuously (or, at random and unpredictable intervals) monitor the behavior of target populations in order, by threat of immediate knowledge of and sanctions to be applied to deviations, to make it conform to forms specified in the promulgated regulations.

In regard to the command element of regulation identified above, a key feature of regulatory law is how frequently, in contrast to actions of the civil and criminal courts, charges against regulated persons or corporations arise from the agencies themselves, and make no claim that particular persons have been harmed.[1] In the justice system, violations are determined *ex-post* (that is, after the fact), following a demonstration of harm to specific persons. That demonstration occurs through a process of adjudication employing strict rules of evidence. In addition, the accused is presumed innocent until proven guilty. Such *ex-post* accusation, adjudication and, if guilt is determined, penalization, not only establishes justice in the particular case, but through demonstration of the consequences, provides *ex-ante* (that is, before the fact) inhibition to other individuals who might be inclined toward violating the rights of others. This whole process is a consistent expression of the classical liberal principle that, whenever possible, government should apply force against persons only in defense of the rights of others (as violators are caught in the act) or in retaliation for violations of such rights. It emerged from centuries of struggle against tyranny and was part and parcel of the establishment of the rule of law.

Regulation, in contrast, is applied *ex-ante.* It applies coercion and penalizes people up front, pressuring them through the process of continuous (or random intermittent) supervision and inspection to act in ways specified by the regulators, denying them actions and uses of their property they would otherwise choose. There is, in this process, no prior demonstration of harm to specific persons resulting from violations of the regulation. What *person* was ever *shown*, for example, by rigorous standards of evidence, to have been harmed by Alar, or Dioxin, or DDT, through the normal, pre-regulation use of these substances? What *demonstrations* of harm to specific persons justified the penalization, by lost income and freedom, of the sellers and users of those and similar substances as a result of the regulatory prohibition of their use? The answer in all of these cases is none.

Of course it is precisely one of the basic arguments for some forms of regulation, that there exists a class of human actions that can be proven by strong scientific evidence to cause harm to others, but where the harm is general, or diffused among other factors, such that the connection between those actions and specific harms to specific individuals cannot be demonstrated by rigorous court rules of evidence. Since, in such cases, court actions would seldom be brought by those harmed, or if brought, would seldom be settled in their favor, it is argued that criminal and tort actions cannot handle this class of evils, and regulation is necessary. Thus the commands, thus the continuous or random intermittent supervision, and thus the substitution of administrative charges of violations for those of private individuals.

All of the examples just cited were chosen to illustrate this asserted class of cases. They are all substances which, it is claimed, can be shown to generate some *statistical* risk of harm to others, such that in some known frequency real individuals will be hurt through their normal, unregulated use. Or, they may harm some element of nature, again in a frequency that does not allow proof in individual cases, and in any case nature has no standing to sue. Infectious diseases also fall into this class. Thus, it is argued, regulation is necessary in order to control, limit or terminate the use of such substances, or control such diseases, and protect and improve the health and well being of the public.

This argument is persuasive on its logic, and constitutes one of the more important rationales for regulation. A few observations are in order, however. First, a huge fraction of current federal, state and local regulatory practices do *not* deal with such cases, and the argument fails to justify them. Second, with regard to most such substances, the evidence establishing their statistical incidence of harm is, contrary to the claim, actually very weak. In addition, it is often developed by the agencies themselves, who have strong incentives to inflate risk estimates precisely to justify regulation.[2] Third, the history of tort law does *not* support the view that it is incapable of handling pollution issues. Last, we would be justified in collectively deciding that a condition in which a substance is so diffused among other environmental factors, and its effect so weak, that its origin and decisive effect in generating harm in particular instances cannot be proven by strict rules of evidence, is precisely the criterion that should preclude the law from coming into play at all.[3]

The most persuasive case in this class is that of communicable disease. It may arguably be too difficult to prove contagion by a specific person to provide *ex-post* penalization through, say, civil or criminal law, such that sufficient *ex-ante* incentive would be provided for universal inoculations. That is, a law making it a civil, or even criminal offense to infect another person with a disease for which an effective vaccine exists, passed with intent to motivate people to obtain inoculations, might not work. Many people might gamble on the chance that they would not get the disease, and therefore not infect others (or that the state would not be able to prove who did it), in order to avoid the expense of inoculation. Hence a law directly requiring such inoculations might be justified. Such a law would be regulatory, since it would directly force people to act in a certain way before they had been shown to hurt anybody.

On the other hand, why should more people comply with a regulation than would comply to avoid possible *ex-post* criminal or civil legal penalization? It would seem obvious *a priori* that criminal or civil penalties could be set at levels sufficient to motivate a large measure of compliance, again reducing the problem of determining vectors so that actual violations could be dealt with by the normal court mechanism. This seems particularly likely given that people naturally wish to avoid illness anyhow, and that the technology of vaccine production and distribution normally keeps prices quite low. Such a method would have the advantage of supplying the necessary public good through a legal mechanism much more in accord with the classical liberal principle that, where possible, even governmental force should be applied only in self-defense or retaliation, as necessary to protect the rights of individuals and punish violations by other individuals *ex-post*. On this reasoning, even the case of contagious disease is not persuasive in justifying regulation.

The Return of the Royal Courts

Accused violators of agency rules are tried in agency tribunals, which exercise judicial or quasi-judicial powers though they are not part of the judiciary. Actually, Congress could well have established them as judicial bodies, since, unlike the franchising of its legislative power, it has clear constitutional authority for creating lesser courts. Its unwillingness to constitute the agencies that way, however, is probably due to the strict rules of evidence and judicial procedures to which they would then have been subject, and the necessity for separating judicial and executive functions. At best, going that route, Congress would have ended up with a separate tier of courts for dealing strictly with regulatory violations and disputes. Precisely to avoid this, Congressmen have acted to grant extensive judicial powers to the agencies themselves, and state legislatures have generally followed the same pattern.

Of course all human action involves decision making, or 'judgment' in the general sense of the term, but not all human judgments have the legally binding effect on others that judicial powers do. The administrative agencies have been granted many such truly judicial powers. Among others, they exercise enabling powers allowing them to permit (or deny) something the law undertakes to be done, as in business licensing or land use zoning, and dispensing powers by which exemptions from regulatory standards may be granted.[4] Where granted the legal authority, they also exercise summary powers, requiring no notice or hearing, when there is no genuine issue of material fact to be tried. This allows them decision, on their own judgment, to apply force against persons or property for specified purposes without a judicial warrant.[5]

It is certainly true that there are limits on the judicial powers exercised by agencies. State constitutions, state and federal enabling laws, and court decisions all specify and limit the judicial authority exercised by regulatory bureaucracies. It has been established that, in accordance with the Constitutional requirements of due process and equal protection of the law, a legislature must declare a policy and fix a primary standard limiting the judicial discretion of an administrative agency. But clearly, this requirement in itself places very little in the way of limits on what the legislative grant itself might be, and tells one little about how the specific powers granted may be exercised.

Administrative agencies exercise powers that may result in private individuals being deprived of life, liberty or property, and the Constitution specifies that this may not occur without due process of law. The question becomes, what does the requirement of 'due process' mean? As it turns out, the law courts have acceded to it meaning much less in administrative agencies than it does in the courts themselves. The key initial decision was precisely that, except in cases of punishment for crimes, due process does *not* mean 'judicial' process (as in the courts), but may be afforded as well by administrative processes.[6] Basically, according to the courts, it simply requires prior notice and an orderly hearing before an administrative tribunal in which the facts are tried, and the opportunity to be heard and defend oneself, and be represented by council, is afforded. The agencies are bound by their own rules of procedure in such tribunals, but are often granted statutory authority to set those rules themselves.

Before a hearing in an administrative tribunal occurs, there must be an investigation by the agency. In the justice system, as required by the fourth amendment, a warrant to search for evidence of a crime can only be issued by a judge on the presentation, by the police, of probable cause (good reason, or evidence) to believe that evidence of a violation exists at the place to be searched. In administrative investigations, however, the agency itself normally has statutory power to issue its own warrants allowing search for evidence. It is also important to note that a court may not normally summon evidence not shown to be relevant to issues in litigation. Unlike the law courts, an agency charged with administration can initiate such an investigation.

The most common form of search in business regulation is agency inspection (for sanitation, safety, emissions, etc.), which may actually take the place of hearings. For some time inspections were assumed to be totally exempt from search warrant requirements. This view was qualified in two 1967 cases, *Camara vs. Municipal Court*, and *See vs. Seattle*, where the Supreme Court held that fourth amendment protections should *not* apply *only* to persons suspected of crimes, but also to privacy interests. The court then proceeded, however, to reduce the legal standard for the issuance of administrative warrants even in cases of potential criminal violations, so that *probable cause was not required.* Instead, they can be issued whenever "reasonable legislative standards for conducting an area inspection exist."[7]

What is more, these cases did not alter the longstanding presumption that warrants were not required for inspections of businesses subject to licensing requirements where the grant of a license was dependent on consent to warrantless searches. Likewise, in *Colonnade Catering Corporation vs. United States* (1970) and *United States v. Biswell* (1972) the court confirmed that regulatory agencies can conduct warrantless searches in intensively regulated industries subject to licensing. Since then, even the state licensing justification seems to have been dispensed with. In *Donovan vs. Dewey* (1981) the court in essence said that, in the presence of a comprehensive and defined regulatory scheme for an industry, so that the firms are aware of the requirement for inspections, the fourth amendment is null and void as far as requiring a warrant before search. In other words, in the view of the court that is supposed to *protect* people's constitutional rights from violation *by* government, Congress is free to void the fourth amendment whenever it wishes by simply passing a law mandating detailed regulation in an industry.

An agency may also have statutory power to issue its own subpoenas, *without any requirement of probable cause*, to compel persons to attend and testify before an investigating body or tribunal. The reasoning of the court in *Oklahoma Press vs. Walling* (1946) is instructive of the judicial philosophy relating to administrative law. The court distinguished between what it termed "actual" searches used in criminal law cases, and "figurative" or "constructive" searches in which an agency demands a regulated firm's records. The implication was that probable cause should rule in "actual" searches but not in mere "constructive" ones. No such distinction is valid, however. A search is a search. Private firm's records obtained in administrative searches can be used in evidence of civil and criminal violations. Fifth amendment protection against self-incrimination applies no less here than in police searches, and the fourth amendment should apply also.

In defense of the court's weak distinction between police and administrative searches, it has been argued that the only evidence of violations of the law might be in the records of the regulated companies. So a strict probable cause requirement could make enforcement impossible.[8] This is an incredible claim. Regulations are supposed to prohibit socially harmful actions and/or mandate socially beneficial behaviors.

To admit that harmful effects are unobservable following violation of a regulation is essentially to admit the inconsequential character of the mandated/prohibited behavior and damn the very existence of such regulations. On this kind of view, however, the constitutional rights of regulated businessmen against unreasonable search and seizure have been systematically denied.[9]

As for the structure and procedures of administrative tribunals, it is important to remember several things about the structure and operation of the law courts for comparison. In the justice system, those accused of serious violations of the law have an initial option of trial by a jury of their peers. The jurors, selected from a pool of private citizens, have no bias in favor of the case of the state. A prosecutor employed by the state attempts, by presenting evidence and testimony of witnesses, to convince the jury of the guilt of the accused. A private defense council tries by the same methods to convince them of the innocence of the accused. The judge, like the prosecutor, is an employee of the state, but of a *different branch*. He or she is not employed by the police, and has the specific function of acting as a neutral arbiter and interpreter of the law, unless the defendant chooses a bench trial. In that case the judge adds the function of the jury in determining, on the evidence, the guilt or innocence of the accused. The whole process works on strict rules of evidence in which there is an initial presumption of innocence, such that guilt must be established by a preponderance of evidence, and in the most serious cases, beyond a reasonable doubt.

To say the least, things are different in administrative law tribunals. In the first place, as regulation expanded, the law courts realized that the vesting of adjudicatory powers in administrative agencies by legislatures could not be construed to deny the constitutional protection of trial by jury. Determined to allow administrative tribunals to operate without such restriction, their solution was to assert that neither the federal or state constitutions guarantee this right except in cases where it already existed when they were adopted. In this interpretation, the constitutional guarantee does not apply to special or summary administrative proceedings created by law subsequent to the adoption of those constitutions.[10] The bottom line is that those accused of violating regulations, even where such violations carry heavy penalties, will look in vain for trial by a jury of their peers in administrative law tribunals.

In such tribunals defense council is allowed, and administrative officials conduct the agency case. witnesses, pro and con, present testimony. Unlike trial courts, however, in administrative law courts the accused are seldom allowed formal pretrial discovery of the prosecution case against them. The place of the trial court judge in administrative tribunals is normally taken by an administrative law judge (previously called a trial examiner) who presides over the hearing and takes the testimony. The administrative law judge, however, is generally appointed *by and for the agency itself*, and the judge's report is normally *not* determinative. It is similar to an auditor's report to a superior, or set of superiors in the agency, who are legally charged with making the final decision. That decision may or may not conform to the recommendation in the administrative law judge's report.[11]

The administrative tribunal is not bound, in its deliberations and determination of guilt or innocence of the accused, by the strict rules of evidence of jury trials. Indeed, as already mentioned, they promulgate their own procedural rules, subject to statutory limits, which can be very wide. Administrative law courts have great leeway in the types of evidence that can be admitted. Indeed, cases often center on opinion or hearsay evidence that would be excluded from trial courts. Legally, it is true, the agency propounding a rule has the burden of proof, and the legal mandate is that a determination of guilt requires a preponderance of evidence. However, proof beyond a reasonable doubt is *not* required.[12] The more fundamental point, however, is that nothing in the operation and structure of these tribunals acts to guarantee that a finding of guilt will actually be made on the mandated standard at all.

In addition, there is no right to appeal unless the enabling statute so provides, hence, in the absence of such provision there is no right of judicial review of the action of an administrative agency. In fact, Congress often deliberately includes clauses in enabling laws precluding judicial (court) review of agency decisions. Even where judicial review is present it is often limited by statute to reviewing the legality of the proceeding, and may not judge the facts of the case. Fortunately, fearing to yield all of their authority over such matters to the agencies, the courts have sometimes, reluctantly, held that review may be made even if no statutory provision is made for such review, and in some cases even when review is statutorily denied.[13]

In all of this it is clear that strenuous effort has been made, by Congress, state legislatures, and the courts, to give administrative adjudicatory procedures the appearance of fairness and due process protection of rights, without the substance. Every standard of evidence and procedure employed by the administrative tribunals is lower than those employed in the justice system. Is it any accident that the accused are found innocent with enormously less frequency in administrative tribunals than in the law courts? The same agency writes the law, investigates and accuses suspected violators, and then acts as prosecutor, judge and jury simultaneously. The similarity of all this to star chamber proceedings is not accidental. It is literally a regression to medieval, monarchist legal practices. Indeed, the entire command and control regulatory process, in which people are penalized up front with no prior demonstration that their actions generate harm to other persons. Search for evidence occurs without judicial warrant issued on probable cause, and basic judicial procedures and protections of the accused are absent or attenuated. It is inherently inimical to civilized standards of law and principles of a free society.

Regulatory Takings of Property

Governmental operations are costly, and can only be undertaken if governments can obtain the necessary resources. Even a government constituted in close approximation to the classical liberal, individualist libertarian theory, elaborated in Chapter 2, such as the U.S. government, must obtain resources to perform its proper function of protecting rights. The same is true for all of the constituent governmental units in the federal system. In accordance with the public goods problem, the acquisition of resources is not likely to be entirely voluntary on the part of all parties yielding such resources to government, even where those resources are used properly to the benefit of all citizens. That is, the resources will have to be taken.

The probability (nay, certainty) exists that even in such a government, positions of authority will frequently be occupied by persons intent on using governmental power to oppress segments of the public to their own advantage. This often involves efforts, through statute or regulation, to redistribute incomes from the general public to themselves, or from some segments of the public to others in return for monetary or political payoffs. It matters not if such activities are rationalized (as they normally are) by an ideology justifying such redistributions, in order, say, to help a 'disadvantaged' group. It also matters not whether a significant fraction of the exponents of the ideology believe it.   Constitutional protections against such activities are necessary to insure the proper public use of resources governmentally taken, and were deliberately included in the document. One such constitutional protection already briefly mentioned is the takings clause of the 5th Amendment.

The takings clause says quite simply that *private property shall not be taken for public use without just compensation* [to the owners]. The clause thereby provides explicit grant of authority for governments at all levels to obtain the resources necessary for proper public purposes, while protecting private property by requiring that owners be compensated for private resources taken. Compensation can come in various forms, as legal scholar Richard Epstein has explained, but basically, the parties yielding such resources must either benefit proportionately from any public good provided or be explicitly monetarily compensated to the full value of the resources taken. *Purely redistributive governmental activities benefiting some at the expense of others are constitutionally precluded on any common sense reading of the clause.*

Private ownership involves a bundle of rights including such things as the possession, use and disposition of the assets owned. Each of these qualities or aspects of ownership is further divisible. Regarding disposition, for example, one may sell the surface area of land one owns yet contractually retain the mineral rights. The variety of governmental actions is likewise such that particular persons may find their property diminished, totally or partially, to a greater or lesser degree in one or more of these dimensions. The market value of such property will decline as a result. The question then becomes one of when the takings clause becomes applicable. The clause itself is unambiguous, however. It simply makes no qualification for small degrees of takings. Indeed, the most straightforward and reasonable interpretation of the phrase "just compensation" is compensation to the full value of the taking, however partial and *whatever* its degree. As Richard Epstein puts it, when the clause says that private property shall not be taken for public use without just compensation, it means private property shall not be taken, *in whole or in part*, for public use, without just compensation.[14]

Government actions may take the property of single persons or of relatively small groups, as when property is taken from those along the route of a highway to be constructed or enlarged. But they may also diminish the property, or the value of the property, held by large groups, through such processes as taxation, regulation, or modifications of liability rules. The courts have made strenuous efforts, stemming seminally from the decision of Justice Holmes in *Pennsylvania Coal Co. vs. Mahori* (1922), to distinguish individual and small group takings from large group takings, in order to remove the latter from the domain of the takings clause, leaving only the smaller classes to be compensable by the state. But there is no legitimate distinction. The inclusiveness of the takings clause has been made clear by Epstein:

> The modern effort to distance the taking clause from general laws cannot be maintained. All regulations, all taxes, and all modifications of liability rules are takings prima facie compensable by the state.[15] [Emphasis in original]

It should be noticed that the takings clause states two requirements to be satisfied in justification of governmental takings. Not only is just compensation required, but the taking can be only 'for public use.' Since the clause would make sense without those three words, their inclusion must have been deliberate. It must have been an attempt to *exclude* some class of takings. In the light of classical liberal political theory, the public use criterion has essentially the same meaning that I gave in Chapter 2 to the general welfare clause limiting Congressional legislative discretion. In this case it restricts the government, federal, state, or local, to coercively acquiring and employing resources only for the provision of genuine public goods, which by their nature would not be provided (or not in adequate amounts) by the private market, and from the governmental provision of which *everyone* benefits in at least rough proportion. This excludes governmental takings for purely private uses, that, while they benefit those private parties to which the resources are directed, either reduce overall well being or leave it unchanged.[16]

One implication of governments, federal, state, or local, being restricted to takings of private assets only for provision of genuine public goods is that, since community well being is improved, often literally in terms of increased aggregate output and real income, those from whom the necessary resources were taken are *already compensated*. The remaining question is whether this implicit, in-kind compensation constitutes *adequate* compensation. Clearly, if the members of the community all yielded resources, and received benefits in relative proportion to their resources yielded and of equal or greater magnitude, explicit pecuniary compensation for the takings would be neither necessary nor justified. Neither would it be necessitated if only a subset of the community bore all or a majority of the cost of the public good, but received an equivalent share of the benefits, as with user fees.

Explicit compensation is necessitated when the resources obtained for public use are taken from a subset of the public, which may share in the benefits proportionately, but bears a disproportionately large share of the cost. In such a case the implicit, in-kind benefits received by those yielding the assets do not provide adequate compensation for the costs they bore. Examples would include such things as the taking by the state of land from a single owner on which to build a prison, or the taking of land from those along a right of way for a highway that benefits the general public. Explicit compensation would also be required under a proper interpretation of the takings clause if the benefits generated by a governmental taking go primarily to others than those yielding the assets. This would be true even if some particular form of redistributive scheme managed, unlike nearly all actual redistributive schemes, to increase, rather than decrease, the size of the social pie.

Regulations are invariably takings, sometimes total but more usually partial, acting to diminish to some degree the rights of the affected parties to control their private assets. Epstein thinks some forms of regulation actually are focused on the provision of public goods, satisfying the public use requirement of the takings clause. They may even provide adequate implicit, in-kind compensation, in his opinion, so that explicit compensation is not required. One example he gives concerns a city ordinance limiting the size, shape and color of business advertising signs. There is a public good provided, according to Epstein, because everyone benefits from the improvement in scenery. The benefit would not be obtained, absent regulation, because each party has a personal incentive to employ a larger, more garish and imposing sign. A private agreement to limit signs cannot be reached due to multi-party negotiating costs and holdout incentives. Epstein also thinks some other forms of regulation are socially beneficial, including railroad regulation, public utility regulation, and the anti-trust laws.[17]

Qualifications and objections can be made to Epstein's argument here. In his sign example, everyone benefits from the scenery provided, but many are simply consumers, not potential advertisers. Applying the regulation to the latter group involves a disproportionate impact, requiring compensation. Also, Epstein is a classical liberal himself, who accepts the notion that governments should, were possible, apply force only in defense of rights or retaliation for violation of rights. As such, he too, easily accepts, on public goods arguments, regulatory solutions that apply force to a person or group, up front, before any demonstration of harm by their specific actions to specific other persons has been made. Many public goods can be governmentally provided by methods consistent with the classical liberal principle. Indeed, the market itself might provide solutions, so that no genuine public good is at issue. One might well suspect that obnoxious signs, depriving people of pleasant views, might *cost* those advertisers customers, thus limiting the use of such signs. It is not obvious that government officials know the optimal size or frequency of advertising signs.

In addition, Epstein's narrow focus on the takings clause prevents consideration of other constitutional problems with the present regulatory process. Satisfaction of eminent domain requirements does not justify the breakdown of the constitutional separation of powers through inclusion of legislative and judicial functions in executive agencies, nor the decay of due process in administrative tribunals. Zoning ordinances, assuming they really are necessary, could be written by elected city councils, rather than unelected zoning boards, and the Federal Trade Commission does not need to have its own courts.

Epstein recognizes, however, that most regulation fails an eminent domain test. Unemployment compensation is a difficult case, he points out, since it is financed by a tax on the workers who are eligible for its benefits, but its impact is disproportionate (since workers actually benefiting are a subset) and it alters employment incentives in ways that reduce, rather than enlarge, the size of the social pie. Oddly, he argues that generalized price controls might meet the constitutional test, even though the rigidities they introduce would reduce aggregate output and income, on the basis that–in peacetime–such generalized harm would result in universal demand for their repeal.[18] Selective price and/or wage controls would require explicit compensation because of their disproportionate impact, however. Such a requirement would surely dissuade the government from their use. It goes without saying that such programs have been employed only because the courts have *not* required compensation from government. Epstein correctly concludes that the great bulk of New Deal and subsequent regulatory legislation is unconstitutional by the properly understood requirements of the takings clause.

One more observation seems pertinent on the subject of regulation as a partial taking of private property. Piecemeal consideration of the character and constitutionality of regulations, such as Epstein undertakes, detracts attention from the massive expansion of regulation as a social control mechanism since the New Deal, its command and control character, and of the ideological rationale supporting that expansion. Given that private ownership consists essentially of the right to determine the use and disposition of assets owned, and that regulation incrementally transfers such authority from the private owners to government, a policy of chronically expanding regulation *is* a policy of incremental nationalization (government confiscation) of private assets.[19]

Notes:

1   Some administrative law cases, such as National Labor Relations Board disputes, charges of wrongful termination of entitlement (income transfer) payments by an agency, and many anti-trust cases, do arise that way.

2   See, for Example, Edith Efron, *The Apocalyptics: Cancer and the Big Lie* (Simon and Schuster, 1984), who has massively documented the degradation of scientific standards of evidence at the Environmental Protection Agency in its self-interested pursuit of regulation of accused carcinogenic chemicals.

3   Again, the point is well illustrated by EPA regulation of alleged carcinogens. There is, in fact, no persuasive evidence that the expanding use of industrial chemicals in America or other technological/industrial nations has added to cancer incidence or mortality, and certainly no evidence that EPA regulation of alleged carcinogens has had beneficial effects on public health For a quick review of the facts, see Joseph L. Bast, Peter J. Hill, and Richard C. Rue, *Eco-Sanity: A Common Sense Guide to Environmentalism* (Madison Books, 1994): Chapter 3.

4   Business and professional licensing by the state is not a modern, but an ancient practice, which the fledgling United States unfortunately inherited from the mercantile nations. There is no valid moral, economic, or constitutional justification for government at any level having authority to grant or withhold right for anyone to enter a legitimate business or profession. Any real problem generated by, say, an incompetent entering a profession, could be dealt with by other criminal, civil, and common law mechanisms. This regulatory practice has in fact simply functioned as a source of bribes for corrupt politicians, tax revenue from licensing fees, and as another device by which existing firms, professionals, or skilled tradesmen prevent entry and restrict competition in order to raise their own incomes.

5   See Ernest Gellhorn and Ronald M. Levin, Administrative Law and Process In a Nutshell (West Publishing Co., 1990): 300-303.

6 See, for example, *Barsky vs. Board of Regents of University of New York,* 347 U.S. 442.

7 Gellhorn and Levin, *Administrative Law and Process:* 143-147.

8 Ibid., p. 133.

9 The ultimate source of all different constitutional treatment of business corporations and persons is the artificial assumption that corporations are legal entities separate and distinct from the persons that own and operate them. This fiction is also why corporations are taxed separately. But it is, however, just a legal fiction. Just as corporate taxes fall upon actual persons, so that their owners, who supply the capital on which all corporate net revenue is earned, are in fact unjustly taxed twice (both before and after distribution of corporate net revenue), searches and subpoenas of corporate records issued or undertaken without probable cause violate the rights of very real individuals.

10 See, for example, *National Labor Relations Board vs. Jones and Laughlin Steel Corporation,* 301 U.S. 1, and Crowel vs. Benson, 285 U.S. 222.

11 See section 557b of the Administrative Procedures Act (1946).

12 Gellhorn and Levin, *Administrative Law and Process:* 264-270.

13 For example, *Johnson vs. Robinson,* 415 U.S. 361 (1974).

14 Epstein, *Takings:* 58. One might argue on utilitarian cost-benefit terms that governmental takings of small value should not require compensation for the simple reason that the cost to the government of establishing the correct value of the compensation will be excessive. But that is simply a reason for government not to indulge in small takings.

15 Epstein, *Takings:* 95.

16 Epstein argues that it even excludes cases where the social surplus is enlarged, but all of the gain goes to those private parties to whom the resources taken were directed.

17 Epstein, *Takings:* Chapter 17. I find reasons for disagreeing with Epstein on all of his chosen examples. See Chapters 4 and 5 below.

18 The 1946 Congressional elections provide a historical incident arguably supporting Epstein's point here. The public acted to massively change the composition of Congress, replacing Democrats with Republicans to a degree exceeding even that of the 1994 Republican landslide. This was done primarily with intent to gain removal of wartime price controls, which most Democratic politicians, and the regulators themselves were determined to retain. However, that very determination shows that the

desire to remove the controls was not universal. Powerful groups can gain even from comprehensive controls that hurt nearly everyone else. In conditions of public ignorance of the connection between the controls and the harm they cause, or the lack of political democracy, they may be retained for long periods of time. The extreme example of Soviet communism illustrates the point.

19 There are those who have long sensed that regulation was a near kin to nationalization the advocacy of which, in addition to the equalitarian ideal, literally defines socialist ideology. They have been laughed at by many advocates of regulation who have sincerely (but incorrectly) claimed not to be socialists. In fact, those sensing the similarity of regulation and socialism were more right than they knew.

Chapter 4

Progressive Era Regulation

Having digressed for two chapters to examine the legal, constitutional and institutional character of regulation and regulatory agencies, it is important to return to the historical story that began in Chapter 1. That chapter ended with discussion of a series of post Civil-War Supreme Court decisions that expanded state and federal regulatory authority. But it was not just the attitudes of the judiciary that changed after the Civil War. Attitudes in Congress and among the general public also changed. The structure of the economy was being transformed as manufacturing and industry grew and technologies advanced. Real incomes rose rapidly, but the accelerating change disadvantaged some persons. Political pressure groups emerged, particularly in the rural midwest. Government schools displaced private education, increasing government influence over public attitudes, and government regulation of business began in earnest.

Robber Barons and Regulation

In the massive industrialization that characterized the American economy in the post-Civil War period, one of the most conspicuous events was the growth of successful firms in nearly every field of industry to sizes and scales of operation never before seen, and seldom imagined. A key element of this phenomenon was that certain firms grew *relative* to their markets, even though the markets themselves were growing, both from the demand sides, as the population and incomes expanded, and from the supply sides, as new firms were created and grew. In the process these efficient firms absorbed or displaced many less successful competitors. The result was that many industries were dominated by a few large firms, though *there nearly always remained a large number of smaller competing firms*. This typical industry structure partly expressed and reflected the existence of economies of scale and scope to the new manufacturing technologies. However it mostly reflected the natural distribution of entrepreneurial ability and managerial talent among businessmen, such that some few in each industry were better than the rest at raising productive efficiency, reducing costs, producing newer or better and lower priced products, and hence in satisfying customers.[1]

Subsequent history might have been rather different had not the next step occurred. For various reasons, partly to avoid confiscatory tax laws and partly from belief by the businessmen that efficiency came from size, rather than vice-versa, the larger firms in many industries began merging into extremely huge firms. In 1880 Rockefeller amalgamated numerous firms it owned into the Standard Oil Trust. In 1890 J. B. Duke merged with other giants of the cigarette industry to form the American Tobacco Company. In 1901 Carnegie Steel merged with eight other steel producers–some themselves the products of prior mergers–to form U.S. Steel, the first billion dollar holding company in the world. In some other industries the largest firms did not formally amalgamate, but attempted to collude to control prices and outputs.

There is little doubt that even before the appearance of the trusts genuine public concern over the power of large business enterprises was emerging, or that the trusts magnified that concern. The size and scale of such private businesses amazed nearly everyone, pleased and excited some by their possibilities, and frightened others. Concern grew that, rather than constituting an expression of successful competition, such large firms represented the appearance of monopolistic domination of the American economy. Various factors acted to inflame and propagate this concern. Some of it came from bitter, less competent competitors within each industry, some from persons in older industries being displaced by newer ones in the dynamic economy. Another source was the relative diminishment of agriculture and disaffection of agricultural interests as the service and manufacturing sectors expanded as a fraction of the economy, and employed an expanding proportion of the labor force.

Socialist ideologies prevalent in the old world that were hostile to classical liberal political and economic institutions had also begun being imported to the U.S. in this period. Many of the adherents of this view became public school teachers or college professors. Combining with the indigenous concern generated by mass industrialization the two views merged into the beginnings of a domestic interventionist ideology since termed progressivism. That ideology was spread among the public and intellectual classes, including the judiciary, resulting in the altered constitutional interpretations of state and federal regulatory authority discussed in Chapters 1 and 2. Subsequently, it was translated into legislative action, much of which took the form of industry regulation.

The period of progressive legislation roughly constitutes the last quarter of the 19th and first quarter of the 20th centuries. It saw the appearance of the anti-trust laws, Interstate Commerce Commission railroad regulation, central banking, public utility regulation of electricity suppliers, professional licensing and entry regulation for medical doctors, and dozens of similar interventions, regulations and restrictions. *Each was justified by its intellectual supporters and political advocates as necessary to correct and control abuses of business in the interests of the general public, and as constituting a governmental response to democratic pressures by that public.* This view of the nature and source of such legislation is now known as the *public interest* theory. For decades, historians, social scientists and intellectuals accepted it uncritically and passed it to the public as the official interpretation.

The progressive period was followed by the Great Depression, which resulted in an even more massive expansion of government regulation, intervention and control, yielding the modern regulatory welfare state. One last huge burst of regulation, this time focused on the environment, health and safety, followed the Kennedy assassination and election of Lyndon Johnson in 1964. By that time, however, accumulating historical and empirical evidence on the nature, origin and effects of regulation had begun to generate second thoughts in certain academic circles.

Regulation and the Private Interests

As early as the 1930s and 1940s certain scholars in the fields of history and political science began to have doubts about the universal validity of the public interest explanation of progressive legislation, and public policy more generally.[2] An influential school of 'political realism' appeared among political scientists that traced public policy to the political action of powerful and organized interest groups. Political realists argued that the claims of general public benefit always used to justify government policies were often, if not normally, cloaks for the self-interests of organized groups that those policies were actually aimed at benefiting. However the influence of this school of thought was limited.

A more enduring shock to academic thinking on the sources of public policy came in 1963 when an influential socialist historian named Gabriel Kolko wrote two books re-examining the economic and legislative history of the progressive period. Kolko found extensive evidence for two propositions. First, examining industry after industry, such as the steel, oil, automobile, telephone and meat packing industries, Kolko found that efforts by the dominant firms and trusts to limit production, raise and stabilize prices, and prevent entry of new competitors through market methods, failed. Competitive conditions prevailed despite the best efforts of the trusts and cartels to 'rationalize' their industries.[3]

Other economists and historians have since found that, not only did competitive conditions prevail, there is little evidence that most of the trusts even tried the theorized standard monopoly practices. Dominick Armentano shows, for example, through detailed examination of the oil, steel and tobacco industries, that Standard Oil, U.S. Steel and the American Tobacco Company all had records of continually *increasing* output and *reducing* prices even after the formation of their 'trusts'. This is the exact *opposite* of the behavior predicted by standard monopoly theory, and indicates the continuing presence of competition in these industries.[4] As Yale Brozen points out, the few trusts that actually did attempt raising prices and reducing outputs, such as the American Sugar Refining Company in the early 1890s and the American Can Company after 1901, quickly lost market share to new entrants attracted into the market, which bid prices back down to competitive levels.[5]

As for the bulk of the trusts that kept struggling to lower prices and raise outputs in order to maintain or strengthen their dominant positions, the effect of the mergers, if anything, was to reduce, rather than enhance, their competitive edge. In nearly all of these industries, the market share of the trusts began declining over time relative to the combined pre-merger shares of the separate firms.[6] In each case, new and efficient firms were able to enter the market and compete successfully. For example, the Morgan interests controlling U.S. Steel alienated

Charles Schwab, who had been Carnegie's right-hand man. Schwab left and built Bethlehem Steel, a company he already owned, into a large and successful competitor.[7] Several other efficient, integrated firms entered the steel industry. U.S. Steel lost market share, and efforts to collude with such new entrants (the Garry Dinners) to stabilize price and output were unsuccessful. Technology kept evolving, output increased rapidly, and steel prices continued dropping.[8]

Standard Oil, which refined 88 percent of the crude oil in the U.S. at its high point in 1879 found its market share declining steadily thereafter. Its competition increased rapidly after 1900 as the Texas oil fields opened up, new firms entered the refining business, and demand switched from kerosene to gasoline. By 1911 there were over 140 independent refiners competing with Standard.[9] Likewise, American Tobacco's share of cigarette sales declined from over 90 percent in 1890, when the trust was formed, to 74 percent in 1907 as the cigarette market grew. Literally thousands of independent cigarette manufacturers and marketers competed with American, making it impossible for the firm to set prices above the competitive level.[10]

The clear *failure* of the trusts and cartels to control prices and outputs and prevent entry into their markets in this period led to Kolko's second hypothesis: *having failed to suppress competition through market methods, executives of the largest firms turned to the political process, and attempted to gain control of their markets through government regulation.* Kolko presented detailed evidence that, despite claims from contemporary politicians and intellectuals that regulation was aimed at protecting the general public, and despite genuine opposition from some segments of the industries to be regulated, such regulation was normally supported, and in some cases even instigated by the dominant firms.

To substantiate the point that much progressive legislation constituted a return to mercantile rent-seeking, benefiting producers and interests in the government at the *expense* of consumers and the public, contrary to the claim of the public interest explanation for such legislation, the most useful set of regulatory acts to examine is those governing the transportation industries. Before doing so, however, it may be useful to briefly examine two other important examples of political rent-seeking in the progressive period. The first concerns the passage of the Federal Reserve Act in 1913, creating the central bank that now controls the American money supply and regulates the banking system.

In Chapter 1 the story was briefly told of the creation and subsequent 1836 expiration (at the hands of President Andrew Jackson) of the Second Bank of the United States. Over the next three-quarters of a century America was probably the only major nation without a central bank. Yet in this period America became simultaneously the greatest manufacturing and industrial nation on earth, with the highest per capita income. It is beyond dispute that a central bank is *not* necessary for the creation and operation of a successful technological/industrial nation. It is true, as previously mentioned, that in that period America suffered periodic monetary and financial instability, with associated economic instability. It is also true, however, that most such instability was a consequence of federal and state interventions such as the Civil War monetary inflation, the Bland-Allison Act of 1878, the Sherman Silver Purchase Act of 1890, and state laws restricting branch banking.

In Europe, certain families of bankers, such as the Rothschild, Warburg, Baring and Lazard families, had operated for long periods of time and become very powerful, often loaning money to governments on both sides in periods of war. In the competitive environment of the United States, J. P. Morgan, John D. Rockefeller, Jr. and a few others had entered this community of wealthy financiers by the end of the 19th century, and the European families were hungrily eying the American market It appears that certain of these people decided cartelization would be preferable to competition, and that a government created central bank, similar to those long extant in Europe, would serve their interests. As pointed out in Chapter 1, central banks were the most successful late mercantile rent seeking institutions. They survived the demise of other mercantile institutions because even democratic governments found them a useful source of revenue allowing escape from the constraints of open taxation.

In 1902 Paul and Felix Warburg emigrated to the U.S., leaving their brother Max in Frankfurt to run the family bank. Both brothers became partners in the Banking firm of Kuhn-Loeb, though Paul appears to have spent most of his time traveling the country to promote central banking.[11] Paul's partner in this enterprise was U.S. Senator Nelson Aldrich, who was in the pocket of J. P. Morgan, and whose daughter Abby was the wife of John D. Rockefeller, Jr. In 1910, after the ideological groundwork had been laid, Warburg and Aldrich decided it was time for plans to be finalized. In the dead of night, and under extreme secrecy, representatives of the powerful banking families boarded trains and traveled to Georgia, where they crossed to Jekyl Island, off the coast, to meet.

The principals at the Jekyl Island meeting were Paul Warburg, Henry P. Davidson, Frank A. Vanderlip, A. Piat Andrew, and Benjamin Strong. Davidson was an executive at J. P. Morgan and Associates. Vanderlip was President of John D. Rockefeller's National City Bank. Andrew was, at the time, Assistant Secretary of the U. S. Treasury, which (along with Senator Aldrich) illustrates the early complicity of government at the highest levels with the proposed cartel. Benjamin Strong was the representative of Morgan's Banker's Trust Company. During the 1920s, as President of the New York District Federal Reserve Bank, Strong became the most powerful person in the Federal Reserve system created subsequent to the Jekyl Island meeting. The starting point was an outline brought by Warburg patterned after the European central banks. The conspirators hashed out the details, and Frank Vanderlip wrote the final version.[12] The next step was for Senator Aldrich to introduce it in Congress.

Unfortunately for these aspiring cartelizers, public and Congressional suspicion of central banks was still strong, and the Aldrich bill did not pass. The defeat appears to have been temporary, however. Only two years later, with the blessing of Woodrow Wilson, the new Democratic President, the Federal Reserve Act was introduced as a Democratic bill and passed Congress handily. Wilson became President because Theodore Roosevelt split the Republican vote by running as an independent on the Bull Moose Party. Some authors claim that Morgan money financed both Roosevelt and Wilson precisely to bring this about.[13] Careful comparison shows the Federal Reserve Act to have been identical in all of its essentials to the Aldrich bill. Frank Vanderlip himself later wrote that the Federal Reserve system had its conception at the Jekyl Island meeting.[14]

Of course one could deny any historical connection between the two events, accepting the standard view that the Federal Reserve Act emerged from the report of the National Monetary Commission created after the recession of 1907 to recommend reform of the U.S. monetary system and headed by Senator Aldrich. But there is no evidence that the commission ever called witnesses or held a meeting (unless one counts Jekyl Island). And it is certainly true that many members of the banking community genuinely opposed passage of the Federal Reserve Act. That opposition may have stemmed, however, precisely from suspicion that a political cartel was in the making, and that they (along with the public) were the intended losers.

Whether the Jekyl Island meeting resulted in the Federal Reserve or not, the meeting perfectly illustrates Kolko's hypothesis. The principals almost certainly had self-interests, not altruistic intent, in mind, believing they could both control and profit from a central Bank they created. Benjamin Strong's presence at Jekyl Island lends enormous *ex-post* credence to that hypothesis. The power and the profitability of the Fed, both to the government and to its operators, is beyond dispute. The Fed obtains revenue for its salaries, expenses and perquisites from interest it earns on government securities and other assets it purchases with base money that it creates from thin air at essentially zero cost.[15] Since it shares a large fraction of its revenue with the U.S. treasury and finances any portion of Federal deficits the government desires, it is loved by both Congress and the executive branch.

On top of this, the Fed's Federal Open Market Committee, which is dominated *by design* by banking interests (the very group the Fed is supposed to regulate), influences interest rates and controls the money stock in ways that allow obvious profit opportunities for those in that community who may be given advance notice. These are the benefits to the banking insiders from the government granted cartel. For their part, the Fed has helped finance the expansion of the federal government relative to the private sector through inflationary debt monetization and monetary expansion that has both taxed the cash balances of the public directly and *raised* corporate and personal tax rates through bracket creep and understated corporate depreciation allowances. Arguably, this not only occurred without, but precisely to avoid, public vote of members of Congress for such tax increases.[16]

A second example of Kolko's hypothesis concerns a famous event that is related in nearly all high school history, civics and American government texts as illustrating the necessity for regulatory legislation to protect the public from predatory business activities. As the story is usually told, a corrupt oligopoly of Chicago meat-packing firms, Swift, Armour and others, dominated the industry at the end of the 19th century. They treated their workers like animals, and in disregard of the public health and safety they employed horribly unsanitary slaughtering and packing processes. Along came the courageous journalist Upton Sinclair, who investigated the conditions in Chicago and exposed them in his novel *The Jungle*. An outraged public thus became aware of the danger and injustice threatening them, resulting first in federal investigations further exposing conditions in the Chicago firms, and then in passage of the Meat Inspection Act of 1906 to secure the public safety.[17]

There are some elements of truth in this story. Slaughterhouses are messy operations even now, and certainly were even more so, then. *The Jungle* did cause public outrage, and Congressional action soon followed. Various agencies of the government investigated the Chicago Meat packers, and subsequently the Federal Meat Inspection Act was passed. There is another side to the story, however. It is significant, as economic historian Lawrence Reed stresses, that *The Jungle* was a *novel*. Sinclair was a socialist ideologue whose intention from the first was to vilify the large Chicago Meat packers.[18] Despite a two year effort at infiltrating the Chicago packing firms and collecting unsubstantiated horror stories from disreputable sources, the best he could do in the way of documentation was to compile such slanderous, unproven charges into an openly fictional story.

It is also important to recognize, as Reed points out, that government meat inspection did not begin in 1906. Federal, state and local governments had been employing meat inspectors to oversee the industry for more than a decade, and none of these inspectors had complained about methods of slaughtering or meat preparation.[19] As Reed says, unless they were *all* corrupt it is hard to credit Sinclair's claims. Some support for Sinclair's view came from a 1906 report by two Washington bureaucrats, Neil and Reynolds. According to Kolko, however, Neil and Reynolds also knew little of the industry and spent less than three weeks in Chicago investigating conditions.[20] When they were questioned by the House Agriculture Committee it was discovered that they had gone to Chicago with the *intention* of digging up dirt on the industry to provide support for the Meat Inspection Act.[21] In contrast, a report compiled by the Department of Agriculture's Bureau of Animal Husbandry the same year on conditions and methods of operation in the Chicago firms found that Sinclair's main allegations were untrue.[22]

As for industry conditions, two factors are important. For one, though the industry was concentrated, it was highly competitive. The Chicago meat packers produced nearly 50 percent of the meat products in the country, but they had hundreds of smaller competitors and had no capacity to charge prices in excess of competitive levels. Any such attempt and they would have rapidly lost market share to their rivals. Second, regarding health and sanitation conditions, it was never shown that the growth of the Chicago meat packing firms had been associated with any increased risks on the part of either industry workers or consumers of meat products, because the opposite was true. The Chicago firms became large not only because they were efficient producers, but in part because they were responsible for innovations such as refrigerated packing plants and railroad cars, the canning process, and the use of chemical preservatives. All of these innovations *decreased* the health risks in the production, transport and consumption of meat products, contrary to the views of ignorant socialists such as Sinclair.

Regarding Kolko's thesis, however, one of the greatest distortions of the standard story concerns the political support for the bill. At that time, the Chicago firms were trying to break into the European meat market. They were experiencing resistance from European competitors who wanted American meat imports to be restricted by their governments. Publication of *The Jungle* followed the notorious "embalmed beef" scandal of 1898, in which it was alleged that adulterated beef had been supplied by the industry to the U.S. army. Even though these allegations–and those in *The Jungle*–were shown to be baseless, they stiffened european resistance to American meat imports and cut sales. The major American packers wanted federal inspection and quality certification in order to satisfy the European governments, but they wanted it to be paid for by taxes on the American public, not through a special tax on the industry itself. In addition, the new requirements of the law raised the costs of their smaller competitors, who operated under less sanitary and riskier conditions than did the Chicago firms. For all these reasons the large firms worked to obtain the Meat Inspection Act of 1906. Indeed, the mercantilist, rent-seeking character of the proposed legislation was so blatant that Upton Sinclair himself came to realize that he had ended up benefiting the large capitalists he hated.[23]

This was all, in fact, a repeated experience for the packing industry. The Meat Inspection Act of 1906 was essentially an amendment adding official federal quality certification and new financing to the Meat Act of 1891. The earlier legislation came about because the reduced costs associated with the new refrigeration technology allowed the Chicago packing firms to undercut the prices of local butchers. The butchers retaliated by attempting to discredit refrigerated beef as unsafe. In response, the big packers, such as Armour, Swift, Morris, and Hammond, lobbied Congress for meat inspection legislation. They wanted it not only to augment their own quality assurances, increasing demand for their products, but because the law made the shipments of each firm public information that they believed they could use to police their private pooling and market sharing arrangements.[24] They were certainly wrong in believing this would allow effective cartelization, since the 1891 act did nothing to either limit entry into the industry or to prevent existing independent competitors from undercutting cartel prices. Nevertheless, both the 1891 and 1906 meat inspection laws were *supported* by the larger firms from a belief that it would help them against their foreign and domestic competitors, contrary to the public interest mythology.

Railroad Regulation

The modern age of regulation in the American economy is often dated as beginning with passage of the Act to Regulate Commerce (often referred to as the *Interstate Commerce Act*) in 1887, which created the Interstate Commerce Commission (ICC). Supposedly, the commission was to regulate railroad rates and operations to protect the public from monopolistic practices and cartel activities. There is little doubt that there was popular, indeed, 'populist' pressure for regulation of the railroads in the post Civil War period. One of the characteristic features of this period was deflation. Prices in general fell from the end of the War almost to the end of the century as the federal government tried to remove Civil War greenbacks from circulation in order to restore gold convertibility. In addition, other nations went on the gold standard in this period, and hence competed for gold stocks. For both reasons there was little growth in the U.S. money stock at the same time as the economy was rapidly expanding. Thus, prices had to fall over time to raise the purchasing power of people's money balances enough for them to absorb the growing quantity of goods and services.

In this deflation some farmers, particularly in the Midwest, who had to ship grain to Eastern and Western markets, became convinced that interest rates, railroad shipping rates, and grain elevator prices had not fallen as much as crop prices, hence they were being exploited by such middlemen. In fact, modern empirical research fails to find any enduring pattern of secular rise in real interest rates or shipping rates in the period. Indeed, Arthur Hadley, writing at the time, reported that railroad rates fell an average of 50 percent between 1865 and 1880.[25] Likewise, John Stover estimates that railroad rates fell 70 percent between 1870 and 1900, while crop prices declined only by about 37 percent on average.[26] Probably the best estimate of crop prices relative to railroad rates over the period is by Higgs. He shows that these relative prices actually rose slightly until the 1890s. They did turn against farmers from 1893 to 1896, but after that, relative railroad rates fell.[27] Nevertheless, the widespread belief in such exploitation at the time generated, among other things, pressure from rural interests for railroad regulation. This was a pressure that the owners and operators of some railroads found useful, and added to, for their own motives.

The charges of monopolistic abuses by railroads must be put into context. Even before the innovation of efficient steam locomotives, and certainly afterwards, railroads drastically *reduced* transport costs between locations and markets they connected. By so doing, increasing the speed with which goods, people, tools and equipment could be shipped–all in the pursuit of profits–they reduced or eliminated the power of local monopolies of all kinds in all locales they served. They were, quite simply, the most potent *anti-monopoly* force ever created to that time. In addition, it was quite impossible for a railroad itself to be a monopoly, since the product they sold was transportation, and their customers *always* had the option of shipping or traveling overland by other methods. Also, in many markets, water transport was available as an alternative. A railroad built into an area could only attract customers by charging lower rates than people would pay to ship or travel by other methods between points along its route, and as other efficient forms of transport developed, such as trucking and airlines, railroads could only retain customers by staying competitive in their prices.

Certainly some locations were served by only one railroad, usually because the market would not support more, but sometimes for less legitimate reasons. The worst example was the thirty year reign of the Big Four (Railroad owners Leland Stanford, Collis Huntington, Charles Crocker, and Mark Hopkins) in California. These men were able to divide up the California market and charge rates for their services that were high by comparison with rail transport outside California, though of course still competitive with alternate transport methods in that state. They only accomplished this much by paying off the California legislature–Stanford was actually Governor of the state for some time–to prevent other railroads from competing with them.[28] In short, the Big Four were a classic mercantile cartel, created by the California state government.

This is not to say that private railroad cartels were not attempted. Indeed, railroading at the time was an industry almost peculiarly subject to such efforts. For one thing, because railroads so greatly reduced transport costs between many locations, and transport costs were a relatively small fraction of the costs of producing and distributing most goods, demand for rail services was often inelastic over a significant range of price. Thus large revenue increases could result from collusive price increases. In addition, the small number of railroads serving any given terminus made collusion appear, to their executives, likely to succeed. Such collusion became widespread in the 1870s as railroads in various regions of the country entered cartel agreements to set and stabilize rates and pool their revenue from traffic between their shared termini.

Inevitably, however, as Kolko makes clear, the private cartelization efforts were not successful over time. Despite the high initial capital investments required, U.S. law made entry into railroading comparatively easy, and any high prices and rates of return generated by cartel action tended to attract competition, adding to supply and causing price to fall. The industry pattern that developed was one of alternating periods of collusion and rate wars. In addition to entry, technological improvements such as coal locomotives and the introduction of common track gages were lowering costs and increasing supply, so that rates, on average, continued to fall and traffic volume to rise, over time, despite repeated cartelization efforts.

Indeed, in a paper containing many insights on the economics of railroading and the origins of the ICC, George Hilton twice states that it was the *instability* of railroad rates, not the level or trend, that irritated the public and motivated the pressure for legislative solutions.[29] Significantly, neither of Hilton's statements contain documentation for that claim, and the bulk of public statements at the time seem to the contrary. More likely this was true only of the railroad magnates themselves. They realized that they simply could not maintain high rates through private collusion alone.

It is true that factors other than the level or trend of prices in rail transport irritated the public. Railroads by nature have large fixed costs relative to variable costs, hence their average costs fall over a large range with increased volume (loads). Consequently, large shippers such as Standard Oil, by reducing the unit costs of service for the railroads, were legitimately able to obtain discounts (rebates). In addition, railroads face more competition at major termini than at intermediate points along a route, hence they frequently charged *lower* prices for *long haul* traffic between such termini than for short haul shipments.[30] The public regarded all such practices as discriminatory. Along with the misperception by agrarian interests that they were being charged monopoly shipping rates, this resentment of misperceived discrimination added to public support for regulatory legislation that the railroads wanted for their own purposes.

In 1886 there were two railroad regulation bills pending in Congress. Congressman John H. Reagan from Texas had been trying to obtain support for his House Bill since 1877, and the Cullom Bill was in the Senate. The 1878 version of the Reagan bill, which had passed the House but not the Senate, outlawed differential rates for large and small customers, outlawed the charging of lower rates for long hauls than short hauls in a continuous trip, and prohibited pooling. It created no commission or rate setting authority and left enforcement to the courts. The bill had actually been written by representatives of shipping interests hostile to the railroads.[31] The Cullom Bill, as Kolko demonstrated, was the product of railroad interests. In the form that passed the Senate in May of 1886 it created a nine member commission with authority to forbid "unreasonable" rates. It also forbad personal discrimination and rebates, but did not prohibit long and short haul price differentials or pooling of freight and earnings. In short, it was a cartel enforcement bill.

The reconciliation that allowed passage of the Interstate Commerce Act the next year basically favored the Cullom version, with some concessions that, as Hilton argues, gave the Act a vague and inconsistent character. Though Representative Reagan felt a commission would be dominated by the railroad interests, he compromised in exchange for a provision forbidding pooling. Cullom accepted section 4, which contained language aimed at forbidding lower prices for long than short hauls on continuous trips, with such exceptions as the commission allowed. But by forbidding the charging of lower prices for long hauls, the bill virtually required the railroads to engage in collusive pricing, since price cuts almost invariably came from rivals at major termini, where customers had alternative carriers to choose between in shipping long haul to other major termini, and not from intermediate short haul points along a route.[32]

As both Kolko and, more recently, MacAvoy, have shown, the immediate effect of the Act was to stabilize the railroad cartels, reducing or eliminating the rate wars and raising average rates.[33] All was not utopia for the railroads, however. The Act did nothing to prevent the entry attracted by cartel prices, and overbuilding worsened. Second, the prohibition of pooling actually made the cartels inefficient. In addition, the Sherman Anti-Trust Act of 1890 specifically forbad "collusion in restraint of trade," which was exactly what the ICC was promoting. Consequently, the ICC and the railroads began a legislative agenda aimed at making the railroad cartels legal. This generated a series of acts strengthening the ICC's cartel enforcement powers. The Elkins Act of 1903, for example, made both parties to a railroad rebate liable to prosecution, making price cutting below the cartel rates more difficult. The Hepburn Act of 1906 not only further restricted the granting of rebates, but extended ICC coverage to express and sleeping car companies.

Some researchers have read this legislative history differently. The Hepburn Act gave the ICC power to set maximum rates, and as the post Civil War deflation ended and the price level began rising, the ICC failed to allow railroad rate increases sufficient to keep railroad rates from falling relative to other prices. Profitability in the industry fell and the railroads responded, as economic theory would predict, by slowing repairs and replacement of capital stock and equipment. Albro Martin and others have interpreted these ICC price restraint actions as favoring shippers, and argued that regulation served the public interest after all.[34]

It may well be true that shipping interests heavily influenced ICC decisions in that period. The very acceptance of the use of government regulation as a mechanism of social control engenders a competitive struggle for control of the political and regulatory process that the larger firms in the industry being regulated may not always win. Corrupt politicians and regulators will, after all, sell their services to the highest bidders. Any control of the regulatory process by the shippers was certainly temporary, however, and the government may have had a far more sinister agenda.

By World War I, due precisely to these rate constraints and certain other financial impediments imposed by the Railroad Valuation Act of 1913, the railroads were in poor shape. The government, relying heavily on the railroads for rapid and reliable transportation of men and material, thus had a handy excuse, provided by its own prior policy actions, to nationalize them. Fortunately, public opinion and political conditions forced the government to return them to their private owners after the war.[35] Shortly thereafter the regulatory process clearly reverted toward railroad cartelization again, in the form of the transportation Act of 1920. This law granted the ICC authority to establish and enforce *minimum* rates, limit entry and allow pooling, thus converting the industry into an officially established cartel.

The Broadening of Transportation Regulation

As the saying goes, "there is many a slip twixt cup and lip." Just as systematic mercantilism was ultimately self-defeating, even for the principals, so too has often been the more fragmentary American cartelization through regulatory agencies. National cartelization of the American railroads under the Transportation Act of 1920 was even more disastrous to the industry than the prior maximum rate regulation had been. Entrepreneurs in the market, attracted by potential profits, have a natural tendency to circumvent such artificial restrictions. In the 1920s Henry Ford's mass production methods had made automobiles cheap enough for mass consumption, and created a rapidly expanding trucking industry. Entry into freight transport by truck was much easier even than into railroading, and as a largely unregulated industry, trucking was highly competitive and rates were low.

For some types of business, trucks and railroads did not meaningfully compete. Trucks had a natural advantage in short hauls between points not connected by railroads, and there are some loads that only railroads could carry given the size and technology of trucking at the time. But more than local delivery business was open to entrepreneurial truckers, and they could compete with railroads for much of their business. With railroad rates held at high levels and technological innovations in railroading being suppressed or delayed by the ICC, shippers whose loads *could* go by truck switched in droves. On top of this, development of aircraft technology resulted in a nascent air transport industry which began to compete with the railroads for mail transport and some high end passenger traffic. As a result of these events, though mostly due to trucking competition, the railroads in the U.S. were dealt a blow from which they have not, to this day, really recovered. The rational political response to this situation, assuming its nature was clearly understood at the time, and that the government really was motivated by public interest considerations, would certainly have been to repeal the Transportation Act of 1920, and perhaps even the Interstate Commerce Act itself, so that the railroads could freely compete. But the ideological, political and historical forces of the day supporting government regulation and cartelization were too strong. In 1929-30 the contractionary monetary policy of the Federal Reserve and the incipient Hawley-Smoot tariff precipitated the Great Depression that was to last for the next decade.[36] In a monumental error of economic theorizing, both the Republican Hoover and Democratic Roosevelt administrations concluded that forcing both prices and wage rates up would raise incomes and prove ameliorative. They failed to grasp that this would simply reduce the purchasing power of money, delivering additional contractionary shocks to the economy and extending the depression.[37]

The most systematic effort of the New Deal to force prices and wage rates up was contained in the National Industrial Recovery Act and the first Agricultural Adjustment Act, both of 1933. The NIRA attempted the deliberate cartelization of all of American nonagricultural industry through trade associations, and the AAA restricted agricultural output by various devices. Both acts were declared unconstitutional by the Supreme court in 1935, in time to limit but not to prevent their contractionary effects on the economy.[38] Though thwarted in its effort at system-wide quasi-fascist cartelization, the Roosevelt administration was determined to impose the same policies piecemeal where possible. So among other similar measures covering banking and industry it passed the National Motor Carrier Act of 1935 and the Civil Aeronautics Act of 1938.

The National Motor Carrier Act, supported by executives of large trucking firms who were subject to the same mercantilist motives that had, in the 1880s, affected many railroad executives, brought the interstate trucking industry under ICC regulation. The detailed regulations limited entry, kept prices relatively high, and controlled internal competitive conditions of all kinds. The Civil Aeronautics Act did the same thing for airlines even more rigidly, so that the nineteen trunk lines that existed in 1938 were the only firms allowed to carry passengers interstate on scheduled routes for the next forty years. Despite the numerous rationalizations for such regulation propagated by the ICC, other government officials, all interventionist liberal intellectuals and even some economists, the interests of the public, who had to pay higher prices for everything transported, were *not* being served. This was made crystal clear by certain political events of the late 1970s and 1980s, which followed important developments within the economics profession.

Notes:

1 The standard Harvard School view in economics is that any departure
from the 'perfectly competitive' market structure consisting of numerous,
identical, price-taking firms represents an inferior market structure. My
views here represent an Austrian/Chicago school perspective that competition is a dynamic *process* consisting of entrepreneurial *activities*, aimed at
reducing costs, improving existing products, innovating new ones, etc. In
a world in which managerial and entrepreneurial abilities are distributed
normally, rather than evenly, real market structures involving significant
concentration of sales and assets in a subset of firms in an industry may
not only be a natural outcome, but be *superior* to the market structure
defined by the perfectly competitive model. Empirical evidence for such a
perspective is provided by Harold Demsetz, *The Market Concentration
Doctrine* (Institute of Economic Affairs, 1973), Sam Peltzman, "The
Gains and Losses From Industrial Concentration," *Journal of Law and
Economics* 20 (October, 1977): 229-263, and Michael Smirlock, "Tobin's
Q and the Structure-Performance Relationship," *American Economic
Review* 74 (December 1984): 1051-1060.

2 See, for example, Leverett S. Lyon and Victor Abramson, *Government and
Economic Life: Development and Current Issues of American Public
Policy* (Brookings Institution, 1940). Lyon and Abramson, writing at the
end of the Depression, seem very much torn between the Public Interest
view of Progressive and New Deal regulatory legislation, and their dawn-
ing realization that private interest activity, neither aimed at nor accom-
plishing the public good, is crucial to explaining much of that legislation.

3 Gabriel Kolko, *The Triumph of Conservatism: A Reinterpretation of
American History*, 1900-1916 (The Free Press, 1963): Chapter 1.

4 See Armentano, *The Myths of Antitrust*, Chapters 4 and 5.

5 Yale Brozen, "The Attack on Concentration," in Yale Brozen, *Is Big
Business the Source of Monopoly? and Other Essays* (The Cato Institute,
1980). In another essay Brozen uses an amazingly simple statistical procedure involving rank correlation of profit rates among industries over time
to demonstrate that the U.S. economy has become much *more* competitive
since the mid 19th century, not less so. See Brozen, "Are U.S.
Manufacturing Markets Monopolized?" in the same volume.

6 One exception was the United Shoe Machinery Company, formed by
merger of four independent shoe manufacturing equipment makers in
1899, which by 1917 attained a vary large share–about 85 percent–of the
market, and maintained that share for several decades though it had about
ten competitors. Another exception was Alcoa, the Aluminum Company of

America, which invented aluminum and maintained a dominant position in the production of primary aluminum ingot long after its patents expired. In both cases these firms maintained their dominant positions through rapid innovation, efficient operation and management practices, and pleasing customers. Both of these firms were *unjustly* convicted for violations of the Sherman Antitrust Act. See Armentano, *The Myths of Antitrust:* Chapter 6.

7 Folsom, *Entrepreneurs vs. The State:* Chapter 4.

8 Armentano, *The Myths of Antitrust:* 103-106.

9 *Ibid.*, p. 78.

10 *Ibid.*, p. 91.

11 Steven Birmingham, *Our Crowd* (Dell Publishing Co., 1967): 400.

12 Kolko, *The Triumph of Conservatism:* 184.

13 Ferdinand Lundburg, *America's 60 Families* (the Vangard Press, 1938): 110-113.

14 Frank Vanderlip, "Farm Boy to Financier," *The Saturday Evening Post* (9 February, 1935): 25.

15 See Charles W. Baird and Alexander Casuto, *Macroeconomics: Monetary, Search and Income Theories* (2nd ed., Science Research Associates, 1981): 168, or Edwards, *Macroeconomics: Equilibrium and Disequilibrium Analysis:* 175-181 and 199.

16 *Ibid.*, 375-386.

17 Thousands of people toured the Chicago stockyards every year, and no public outcry against conditions there resulted. It is a tribute to the power of graphic literary depiction that Sinclair's novel was able to generate such an outcry.

18 Lawrence W. Reed, "Of Meat and Myth," *The Freeman* (November 1994): 600-602.

19 This was the testimony of Congressman E. D. Crumpacker of Indiana, U.S. Congress, House Committee on Agriculture, *Hearings on the So-called "Beveridge Amendment" to the Agriculture Appropriation Bill,* 59th Congress, 1st Session, 1906, p. 194, as cited in Reed, "Of Meat and Myth."

20 Kolko, *The Triumph of Conservatism:* 105.

21 *Hearings*, p. 102.

22 Reed, "Of Meat and Myth" : 601

23 Upton Sinclair, "The Condemned Meat Industry: A Reply to Mr. J. Ogden Armour," *Everybody's Magazine* 14 (1906): 608-616, particularly pp. 612-613.

24 Gary M. Walton and Hugh Rockoff, *History of the American Economy* (6th ed., Harcourt Brace Jovanovich, 1990): 425.

25 Arthur T. Hadley, *Railroad Transportation; its History and its Laws* (G. P. Putnam's Sons, 1885): 17.

26 John F. Stover, *American Railroads* (University of Chicago Press, 1961): 100.

27 Robert Higgs, "Railroad Rates and the Populist Uprising," *Agricultural History* 44 (July 1970).

28 See Oscar Lewis, *The Big Four* (Alfred A. Knopf, 1938).

29 George W. Hilton, "The Consistency of the Interstate Commerce Act," *Journal of Law and Economics* 9 (October 1966): 87-113.

30 For a clear and forceful discussion of these matters see Armentano, *The Myths of Antitrust*: 70-73.

31 Hilton, "The Consistency of the Interstate Commerce Act": 104, n. 83.

32 *Ibid.*, pp. 105-109.

33 Gabrial Kolko, *Railroads and Regulation* (Princeton University Press, 1965), and Paul MacAvoy, *The Economic Effects of Regulation: The Trunkline Railroad Cartels and the Interstate Commerce Commission, 1870-1900* (MIT Press, 1965).

34 Albro Martin, *Enterprise Denied: Origins of the Decline of American Railroads, 1897-1917* (Columbia University Press, 1971).

35 Both World Wars I and II provided excuses for those of dictatorial inclination in the U.S. government to impose their proclivities on the economy, and this was accepted by the public as necessary due to the emergency conditions. In fact the controls *hampered* the war effort in both cases. After both wars, there was a strong reversion to a more libertarian perspective, and a backlash against the wartime controls. In neither case, however, was the reversion complete. See Chapter 1, note 14, and Chapter 3. note 18, above.

36 The seminal work on the monetary element and the role of the Federal Reserve in the Great Contraction is, of course, Milton Friedman and Anna Jacobsen Schwartz, *A Monetary History of the United States, 1867-1960* (Princeton University Press, 1963). Friedman and his followers concede

some real elements in the contraction, however, such as the tariff, in addition to the monetary element. See, for example, Alan H. Meltzer, "Monetary and other Explanations of the Start of the Great Depression," Journal of Monetary Economics 2 (1976): 455-471. The common element in all factors generating the depression–and preserving it for a decade–was harmful government intervention.

37 Anyone familiar with the basic economic concept of demand elasticity (as even Roosevelt administration economists must have been) knows that forcing a price up need not even cause *nominal* revenue to rise, much less *real* income. Given this elementary knowledge, the very notion of creating industrial cartels (or agricultural restrictions) with intent of contracting real output, in order to raise prices during a depression that is already characterized, definitionally, by excessively *low* real output and income, is so ghastly and stupid as to be nearly beyond belief.

38 See Michael M. Weinstein, "Some Macroeconomic Impacts of the National Recovery Act, 1933-1935," in Karl Brunner, ed., *The Great Depression Revisited* (Martinus Nijhoff, 1981): 262-285, and Gene Smiley, "Can Keynesianism Explain the 1930s?" *Critical Review* 5 (Winter 1991): 81-114.

Chapter 5

The Economic Theory of Regulation

One of the most important developments in economic theory in the second half of the 20th century occurred when, largely out of frustration, economists began applying economic modeling techniques to the understanding of the political process. Two of the most prominent economists in the profession, George Stigler and James Buchanan, have been awarded the Nobel prize for their contributions in this area, Stigler in 1982 and Buchanan in 1986. Two separate strands of this literature have developed, roughly contemporaneous with the contributions of Kolko in the History profession. One is known as the economic theory of regulation, after Stigler's seminal paper, and the other is known as public choice theory. Both are special interest group theories of democratic legislation, and they can now be essentially read as one literature.

Electric Utility Regulation and The Public Interest

The origin of the economic theory of regulation is usually dated from Stigler's famous paper in 1972.[1] In fact, the story must be pushed back at least a decade. For some time, economists studying regulation empirically, had become increasingly uneasy with the public interest rationale for regulatory legislation. When such legislation began in 1877 and expanded in the 1930s, it was easy for its political and ideological advocates to engage in utopian theoretical claims for its prospective benefits. But most economists are inclined toward *checking* theories. As evidence accumulated over decades on the operation and behavior of regulatory agencies, it became increasingly difficult for them to justify that behavior as serving the general public good. Even defenders of regulation, in the economics profession, found it necessary to modify the public interest rationale for such legislation by arguing that regulatory agencies may often be captured over time by the industries they regulate, and begin promoting industry, rather than general public interests.[2]

The final straw came with a 1963 paper by Stigler and Claire Friedland examining the effects of electric utility rate regulation on electricity prices.[3] Stigler and Friedland noted that formal rate regulation began with the establishment of state regulatory commissions in Wisconsin and New York in 1907. By 1915 two-thirds of the states had such commissions and over three-quarters had them by 1932. This made it easy to compare prices across states at points in time when some were practicing rate regulation and others were not, and to observe prices over time, to find the effects of regulation. Of course the claim of the regulators, utility executives and intellectual advocates of regulation was that the regulation was preventing monopoly pricing on the part of a set of firms that were, by virtue of large economies to scale, natural monopolies. That is, the first firm reaching the appropriate scale would have the lowest costs. Hence it would supply the entire market (all others having been eliminated) and charge a monopoly price. No competing firm would enter the market because to do so at the appropriate scale would add so much supply as to force price below costs.

Stigler and Friedland's data, from 1917 and 1922, did indeed show that revenues per Kilowatt Hour were lower in regulated than in unregulated states, but it turned out that they were lower in those states *both before and after regulation.* Testing for the effect of other variables such as population density, fuel prices, the proportion of power generated by (cheaper) hydroelectric sources, and per capita income of customers in a multiple regression for the years 1922 and 1932, they found that such variables fully accounted for price differences among the states, and regulation had no effect. Since regulation is supposed to eliminate monopoly profits along with the monopoly price, Stigler and Friedland also tested for the effect of regulation on rates of return, and again found no statistically significant effect.

Stigler and Friedland's results shocked the profession, and other researchers subsequently found little effect of utility regulation in lowering rates.[4] To cap it all off, a few years later Harold Demsetz demonstrated that there was no necessary theoretical connection between large scale production economies and the emergence of a monopoly price in an industry. His essential insight was that, in the absence of a state monopoly franchise, the number of producers is independent of the number of bidders who may contract to supply goods or services (such as electricity) to prospective customers. Scale economies in production imply only that bids submitted will offer larger quantities at lower prices. In the presence of large scale economies in production the lowest bidder will be the sole firm, but as long as the cost of forming contracts is small and producer inputs are available at market prices, the price will be competitive.[5] To see what Demsetz was talking about, one need only consider the current constant bidding for contracts with customers by alternate potential suppliers of long-distance telephone service now that the government franchised and protected monopoly in the provision of such service has been eliminated. The question Demsetz' argument raised was well expressed in the title of his paper: *Why Regulate Utilities?*

Meanwhile, Stigler's research led him to initiate the theory of regulation as a form of *private* rather than public interest legislation. But that theory implies that the special interests behind regulatory legislation expect to *get* something, which implies some efficacy to regulation after all, *contrary* to the result of his own 1963 paper. That oddity led economist Greg Jarrell to revisit the electric utility industry in a study published in 1978.[6] Jarrell pointed out that, due to the use of city streets by electrical firms, prior to the onset of state rate regulation, municipalities had regulated utilities through the granting of franchises. The common practice had been to grant such franchises freely to virtually all aspiring electricity providers, creating conditions of open entry at low cost. That some economies to scale were present was indicated by a tendency toward consolidations over time. The common argument for replacing municipal regulation with state regulation was that the city governments lacked the moral fiber, will and capacity to control such large consolidated utility firms.

Jarrell was familiar with Demsetz' argument, however, and suspected both that consolidation in this period did *not* mean the end of competition, and that state monopoly franchises and rate regulation may have emerged *not* from consumer demand, but from pressure by producers wishing to obtain monopoly profits unattainable in the competitive environment. A simple test occurred to him, since the public interest theory implies that monopoly prices and profits would have existed *prior* to state regulation, particularly in early regulation states, and effective state regulation *in the public interest* would have resulted in price and profits falling. The economic (or special interest) theory of regulation, in contrast, implies the opposite sequence of events.

Jarrell noted that only five states had state regulation of utilities before 1912, but twenty-five more initiated such regulation by 1917. Most of the remaining states instituted state regulation over time at a slower pace. Designating those twenty-five states regulating between 1912 and 1917 Early Regulation (ER) states, he compared prices and profits in their electrical utility industries before and after regulation with those in states that regulated after 1917 (LR). What he found was that, adjusting for other demand determinants, ER states in 1912 had unit electricity prices that averaged 46 percent lower than those in LR states, but by 1917 they were only 20 percent lower. Hence between 1912 and 1917 ER states had experienced a roughly 26 percentage point *increase* in electricity prices relative to LR states. The same picture emerged from comparison of profits. In 1912 ER states had an average 38 percent *lower* gross profits per KWH than LR states, but by 1917, after the ER states had initiated state regulation, the gross profits of ER and LR states were the same.

Jarrell concluded that state utility regulation began where conditions were most *competitive*, not most monopolistic, and the utilities, not the consumers, were the gainers from regulation, contrary to the ubiquitous claims of advocates of the public interest theory of regulation. Another conclusion Jarrell reached was that the early municipal regulation of utilities, which basically consisted of a policy of open entry, had been effective in maintaining competitive conditions after all. Apparently, Stigler and Friedland's use of 1917 and 1922 data in their 1963 paper, which led them to the conclusion that utility regulation had had no effect in *reducing* industry prices and profits, had caused them to miss the actual earlier effect of such regulation in *raising* prices and profits in formerly competitive electricity markets.

The Economic Theory of Regulation

Stigler developed the economic theory of regulation in specific rejection of the public interest theory that regulation necessarily results as a public sector response to voter pressure and aims at protecting the public from monopolistic or oligopolistic predators. It is an *economic* theory because it employs the economic approach to analyzing man and society. First, it assumes that the various parties, voters, regulators and industry decision makers, all act from self-interest motives. Second, it assumes that they wish to maximize their gains. Third, it seeks to explain regulation as an equilibrium outcome of the supply of and demand for regulation. Finally, it attempts to identify the parties constituting and factors determining supply and demand and derive empirically testable predictions from the model.

Such an approach does not *a priori* exclude all public interest outcomes, since members of the general public can certainly express their own interest through voting. Stigler made it a primary thesis, however, that as a rule, regulation would be acquired by the industry, and would serve its benefit. The central fact behind the demand for regulation by such firms, he argued, is that the state has the valuable and unique power of legal coercion, which they can use in four ways to transfer income from the public to themselves. First is the possibility of obtaining a direct subsidy. This is seldom sought, Stigler argued, because the gains from such subsidies would be dissipated by entry of new firms (which rents in the form of a subsidy would attract) over time.[7] Second is the control over entry itself, such as employed by the CAB to prevent entry of new trunk airlines. Third is the power to affect substitutes and complements. In Stigler's lucid example, butter producers will wish to use government regulatory power to suppress margarine production and encourage bread production, since both of these events would increase demand for butter.[8] Fourth is the power to fix prices.

In a crucial observation, Stigler noted that the democratic political process places limits on the use of regulation for cartelization policy. Other interests–perhaps directly opposed to industry interests–will be felt and must be considered by the government regulators. Consequently, cartel regulatory policy will *not* be applied in a pure industry profit maximizing way. Nevertheless, in the democratic process, Stigler argued, the preferences of industrial or occupational groups will tend to dominate the general public interest for several reasons. For one, democratic voting is simultaneous and intermittent, leaving representatives with wide discretion for long periods In addition, uninformed voters cannot be excluded, and on regulatory (and other) issues many voters are uninformed. This is because the losses to each consumer/voter generated by the regulatory redistribution to a particular industry are small enough to provide little incentive for such voters to inform themselves

The industry must pay the potential political suppliers of regulation with votes and resources for regulation it desires, but it faces problems in doing so. After all, an industry generally consists of independent firms, and a campaign for regulation must be organized. Such efforts, Stigler pointed out, face the problem that firms in the industry not contributing resources to the lobbying effort will also gain from any regulation supplied, hence many may "free ride" on the contributions of others. This makes it difficult to organize and fund such lobbying efforts. Though Stigler did not specifically note this point, any efforts to organize counter-lobbying efforts by members of general public who will lose from regulation face a worse free-rider problem than do the producers, because there are more consumers and each has only small incentive to contribute resources. For this reason also, producer interests will often win such political battles.

Stigler's paper set off a tidal wave of research in the profession. The most important theoretical development came in 1976 when Sam Peltzman rigorously formalized and generalized Stigler's model.[9] Neither Peltzman nor Stigler made any distinction between legislators and regulators, modeling them as essentially the same persons for simplicity. Peltzman specifically assumed that legislator/regulators rationally attempt to maximize votes by trading off wealth between producers and consumers. In this process there are diminishing returns in terms of votes obtained from favoring either group too much at the expense of the other. The sort of voter ignorance, externality and group size considerations made by Stigler were given rigorous formulation in the regulatory profit and utility functions of the model.

Graphically, the basics of Peltzman's model are easily illustrated. Assuming linear demand, the profit function is related to the price set by the regulators in the 'hill' shape shown. Point A shows the price at which the profits of the regulatory cartel would be maximized. This is equivalent to the profit maximizing price in the rent-seeking graph of Chapter 1. Point C in contrast is the zero regulation outcome, in which the competitive price would prevail and economic profits in the industry would be zero, as long as private cartelization efforts were not successful. Since higher regulated prices diminish public support for the regulators at an increasing rate, and lower prices diminish industry support for the regulators at an increasing rate, the utility curves of the regulators have the shapes shown. Vertically higher curves represent higher vote and satisfaction levels for the regulators, and happiness maximizing regulators will set industry price at point B.

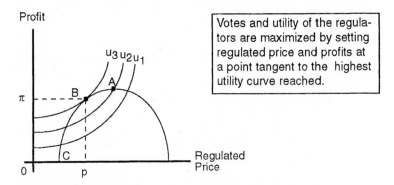

Graph 5.1:
Peltzman Theory of Constrained Regulator Utility Maximization

The crucial result of the model is precisely that the regulated price will *not* be the monopoly profit maximizing price as shown in the rent-seeking graph of Chapter 1, but somewhere between that price and the unregulated zero-profit price. This is due to the necessity of considering both consumer and producer interests, as Stigler had intuited. Another conclusion drawn from this by Peltzman and others is that regulation will be more likely to occur in perfectly competitive industries operating at point C before regulation and monopolistic industries operating at point A before regulation. In contrast, regulation should seldom occur in oligopolistic industries operating at intermediate prices, since the gains to regulators from regulation of such industries will be minimal. In evidence they cite regulation of competitive producer groups such as barbers and medical practitioners on the one hand, and electric utilities on the other.

Note that this argument implies *public interest* outcomes where the industries were effectively privately monopolized or cartelized before regulation. There are counter observations, however. Indeed, the example of public utilities arguably counts *against* this theoretical claim of Peltzman's. The electrical utilities were generally not monopolies *before* regulation, but only *after*. Nor were they effective cartels. As Demsetz and Jarrell found, the typical industry structure in local electrical markets prior to state regulation was concentrated, but open entry left price competitive. The same was true of the railroads, as shown in Chapter 4. Market structure was normally oligopolistic, but the typical cartel failed. It would appear that oligopolistic industries are in fact frequently regulated, because the instability of cartels makes potential gains from government price control and entry barriers large, and the small number of firms makes costs of organizing low.[10] All this is clearly in accord with a *proper* interpretation of the Model.

Numerous other researchers have extended and applied the economic theory in explanation of diverse regulatory phenomena. It has been recognized, for example, that the conflict over the initiation and control of regulation may in some cases not be so much between a single industry and the general public as between industrial groups, as when the primary buyers of the output of an industry are firms in another industry. It was already pointed out in Chapter 4 that large shipping firms may well have been able to affect decisions of the ICC at times, so that its regulation was *not* always uniformly pro-railroad. In a similar vein, there is sometimes a conflict over the existence or form of regulation between firms within an industry. For example, when firms in an industry vary in the accident or injury risks their workers face, or in their costs of reducing such risks, safety regulation may be a method by which the low cost firms attempt to gain a competitive advantage over their high-cost rivals and force them out of the industry.[11] On the other hand, many forms of regulation are clearly aimed at benefiting *high-cost* firms at the expense of their *low-cost* rivals.[12]

Numerous historical episodes and instances of regulation have been modeled in interest group terms. The work of Ekelund and Tollison was heavily relied on in the writing of Chapter 1 above. Marvel used this theory to explain the origin and form of the British Factory Acts.[13] Boudreaux and DiLorenzo recently explained the passage of the Sherman Antitrust Act of 1890 as an outcome of special interest group pressures.[14] Shugart and Tollison explained the liberalization of corporate chartering laws between 1837 and 1913 in interest group terms.[15] This raises the point that the economic theory of regulation must be able to explain periods of *deregulation* as well as regulation, which will be the important to the next section of this chapter.

Other extensions of the economic theory of regulation have involved attempts to separate Stigler and Peltzman's legislator/regulators and model the operation of regulatory bureaucracies. One issue here is the principle-agent problem, discussed already in Chapter 2, concerning the extent to which regulatory bureaucracies efficiently represent the interests of their legislative principals, and at another remove, the interests of the voters, who are the principals to which *legislators* are agents. I made clear in that chapter my disagreement with those economists who argue that either regulators or legislators themselves are perfect agents. The whole process of franchising legislative power to unelected executive branch personnel seems *designed* to insulate them from democratic pressures and establish effective, discretionary governmental power to command and control the property and actions of private persons. In an important 1974 paper, Richard Posner noted that one reason an independent judiciary, insulated from political pressures, was designed into the Constitution was to reduce the extent and effectiveness of special interest groups in obtaining redistributive legislation. As such, the delegation of legislative power to executive branch agencies counted as evidence in *favor* of the economic theory of regulation.[16]

Posner was seriously concerned with evaluating the scientific status of the economic theory of regulation, however, and pointed to several defects he perceived. First, he argued that, from a scientific perspective, its very explanatory power was a problem. It seemed to him hard to define evidence that could *falsify* the theory. That is, almost any historical episode of regulation could be explained in its terms. A second weakness Posner saw was that counter examples to the prediction of the economic theory exist, since, in his opinion, the social regulation of the late 1960s and early '70s had no obvious special interest group origin. The problem here is that Posner's second observation contradicts the first. In addition, he does not seem to see that Stigler's argument allows for some public interest outcomes. Peltzman later made this point much clearer.

Posner pointed to two other weaknesses he saw in the interest group theory of regulation without realizing that one of them explained the other. First, he asserted (correctly) that nothing in the theory predicts that interest groups will fail to use the socially lowest cost methods for achieving an income transfer from the public to themselves. Yet direct cash transfers, which have much lower social costs than government cartlization, are seldom employed. Thus the theory would seem *not* to explain an important observable aspect of regulation. Apparently he rejected Stigler's own explanation for this phenomenon, though he did not mention it. Then in another part of his paper Posner made the following observation.

An important, but as yet unexplained, datum is the characteristic
public interest rhetoric in which discussions of public policy are conducted and the policies themselves framed. The use of language that,
if the economic theory of regulation is correct, is utterly uninforma-
tive and indeed misleading is not costless; presumably it is employed
only because there are offsetting benefits. These benefits must have to
do with increasing the costs to members of the public of obtaining
accurate information about the effect of the actions of their legislative
representatives on their welfare.[17]

Gordon Tullock has since explained the obvious connection between
these phenomena. Special interests seldom seek direct cash transfers simply because *the naked redistribution would be too obvious.* It is necessary
to confuse the average voter/consumer and reduce political opposition by
giving redistributive political efforts a public interest cover.[18]

Still, Posner has identified a crucial weakness, and Tullock has only
partly corrected it. Advocates of the economic theory have largely failed
to analyze the pervasive efforts of legislators, regulators, and rent-seek-
ers to cloak their actions in public interest rhetoric and model its effects
on the form and extent of regulation. Nor have they asked the significance of the public interest doctrine as a crucial element in a larger
interventionist/redistributionist ideology–welfare liberalism–propagated by the intellectual class incessantly through books, news media, college courses and K-12 schools.[19] This relates to the point above about
legislators and regulators as agents, because it seems likely that, in the
absence of the misleading public interest claims and the political insu-
lation of regulators, the democratic mechanism would be a more effective restraint on redistributive special interest legislation than advocates
of the economic theory of regulation presume. Both the institutional
structure of the regulatory mechanism and the massive propagation of
false public interest claims aim precisely at suppressing such democratic restraints.

In the same vein, note that *no* effect of the discovery and propagation of economic knowledge on the extent or nature of regulation is
included in the economic model of regulation (though the model could
certainly be modified to show such effects). Why in the world have
economists, including those such as Stigler and Peltzman, done what
they do? Does the development and propagation of economic theory
and evidence, in the halls of Congress or among the educated populace,
have *no* effect on public policy choices? As the next section will show,

however powerful the entrenched special interests, in at least some cases it almost certainly does.

Transportation Deregulation in the Carter/Reagan Era

It is now time to continue the story of transportation industry regulation begun in Chapter 4, because so many lessons can be learned from subsequent events. Developments in the industries themselves, accumulating empirical studies on the operation of the industries, and the development of the economic theory of regulation resulted in significant deregulation of those and other industries, such as telecommunications, cable television, and financial services, during the Presidencies of Jimmy Carter and Ronald Reagan. All of these industries had sought and gained regulation for redistributive motives, as had the transportation industries. Telephone service was competitive, for example, until the Bell corporation sought and obtained an exclusive government franchise, and the recent breakup of Bell and deregulation of long distance service simply partly reversed that prior regulatory action. Cable television, of course, has been based on municipal franchises of monopoly from the beginning, though not from any technological or economic necessity. It is important to explore both the causes and consequences of the recent deregulatory episode, focusing on the transport industries for brevity and clarity.

Aircraft development was rapid following the flight of the Wright brothers at Kitty Hawk in 1903, but World War I provided a large stimulus to aircraft technology and manufacture. Following the war, military craft were dumped on the market at low prices. In 1918 the Post Office Department began employing Army pilots for mail delivery between New York and Washington. The casualty rate was very high, and a few years later a commission appointed by President Calvin Coolidge recommended transfer of the airmail operation to private contractors. This provided stimulus to the growth and operation of private mail-passenger airlines. The Hoover administration continued this practice. In 1934 President Franklin Roosevelt was convinced by U.S. Senator Hugo Black (a future Supreme Court Justice) that the airmail contracts were crooked, and Roosevelt capriciously gave the job to the Army Air Corps. In only a week there were dozens of crashes in which twelve pilots died, and the average cost of mail delivery turned out to be four times as high as under private delivery. Contracts to private firms quickly resumed under a new law, the Air Mail Act of 1934.[20]

The law was a mish-mash, which required competitive bidding on the one hand, but vested regulatory control of the industry in four separate agencies on the other. It forbad excess profits by the airlines, but also subsidized losses, resulting in ridiculously low bids for mail contracts. Under competitive pressures during the Great Depression, the airlines formed the Air Transport Association and lobbied for more coherent federal regulation. In 1938 Congress passed the Civil Aeronautics Act giving the airlines their own regulatory agency, the Civil Aeronautics Board, to create and enforce their cartel. The CAB was granted power to require certification for an airline to operate, and to set and enforce rates. The 19 existing 'trunk' lines carrying passengers were granted certificates, and from that time forward *no entry* was allowed into the scheduled interstate passenger business, despite enormous growth in the economy and, consequently, in the demand for air transport services. In fact, mergers and acquisitions reduced the number of trunk lines to 11 by 1961.[21]

Between 1943 and 1950 the CAB did authorize 21 firms (Bonanza, Ozark, Piedmont, and others) to provide subsidized local feeder service connecting smaller communities with larger cities. These firms had monopolies over their routes, and were forbidden from competing with the trunk carriers, though they did pick up some routes the majors dropped. After 1950 no new feeders were certified, and attrition reduced the number to 13 by 1965.[22] The story is similar for the "nonsked" airlines, which initially able to escape the CAB regulation and enter the industry by not operating fixed schedules and routees. Some 150 nonskeds were in business by 1947. As Mary Bennett Peterson explains, these firms cut unit costs and prices by making fast adjustments in air traffic movements, and took a significant amount of business from the trunk lines.[23] The predictable political response by the majors resulted in a change in the law in 1947 bringing the nonskeds under ICC entry and price regulation. By 1959 only 50 of these firms still existed.

The pricing policies of the CAB appeared almost as blatantly cartel oriented as its entry restrictions. The situation was confused somewhat by the CAB practice of holding rates above marginal cost on long and medium haul trips while holding them below cost on short-hauls, so that profits on the former were subsidizing the latter. But the CAB frequently *refused* requests of trunk lines competing for business on particular routes to reduce fares, as would be predicted of a cartel enforcing agency. That the CAB was generally holding air fares *up,* not down, became clear to economists, however, from observation of the California market. In California between 1946 and 1965 sixteen different firms entered the market (and some subsequently left) carrying passengers *solely instate.* As such they escaped CAB rate and entry regulations, and competed with CAB certified trunk lines for traffic between major California cities.

Even worse from the perspective of the airline cartel, the California firms were subject to little state regulation, because the California Public Utilities Commission could not legally control the fares of the instate firms. The most successful of these indigenous California firms was Pacific Southwest Airlines (PSA), which was consistently able to provide safe and reliable service while charging lower fares than the CAB regulated trunk lines. Often, PSA carried more passengers than any other carrier in all three of the largest California markets. Studies of this situation by economists such as William Jordan largely settled the debate within the economics profession over whether the CAB was holding rates up or down overall.

The change in attitudes among economists due to such empirical studies of regulated industries and to the development of the economic theory of regulation, occurred in conjunction with other events that were changing the political economy of regulation. For one, it was becoming clear to executives of many of the CAB certified airlines that they were no longer benefiting from regulation. Certainly they were aware that PSA was forcing rates down in California, but that was only one instance of a broader process. *It appears that even the best and most stringent set of regulatory controls can only create and maintain cartel profits for a period of time, after which internal and external competitive pressures act to dissipate such rents.*

Forbidden from engaging in price competition with one another on particular routes, for example, the trunk lines had for decades substituted competitive improvements in service quality, which tended to reduce their price-cost margins. In addition, much of the rents originally gained for the airlines by CAB entry restrictions and price controls were being absorbed over time in wage increases by airline unions. Consequently, as they became aware of deregulation sentiment in the economics profession and on Capital Hill, airline executives themselves became split on the continuance of regulation.

A third change favoring deregulation was the appointment by President Carter of Alfred Khan as Chairman of the Civil Aeronautics Board. Carter, as a private peanut farmer before becoming Governor of Georgia, had experienced regulation from the side of the fence opposite that faced by most politicians. Khan was a distinguished economist who had written one of the most widely used texts on economic regulation. With the President's blessing he immediately began a campaign of deregulation both through changes in agency rules and by supporting legislation to formally deregulate the transportation industries, beginning with the airlines. For the first time, Congress was faced with an Administration, most economists, many of the firms in the industry, and even the head of the regulatory agency itself, all favoring deregulation. Even some 'consumer' groups, such as Ralph Nader's, were convinced by the evidence to support deregulation. Opposition came, of course, from the airline unions, regulators fearing for their jobs and power, the national liberal news media, and many leftist intellectuals who saw regulation itself and its public interest rationale being threatened if deregulation occurred anywhere. The accumulated evidence and testimony before the committee and the fact that the bill came from a Democratic rather than Republican President was too much for the opposition, however, and the Airline Deregulation Act passed in 1978.

The Act removed entry restrictions and allowed the airlines to reduce prices ten percent without notice to the CAB, and up to 70 percent with a 45 day notice. The moment of truth for the regulatory ideology arrived. Had the CAB been holding air fares down, in protection of the public, or up, to the benefit of the firms? Was the CAB preventing entry or not? The answers soon came. Several new airlines entered the market and began competing for business. Even before that, prices began dropping. Fares dropped 20 percent in 1978 alone, and from 1979 to 1984 dropped another 13 to 15 percent. Despite intense competition during and aggravated by the double-dip recession of 1980 and 1982, the safety record of the industry continued to improve. This was contrary to the predictions of some opponents of deregulation, who thought that price and cost competition would come at the expense of safety.

Such opponents had also predicted a reduction in service in some communities as firms dropped less profitable routees, and some such routees were dropped. Feeder lines took up the slack, however, and almost no communities lost service. This demonstrated the absurdity of the ICC argument that in order to maintain service to smaller cities it was necessary to charge prices below marginal cost on short-hauls and subsidize such flights from revenues obtained by setting prices above marginal cost on long distance travel. That argument had probably never been anything but cover for a strategy for setting average prices at high levels and confusing the evidence to outside critics.

Not everything took place as economists had predicted. For one thing, following a period of intense competition many of the new airlines and some of the old ones left the business or merged with other firms, and the industry reconcentrated in terms of number of firms, though most of the assets stayed in the industry. Apparently current air travel technology mandates a fairly concentrated industry, though that certainly does not mean an uncompetitive industry. Some economists such as William Jordan, however, had thought the industry would be much less concentrated under deregulation than it has turned out to be.[24] But the remaining firms are survivors, and are much more efficient than prior to deregulation.

Another surprise was the development of the Hub and Spoke system, in which many big city terminals are dominated by a single trunk line, fed passengers arriving for long-distance travel on feeder lines from smaller communities in the region. Some studies do show that fares are somewhat higher for similar trips at Hub terminals than at non-Hub terminals served by more airlines. They also show, however, that the service is better at the Hubs. A single airline can coordinate schedules better so that waits between connections are shorter than where passengers have to change airlines. Also, less baggage is lost when it does not have to be transferred between airlines. There is nothing unfair or exploitative *a priori* about charging a slightly higher price for a better product.

On the downside, congestion at airports increased, though this was precisely a consequence of the vast expansion of flights as the price of air travel was brought within reach of the ordinary person, and not just the business traveler. Worse, the air traffic control system run by the Federal Aviation Administration (FAA) is operating with increasingly antiquated equipment, subject to increasing breakdowns. The only failure here, however, is the failure of deregulation to be extended to airports themselves and to air traffic control, so that those functions can be efficiently provided by the market. Whether the strains in the regulated portions of the air transport system will eventually result in their deregulation, or in the reregulation of the airlines, remains an open question.

The immediate beneficial consequences of the Airline Deregulation Act confirmed the worst fears of regulation advocates by adding impetus to further deregulatory legislation. In 1980 Congress passed the Motor Carrier Act of 1980, removing ICC entry restrictions into interstate trucking, prohibitions on carriers serving intermediate points along a routee, and on return trip hauling, as well as many pricing controls. These and other regulations removed by the 1980 law were part of a complex cartel enforcement system for the truck lines developed under the original National Motor Carrier Act of 1935. They had been supported ideologically by an explicit argument that too many firms created destructive competition, which would endanger safety and eventually generate private cartelization of the industry by a few surviving firms. The effect of the ICC regulations perceived by economists studying the industry, however, was to restrict the supply of ground transport services, create vast inefficiency in truck freight through restrictions on internal competition, and redistribute income to the favored carriers from shippers and the consuming public.

As with the regulated airlines, evidence on the inefficiency and harmful effects of trucking regulation came partly from comparison with unregulated firms. Motor carrier transport of agricultural products was exempted from ICC rate regulations, and many firms operated in this sector free of ICC jurisdiction. Comparison revealed that the average revenues of the unregulated carriers were 58 percent lower than those of ICC regulated firms carrying general freight, and that their average costs were also much lower.[25] Also, after truck transport of poultry was deregulated in 1952, an Agriculture Department study found that shipping rates for poultry fell over 30 percent while service quality improved.[26]

That ICC certification and rate regulation was hurting, not benefiting the public, became unambiguous from the immediate effects of the 1980 deregulation. During the first year over 2,400 new firms entered the business of interstate freight transport, and shipping rates fell significantly.[27] Profits in the industry plummeted, as one would expect from such entry. Failure rates rose as less efficient firms lost out, but under the intense competitive pressure, schedule reliability measurably improved. Safety in the industry also improved. The Department of Transportation (DOT) recently reported that the fatal truck accident rate fell from 6.56 per hundred million miles in 1976 to 4.34 in 1987.[28] Advocates of transportation regulation seem never to understand that safety is important to *demanders* of transport services, who will switch away from unsafe transport providers, and improvement in that variable is one of the ways suppliers compete to attract customers.

Railroads, the industry with which transportation regulation began, were also partly (but only partly) deregulated at the same time as the trucking industry under the Staggers Rail Act of 1980. Over time, ICC regulations had created vast inefficiency and severely hurt the industry. Rates on most commodities were held above marginal cost. The railroads were unable to quit unprofitable routes and consolidate. Strong unions, essentially forced on the firms by the government through a series of laws beginning in 1888 and culminating in the Railway Labor Act of 1926, made labor costs excessive. Regulation had severely inhibited technological advance, managerial improvements, and productivity growth in the industry. The 1980 act partly alleviated conditions by removing rate controls entirely on many commodities shipped by railroads, and allowed the firms to negotiate contract rates on all commodities.

Deregulation has been only partial in all of the transportation industries, and the same is true of the other industries deregulated in this period. The magnitude of the deregulation should not be understated however. Clifford Winston reports that in 1977, 17 percent of U.S. GNP was produced in fully regulated industries, and by 1988 this had fallen to 6.6 percent.[29] Even this partial deregulation has had immense benefits for the U.S. Economy, in which transport costs are a component of the final price of nearly all products. John Taylor reports a Brookings Institution study that found annual savings of $20 billion a year since 1980 from interstate truck deregulation alone. Surveying studies of the effects of deregulation generally in the 1970s-1980s, including deregulation of transportation, telecommunications, cable television and banking, Winston concluded that society had gained at least $36-$46 billion in 1990 dollars as a result.[30]

It is important to note, however, that this deregulation was not only partial in the industries affected, but was merely a temporary retrenchment following an immense wave of social and environmental regulation that occurred in the 1960s and 1970s. This odd conjunction of contracting industry regulation and expanding *social* regulation in the 1970s and 1980s may in part be explained by the economic theory of regulation itself.

Peltzman, in an effort to see if his own theory could explain episodes of deregulation, has proposed a life-cycle of regulation. Firms seeking rents through the political process generate regulation, which transfers income as intended, but the rents erode over time because the regulators cannot entirely prevent the competitive forces from operating. Eventually deregulation becomes politically profitable.[31]

What is missing from the life-cycle version of the Economic Theory of regulation, as from all versions thus far, is *any explanation of the role of ideology and/or economic teachings.* The disaffection of some members of these industries–particularly the airlines–was certainly important in generating political conditions in which deregulation was possible. It would almost certainly never have occurred, however, without the dozens of devastating studies of regulated industries by professional economists, without the development and spread of the economic or interest group theory of regulation itself, or without the economists who influenced Jimmy Carter, particularly Alfred Khan.

Clifford Winston has pointed out that political scientists and lawyers studying the deregulatory episode have recognized this crucial role of economists. Martha Derthick and Paul Quirk have argued that deregulation would never have occurred had it not been supported by microeconomic research.[32] Steven Breyer, who worked for Senator Edward Kennedy during the debates, and Michael Levine, who worked at the CAB, expressed similar opinions.[33] Clearly the structure of self-interests is important in explaining regulatory or deregulatory episodes and trends. Just as clearly, however, so is the power of ideas and the state of knowledge.

A small postscript concerning recent events relating to the subject matter of this chapter may be useful. First, in 1996, after nearly two decades of having its functions and power divested, the radical Republican Congress elected in 1994 abolished the Interstate Commerce Commission. Second, industry deregulation has begun to be extended to electric utilities. Utilities have been increasingly connected through local networks or "power pools" since the 1920s, and for decades, the only barriers to consumers having the ability to shop around and buy power from the cheapest source in a competitive market have been legal and political, not technological or economic.[34] Gradually those political barriers are beginning to crumble in California and elsewhere. As they collapse, the last vestiges of the theory of natural monopoly will fall with them, along with the whole notion that utility regulation was created or maintained in the public interest.

Notes

1 George Stigler, "The Theory of Economic Regulation," *Bell Journal of Economics and Management Science* 2 (Spring 1971): 3-21.

2 See, for example, David B. Truman, *The Government Process: Political Interests and Public Opinion* (Knopf, 1951).

3 George Stigler and Claire Friedland, "What Can Regulators Regulate? The Case of Electricity," *Journal of Law and Economics* 6 (October 1963): 1-16.

4 For example, Thomas Gale Moore, "The Effectiveness of Regulation of Electric Utility Prices," *Southern Economic Journal* (April, 1970): 365-375.

5 Harold Demsetz, "Why Regulate Utilities?" *Journal of Law and Economics* 11 (April 1968): 55-65.

6 Gregg A. Jarrell, "The Demand for State Regulation of the Electric Utility Industry," *Journal of Law and Economics* 21 (October 1978): 269-195.

7 Stigler's argument is clearly defective here, because it does not explain why industries would not simply combine benefits 1 and 2, that is, obtain a subsidy and protect the rents from dissipation by having government bar entry. Clearly a better explanation for the frequent aversion of rent-seeking firms to direct cash subsidies is needed. See below.

8 Stigler could well have made reference here to the Supreme Court case of *McCray vs. U.S.* (1904), discussed in Chapter 1 above.

9 Sam Peltzman, "Toward a More General Theory of Regulation," *Journal of Law and Economics* 19 (August 1976): 211-240.

10 It is odd that Peltzman would argue this way, since in other research he has shown himself among those most aware of the strenuous competition and efficiency of operation that actually characterizes most concentrated industries. See Sam Peltzman, "The Gains and Losses from Industrial Concentration," *Journal of Law and Economics* 20 (October 1977): 229-263.

11 M. T. Maloney and R. E. McCormick, "A Positive Theory of Environmental Quality Regulation, " *Journal of Law and Economics* 25 (April 1982): 99-124.

12 One of the best examples here is the minimum wage law. Low wage rates
   in the Southern, largely agrarian states have, since the Civil War, been
   causing Southern workers to move north where wage rates were high due
   to industry and unions. This has put downward pressure on union wage
   rates in the North. Concomitantly, industry in the North has been moving
   South seeking reduction in labor costs. This is an efficiency enhancing
   redistribution of resources that would, over time, tend to equalize wage
   rates and rates of return between the two regions. The primary motive of
   the Northern Congressmen promoting the minimum wage law in 1938,
   however, as revealed by the Congressional debates, was to stop this
   process by artificially raising labor costs in the South. See Thomas
   Rustici, "A Public Choice View of the Minimum Wage," *Cato Journal* 5
   (Spring/Summer 1985): 103-131.

13 Howard P. Marvel, "Factory Regulation: A Reinterpretation of Early
   English Quality Regulation," *Journal of Law and Economics* 25
   (April1982): 99-124.

14 Donald J. Boudreaux and Thomas J. DiLorenzo, "The Protectionist Roots
   of Antitrust," *Review of Austrian Economics* 6, No. 2 (1983): 81-95.

15 William F. Shughart and Robert D. Tollison, "Corporate Chartering: An
   Exploration in the Economics of Social Change," *Economic Inquiry* 2
   (October 1981): 585-599.

16 Richard A. Posner, "Theories of Economic Regulation," *Bell Journal of
   Economics* 5 (Autumn 1974): 335-358.

17 Posner, Ibid., p. 355.

18 Gordon Tullock, "The Backward Society: Static Inefficiency, Rent
   Seeking, and the Rule of Law," in James Buchanan and Robert Tollison,
   The Theory of Public Choice II (University of Michigan Press, 1984):
   224-236, particularly pp. 228-229.

19 As one example typical of thousands of dogmatic public interest claims
   for the origin and effects of regulation that are made in apparent utter
   ignorance of the last 30 years of development in the theory and empirics
   of regulation in the economics profession, consider Manuel G. Mendoza
   and Vince Napoli, *Systems of Society* (6th ed. D.C. Heath and Co.,1995),
   p. 350. This text is widely used in College level introductory social science survey courses.

20 This story is told in more detail in Mary Bennett Peterson, *The Regulated
   Consumer* (Green Hill Publishers, 1971): 130-132.

21 William A. Jordan, *Airline Regulation in America* (Greenwood Press, 1970): 15. Jordan's book is one of the most detailed and influential studies of airline regulation of the period.

22 Jordan, *Airline Regulation in America:* 1

23 Peterson, *The Regulated Consumer:* 136-137.

24 Jordan, Ibid., p. 27.

25 Richard N. Farmer, "The Case for Unregulated Truck Transportation," *Journal of Farm Economics* 46 (1964): 398-409.

26 Reported in George W. Hilton, "Transportation Regulation and Private Carriage," in *Conference on Private and Unregulated Carriage* (Northwestern University Transportation Center, 1963): 13, 26-27.

27 Unlike the airline industry, the interstate trucking industry has not reconcentrated. The number of firms has expanded from 18,045 in 1980 to 45,791 in 1990, according to the DOT.

28 According to John C. Taylor, "Regulation of Trucking by the States," *Regulation: The Cato Review of Government and Business* No. 2 (1994): 44.

29 Clifford Winston, "Economic Deregulation: Days of Reckoning for Microeconomists," *Journal of Economic Literature* 31 (September 1993): 1263-1289, specifically 1263.

30 Winston, "Economic Deregulation": 1284.

31 Sam Peltzman, "The Economic Theory of Regulation after a Decade of Deregulation," *Brookings Papers on Economic Activity: Microeconomics* (1989): 1-41.

32 Martha Derthick and Paul J. Quirk, *The Politics of Deregulation* (The Brookings Institution, 1985).

33 See Steven C. Breyer, Regulation and its Reform (Harvard University Press, 1982), and Richard C. Levin, "Railroad Rates, Profitability, and Welfare Under Deregulation," *Bell Journal of Economics* 12 (Spring 1981): 1-26.

34 See Matthew C. Hoffman, "Power Moves," *Reason* (June 1994): 52-54, and Vernon L. Smith, "Regulatory Reform in the Electric Power Industry," *Regulation* No.1 (1996): 33-46. The same issue of Regulation also contains other excellent essays on the subject.

Chapter 6

Labor Regulation and Cartelization

A major set of laws that emerged from the progressive movement and had its historic origins in the post-Civil War period of rapid industrialization is those regulating labor relations in the United States. Given the argument of the last two chapters about the character of progressive era regulatory legislation as it applied to industry, it seems important to ask whether this labor legislation was written in the public interest, or had a rent-seeking, special interest character. Initially one might think that the public interest was paramount. Far more members of the public are employees than are employers. Were not workers subject to massive exploitation by rapacious capitalists in the 19th century? Would they ever have reached modern living standards without unions, which depended for much of their growth on such legislation? Let us see.

Unions and Labor Legislation

It is important to start with basics in discussing labor unions and labor legislation. There is nothing in the classical liberal principles of a free society that precludes the formation and existence of labor unions. Under the principle of free association, which is virtually a defining quality of personal freedom, a worker would have every right to hire an agent to represent him/her in bargaining with a firm over wages and working conditions. Indeed, any number of workers would have the right to form an association and employ the same bargaining agent or agents. But prospective employers, who are also free citizens with the same rights of free association and non-association, could freely choose to bargain or *not* to bargain with union agents, unless they had, through prior voluntary contract, freely obligated themselves to do so. Even the strike cannot be ruled out on first principles. By the right of free association and non-association, workers may collectively withdraw their employment as a bargaining strategy unless they have voluntarily contracted with the employer not to do so. *Neither union members nor employers, however, would have any right to forcibly prevent each other from bargaining freely and forming employment contracts with other workers or firms.*

There are economic advantages to such voluntary unionism. For one thing, by acting as certifying agents for highly skilled workers, who by virtue of their greater skills would have higher marginal products on average than other workers, unions could obtain a positive wage differential equal to the average productivity differential of their members over non-union workers with the same type of skills. Unions could also perform training functions to raise the productivity of their members, and valuable functions in establishing grievance procedures and communication lines between management and labor. By offering a single bargaining agent for a group of workers, a union may even reduce bargaining costs for the firm. For such reasons, contrary to union mythology, some firms voluntarily created company unions in the 19th century, and others welcomed external unions, though it is true that many firms wanted neither.

Historically, the earliest unions were mostly craft unions. Union organization began in earnest during the post-Civil War period of accelerated industrialization. Even before the war, workers were being drawn off the farm *by the relatively high earnings to be obtained in mining, industry, transportation and trade.* In 1840, over 62 percent of all employment in the U.S. economy was agricultural employment. By 1900, the share of agriculture in total employment was down to 40 percent.[1] Others were entering the U.S. as immigrants, also drawn, to no small extent, by the *higher* potential earnings available here than in Europe.[2] Thus the large-scale labor force was emerging as a natural supply response to an expanding demand for industrial and retail employees.

Quite naturally, some workers felt disadvantaged in bargaining with firms over salary and working conditions, and suspected that they were being paid less than they deserved. In any case, everybody would *always* like to earn more than they are, and some workers were easily convinced that union organization, backed by the strike threat, would allow them to make significant wage gains. Unfortunately, in this process, unions seldom adhered to the voluntary union model described above. It must be remembered, from Chapter 1, that guilds of skilled workers were among the important organizations seeking rents through government granted and enforced supply control and entry restrictions under the late medieval mercantile system.

Those same attitudes manifested themselves early in union history. Unions attempted to construct themselves as labor cartels, able to control and restrict the supply of labor available to firms or industries and force wage rates above market levels. Lacking state enforcement of their cartelization efforts, however, in labor disputes of the day unions often augmented the strike with physical intimidation of non-union replacement workers, and violent destruction of company property. Companies hired armed guards to protect replacement workers and company property, and violent confrontations sometimes occurred.

One of the great misconceptions generated by the labor mythology is the extent of unionism in the 19th century. The simple truth is that, given the individualist ethic of the day, the *vast* majority of workers did *not* wish to be unionized. Union membership only reached 3 percent of the labor force by 1900. As long as workers are free, in the absence of a voluntarily accepted closed shop contract between a company and a union (binding the firm to employ only union members), to join or not join a union to obtain a particular employment, it appears that union membership would not exceed 6 or 7 percent of the labor force. That proportion was reached early in the 20th century and endured until 1917. Government attitudes toward unionism, however, were changing. For some time unions making efforts at private labor monopolization were viewed by the Federal courts, correctly, as combinations in restraint of trade, subject to prosecution under the Sherman Antitrust Act of 1890. Consequently, unions sought exemption from the Sherman Act.

As the Progressive movement gained power, more and more politicians began to see the potential for mass votes and campaign contributions from providing aid and support to organized unionism. They also lost their moral objection to the coerced income redistributions from the employers and consuming public that would result. In 1914, when

Congress passed the Clayton Antitrust Act, it began providing unions with the antitrust exemption they sought, an exemption that would have been unnecessary if unions were not *in fact* aspiring labor cartels. Unfortunately for the unions, subsequent Supreme Court decisions largely annulled the pro-union provisions of the Clayton Act. During World War I, progressive intellectuals appointed by President Wilson to the War Labor Board used their virtually dictatorial power to force firms in many industries to unionize, and the unionized fraction of the labor force reached 12 percent. It began declining immediately after the war, however, and despite the Railway Labor Act of 1926, mandating collective bargaining for all interstate railways, the union share was back down to 6 percent by 1930.

This was the beginning of the Great Depression, however, and of the great period of pro-union legislation. At least six such laws were passed, but two are of primary importance in structuring the current legal environment of labor markets. In 1930 *Republican* President Herbert Hoover signed the Norris-La Guardia Act, which had three main provisions. The first was to make "yellow dog" contracts in which firms ask, as a condition of employment, that workers agree not to join a union, legally unenforceable. Previously, firms were free to ask for non-union oaths, just as unions were free to ask the firm for a closed shop agreement, and both forms of contract were enforceable in the courts.

The second provision of Norris-La Guardia restored and extended the exemption of unions from antitrust prosecution under the Sherman Act that had begun with the Clayton Act. The third provision removed the power of federal courts to issue equity injunctions in labor disputes. In addition, the Act prohibited the courts from issuing injunctions against unions for breach of contract. The effect of this law, in providing *special* privileges and exemptions for unions and union members that are not provided to other citizens under the law, is clear.

The single most important labor law of this century, however, was the National Labor Relations (or Wagner) Act of 1935. The first thing the Act did was to make illegal many perfectly legitimate employer methods of resisting unionization of their labor force, defining them as "unfair labor practices." The central element of the Act, however, was to allow any firm to be unionized by simple majority vote of the employees, such that the union becomes the exclusive bargaining agent for *all* of the employees, including those who vote against and do *not* want representation by the union. Elections are conducted and all provisions of the law are enforced by a political regulatory agency, the National Labor Relations Board. Despite pious statements that the law is to give effect to the right of employees to associate freely in forming unions, the law obviously violates the rights of free association and non-association of employers, their agents, and employees not desiring unionization.

The effects of the Act were immediate and dramatic. Massive labor organizing occurred over the next two years, and in a period of extreme job scarcity and enormous unemployment, such that opportunities to change jobs to avoid unpleasant circumstances were essentially nonexistent, literally millions of workers who did *not wish to be unionized* were forced into unions through certified NLRB elections. In 1937, after the election of 1936 had safely seen Franklin Roosevelt reelected, the unions initiated a massive series of strikes to force wage rates up. *As a predictable result of these pervasive forced wage increases, the economy, which had been recovering since 1934, was shocked back into deep depression in 1938.* The unemployment rate increased between 3 and 5 percentage points, depending on the data source used [3]

With 11 percent of the labor force shifted into the military, World War II mobilization finally ended the depression, and unionization efforts continued after the war. Federal government support of unions declined when Republicans took over Congress in 1946. Congress passed the Taft-Hartley Act of 1947, modifying slightly some provisions of the Wagner Act, but retaining all of its basic provisions and regulatory structure. The fraction of the labor force unionized increased to a maximum of 25.5 percent in 1953, after which it began a slow decline. In the 1960s, another burst of federal support for union activism, from Presidents Kennedy and Johnson, simply accelerated their decline. The unionized fraction of the labor force is now, in the 1990s, down to 17 percent or less, and is still declining.

The Union Ideology and Mythology

Despite the fact that most labor legislation of this century was manifestly *not* aimed at benefiting *firms* in a specific industry, and indeed has not only had a generally anti-capital but *anti-capitalist* character, the relevance of the economic theory of regulation is clear. First, this legislation was openly redistributive. The stated intent of the laws was to benefit organized workers, a special interest group that was a small proportion of workers, at the expense of their employers. It was a fairly large special interest group admittedly, which therefore arguably faced a massive free rider problem and hence took a long time to organize and attain its political goals. That also, however, accords with predictions of the special interest model of regulatory legislation.[4] In addition, the eventual competitive erosion of rents obtained through regulation, and consequent decline of unionization, is in accord with the life-cycle version of the special interest theory.

It seems, however, that the economic theory must be amended in one way to explain labor legislation. The union struggle was political, economic, physical, and organizational, but above and behind all, it was ideological. Union advocates did not say to other workers, "Join us in forming a labor cartel and coercively excluding our non-union competitors in order to force wage increases from employers, and we will cut you in for equal shares. Otherwise *you* will be forcibly excluded, injured, or killed." They seldom openly said to politicians, "Help us redistribute income forcibly from businessmen and the public to ourselves and we will reward you with campaign contributions, bribes and bloc votes." Instead they said to all, "Help us because it is just; because we are being underpaid and ill treated, and deserve redress." As Posner said, such rhetoric must have a function. Whether true or false, the propagation of such moral and ideological claims by unionists and their intellectual and political supporters was crucial to the eventual political and organizational success of unions.

Several elements of the union ideology and mythology seem important to list and evaluate. First is the claim that in unregulated labor markets workers individually have inferior bargaining power, such that firms are able to exploit workers by setting and maintaining wage rates at subsistence levels. Associated with this is the modern, post World-War II historical claim, made by virtually all labor leaders, that workers would never have achieved modern living standards absent unions and labor legislation. A third element of the union ideology that has always been paramount, is that "the enemy is the Company." That is, the struggle is between labor *as a class* and the owners of capital *as a class*. A fourth claim, again historical and mythological, is that the firms initiated violence far more often than did the unions.

The notion–however natural to individual workers–that firms have all the power in setting wage rates, while workers individually have none, has little basis in fact. As already pointed out, workers in the 19th century industrial labor force were *attracted* into such employments by the *superiority* of compensation and conditions there to alternate–primarily agricultural or pastoral–available employments. And within the industrial sector there were thousands of different private firms. It is difficult to believe a worker could be exploited for any enduring period when he or she could simply change employers or jobs, and historically people *frequently did so.*

Firms could not and cannot make any worker accept a wage. If they offer a wage that is too low, workers leave for better employments, and the wage must be raised to retain the necessary number and quality of employees. If only one local employer existed (a highly unusual condition even in those days), and for some reason, such as high transport costs from an isolated location, workers could not leave in response to artificially low wages, sooner or later the high returns earned by the firm would attract *capital* to the region. That is, one or more other firms would enter the local market and compete for the underpaid labor, bidding wage rates up. As a general proposition, as long as capital and labor are free to move, neither can exploit the other for an enduring period.[5] It seems likely then, that any exploitative underpayment of workers in the 19th century was intermittent, localized and transient.

One of the difficulties in evaluating union claims of widespread underpayment and labor exploitation in the 19th century, is precisely that they *never* define what *constitutes* underpayment or exploitation.[6] This failure is deliberate, since providing such objective definitions would immediately subject union advocates to calls for empirical proof of their claims that such exploitation was or is common. This they wish to avoid at all cost. Likewise, their effort to obtain power through government *regulation* to control labor supplies and redistribute income to themselves has the same motive. Civilized, constitutional standards of law require that if one person is accused of unjustly harming another, redress or punishment through government force must follow *proof* of that fact in accordance with rigorous standards of evidence in a court of law. One of the primary reasons for employing regulation as a form of law is precisely to institute redress of an ideologically theorized social injustice, allowing some to gain at the expense of others who are to be punished and coerced by the law, *without* being subject to that necessity.[7]

The best we can do in empirically evaluating claims of exploitation and underpayment is to employ economic theory and methods. As a fundamental, economists recognize that firms employ people to *do* something; that is, to add to the firm's output of goods and services. The market value of the output added to the firm's total production per time period by the marginal employee sets an upper bound on what the firm can afford to pay that employee. As a firm with a given capital stock hires additional workers, reducing the capital-labor ratio in production, marginal product tends to fall for each successive employee hired. Profit *maximizing* firms competing for scarce labor in competitive markets add employees until, for the last person hired, the wage equals the value of the marginal product.[8]

If firms generally pay workers a wage (actually, the dollar value of both wage and non-wage compensation) equal to the *value* of their marginal products, then the *purchasing power* of worker's wages, that is their literal value in terms of goods and services, will equal worker's physical marginal products. The key argument here is that *the productivity of employees in any given production period is the prime determinant of their real compensation.* It follows that, if firms do research and development that improves technology and/or invest in increased capital, and workers invest in improving their skills, so that productivity rises over time, real employee earnings should rise proportionately. The union theory that, absent unions, workers will be exploited and paid only a subsistence wage, makes no such prediction. The post-Civil War period of nascent unionism in which rapid industrialization was raising labor productivity would seem to be a good test case.[9]

Fortunately, reasonably good data actually exists for this period. Table 6-1 in the appendix to this chapter shows average, real annual earnings of non-farm employees (adjusted for changes in the value of money using the 1914 Consumer Price Index) for each of the thirty-five years from 1866, the year after the war ended, to 1900. Real earnings per non farm employee grew 78 percent over the period, from $322 in 1866 to $573 in 1900. This amounts to a 1.659 percent average annual compound rate of increase.[10] Since the proportion of the labor force unionized at the time was trivial, this real earnings growth cannot be attributed to unions. Just as clearly, *any claim that workers were suppressed by ruthless exploitation to a subsistence level of real income prior to the emergence of large scale unionism is nonsense.*

A suspicion may still exist that a *jump* in employee real earnings at the time of mass unionization may have been necessary to lift workers to modern living standards (we will see that, in fact, the opposite happened). However, if we run the post-Civil War growth rate forward for 50 or 60 years from 1900, calculating $573(1.0659)^{50}$ and $573(1.0659)^{60}$, the resulting estimates of 1950 and 1960 income for non farm employees are actually slightly *larger* than the *actual* incomes for those years when those are also expressed in 1914 dollars. The imputed 1950 income is $1,305 while the actual 1950 income was $1,154, and the imputed 1960 income was $1,538, while the actual 1960 income was $1,422. *Clearly, the assertion that in the absence of mass unionism the market could not have raised worker's real incomes to modern levels is without foundation.*

To further examine the affects of unions on employee wages, it would be useful to compare the post-Civil War period with a similar historical period in which a large fraction of the labor force was unionized. Accordingly, Table 6-2 in the appendix to this chapter shows real annual earnings of non farm employees for the thirty years of the post-World War II period from 1948 to 1977.[11] This was the classic period of mass unionism in the United States, over which the unionized fraction of the labor force averaged more than *ten times larger* than it did in the post-Civil War period. If unions are as beneficial to the real earnings of workers *as a class* as union leaders and their intellectual sycophants have always claimed, one would expect such earnings to have grown more rapidly in the second period than in the first. *In fact, growth in real annual earnings of non farm employees averaged only 1.45 percent per year from 1948 to 1977. This is well below the nearly 1.66 percent annual compound rate of growth over the post-Civil War period.*

In the second period unionism actually seems to be just as insignificant a factor in generating rising real incomes as in the first. This can be seen from Graph 6.1, which plots index number values for aggregate, average, hourly real output of non-farm employees and hourly real earnings for such employees over the 1948-1977 period. The data employed in the construction of the hourly real earnings index included employer contributions for social insurance and private benefit plans. The close correlation between the two variables is visually clear, and the mathematical correlation is .996, which is statistically indistinguishable from a perfect correlation of 1. Clearly, the productivity of labor is such a strong determinant of its compensation that there is little room for unions as an explanatory variable. Some may wish to argue that unions, somehow, are crucial to raising productivity, but they would have to explain why worker productivity and real earnings grew so strongly when unions were largely absent.[12]

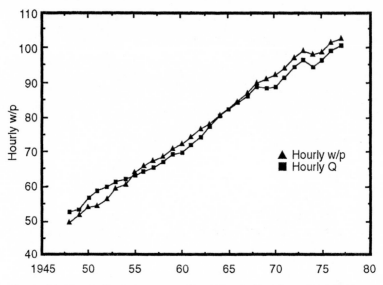

Graph 6.1: Hourly Real Output and Real Hourly Earnings, 1946-1977.

It is important to recognize the limits of the arguments and evidence just presented. For one thing, one should be wary of concluding that large scale unionization *reduced* the growth of employee real incomes in the post World War II period relative to the post-Civil War period. Even though there is good reason for believing that, by forcing wage rates above market levels unions absorb investment capital and reduce real economic growth, there are other factors. Despite their similarities, the degree of unionization was not the only difference between the two historical periods. In much of the first period, the gold standard was in operation, in contrast with the Federal Reserve fiat money system of the second. Also, levels of federal taxation, expenditure, and industrial and social regulation, were negligible in the earlier period in contrast with the latter. All of these institutional changes have probably hurt economic growth in the post World War II period. Nevertheless, there is no support in this data for union claims of systematic labor exploitation in the 19th century, or for the claim that the large real income gains of ordinary workers over time are due to unions.

The third and fourth elements of the union ideology are closely related. The claim that the interests of workers as a class and capitalists as a class are inherently opposed, borrowed by the unions from socialist ideology, is intended solely to maximize public support and suppress opposition to unions. It has no support in either economic theory or the actual history of labor organization and union action. For one thing, though labor and capital as inputs are substitutable as long as their proportions are least marginally variable in production, they are essentially *complementary* factors, working *together* to generate output and income. In addition, no law ever prevented a worker from purchasing stock, or starting a business, and many have done so. Labor and capital have never been rigid categories in America, where vertical socioeconomic mobility is the rule, not the exception. Similarly, another way of seeing the silliness of the supposed inherent antagonism of labor and capital, is to note the huge fraction of corporate stock that is nowadays owned by *union and other worker pension funds,* such that workers have a direct pecuniary stake in the profitability of corporations. Union and other workers, to a very significant extent, *are* the capitalists.

The most important observation on this issue, however, is probably that, in the history of union organization and action, the most fundamental ongoing struggle, resulting in the most violent confrontations, has been that between union and *non-union* workers. Contrary to all union claims that union negotiations for wage increases are aimed at redressing underpayment, when they fail to reach an initial agreement, and a strike signals the presence of employment opportunities at the employer's wage offer, other workers almost invariably offer to fill those employments. That would manifestly *never* be the case if the employer's wage offer were exploitively low.[13]

It is simply not possible to make sense of the picket line and other intimidation tactics of unions *except as an effort to exclude other workers* who see opportunities to *improve* their living standards (or they would not be willing to shift from their current employments), even though the wage rates they would obtain are *below* those being asked by the union. The observable antagonism and struggle between organized and unorganized labor makes nonsense of the ideological claim of a categorical labor/capital struggle. But economically it is obvious: *suppliers compete primarily with other suppliers* for the business of demanders, and only when they are the *only* supplier from whom the demanders can buy, can they force the price up. Union gains necessarily imply and require the exclusion of other, competing, workers.

Part of this same myth is the claim that unions have been more frequently the victims than the instigators of violence. Charles Baird reexamined the history of the three most infamous examples of labor violence in the 19th century: the Haymarket riot of 1886 in Chicago's Haymarket Square, the Homestead strike at Carnegie steelworks in Homestead, Pennsylvania, and the Pullman strike of 1894. In each case he discovered and demonstrated that the standard histories were grossly distorted toward the union view, and that the unions had in fact initiated the violence.[14] It was most frequently directed against non-union workers and corporate security forces. State and local police officials were also often threatened, shot or bombed, and though union workers sometimes realized they needed corporate assets, large scale destruction of corporate property was frequent.

It is important also to note that, just as the strike is actually seldom resorted to, but the strike *threat* is chronic and persuasive, when strikes do occur union violence need not be overt to be effective. Forms of intimidation of competing employees and company agents short of outright violence, such as threats, car chasing, tire slashing, and so on, are far more common than outright physical assaults. Indeed, picketing itself is *inherently* intimidating, and *intentionally* so, which is why the federal courts, for a period of time early in this century, intentionally and quite correctly placed limits on its use.

Union violence and company property damage in strikes was so common that the federal courts increasingly granted equity injunctions to firms, prohibiting the violence and sometimes stopping the strikes. Eventually, of course, the unions succeeded in getting that power removed from the courts through the Norris-La Guardia Act. In an exhaustive study Sylvester Petro showed that the courts were very careful and fair to the unions in their issuance of injunctions. Unions, in contrast to firms, almost never *sought,* much less gained, equitable relief from the courts against the employer depredations they allege to have been so common.[15] In fact union violence and intimidation are a chronic element of labor disputes to this day.[16] The press, however, partly because it is *itself* highly unionized (some of the most violent strikes in this century have been printer's union strikes), and also because of its liberal bias, seldom reports such acts, as if they are not important.

Even worse, since the Great Depression, Congress and the Federal courts have actually *sanctioned* the use of violence by unions in labor disputes. Unions have been exempted from the federal extortion statutes, for example, on the basis of an implicit judicial philosophy that their intended ends (raising wage rates) justifies the means.[17] The only good news in all this is that union tactics have alienated them from public support and are self-destructive. The direct consequence of their legalized labor cartel activities has been a progressive decline in union representation in the American labor force as they price themselves out of employment. This will continue unless union organizing and price-fixing power is reinforced by a new set of laws and legal privileges.

The Economics of Union Action

The discussion thus far may leave the reader puzzled. If union organizing, strike action and collective bargaining augmented by favorable labor legislation have not made workers better off, then what has been its point? Why have such efforts been ongoing? In part the answer is simple: to say that unionization has not made *labor* better off *is not* to say that it has not made *union members* (or at least a subset of union membership) better off. Indeed, that employed union members generally make more than employed non-union workers in the same trades or fields is beyond dispute. Two things become necessary to explain: First, how this positive income differential in favor of union workers is created and maintained. Second, if it is indeed the result of a forced redistribution aided by regulatory action, at whose expense is it generated? Here again, it turns out that such regulatory rent redistributions only partly work, and work only for a limited period of time.

While the Wagner Act made yellow dog contracts unenforceable, it left unions legally free to operate under closed shop contracts, in which only workers who were union members could be employed by the firm. Such contracts are a powerful exclusionary device, since the union is able to control and limit its own membership, and hence could strictly control the supply of labor to any firm or industry operating under such a contract. In the 1946 midterm elections, however, the Republicans took over Congress, and in 1947 they passed the Taft-Hartley Act, one provision of which made closed shop contracts illegal. However, unions can still employ the somewhat weaker *union shop* contract, under which a person can be employed without being a member of the union, but must subsequently join and pay dues. These contracts are legal in thirty states, but twenty one others have passed right-to-work laws, under which employees *cannot* be forced to join the union.

Even in right-to-work states, however, non-union workers in NLRB unionized firms are forbidden from negotiating for themselves. Hence the union, as sole negotiator for all workers, has a government granted monopoly power in wage negotiations, which it can employ to force wage rates above competitive levels. It is also important to stress another institutional feature of modern American unions, and that is their large size and industry-wide (and sometimes even cross-industry) character. As Morgan Reynolds stresses, the typical union is not orga- nized around a single firm. The memberships of less than fifty large unions together constitute more than 90 percent of the union workers in the United States. The national organization, not the local, controls the union, and collective bargaining is often industry-wide.

Unions typically employ two strategies to force employers to pay increased wage rates and benefits. The first is to restrict the supply of labor available in the industry. A costly strike combined with intimida- tion of non-union competitors as a negotiating tool, whether actual or merely threatened, is only the most obvious method to achieve this. Closed shop contracts combined with membership limits are another method. Long apprenticeships in trades can be employed to reduce the supply of skilled workers available over time, and legal restrictions on immigration are another tool.

The initial effects of such supply restrictions are shown in Graph

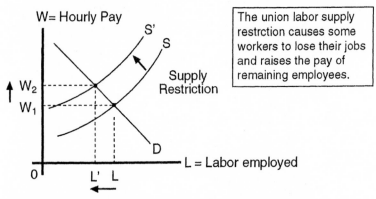

Graph 6.2: Initial Effects of a Union Labor Supply Restriction

6.2. Assume the competitive wage for workers of a particular type and skill in an labor market (which may include, on the demand side, firms from many industries) is W_1 under competitive supply and demand conditions, and that the equilibrium quantity of employment is L. If the union is able to constrict the labor supply to S', they can negotiate for, and employers will accept, a wage equal to W_2 to clear the market. It is vital to note that, *since the demand for labor* (as for any other good or service in the market) *is an inverse function of its price, other things equal, the quantity of employment must decline as a consequence of the wage rate increase.* Hence the gains made by those union members, or other workers represented by the union who retain their employment come partly at the cost of lost income to other employees of the firm or industry.[18] Note also that there is no guarantee that total labor compensation will rise. *Since the increase in the wage is associated with a decline in employment, total labor compensation in the industry may (initially) rise, fall, or remain the same.* It will rise only if demand is inelastic.

The second strategy is simply for the union to employ its bargaining power to force the firms to contractually set the wage at W_2 and let the firms reduce the quantity of labor they demand to L'. Mathematically and graphically these strategies seem identical in effect. If the union restricts employment to quantity L' then wage W_2 is the only one that clears the market, and if the union forces the firms to pay wage W_2 then L' is the only equilibrium quantity of employment. In practice, however, restrictive control over labor supply is required even in the second case, to force the firm to accept the high wage. In effect, the two methods are essentially indistinguishable.

In either case, it is important to understand that, since wage costs are a large fraction of all costs even in competitive industries, the costs of employers are increased significantly when they are forced by unions to pay above market wage rates and benefits. This has the effect of reducing supplies in the markets for the *products* the firms are employing the workers to produce, so that prices must rise for those products. Thus *part of the gain for union workers who retain their employment, comes at the expense of consumers of the final products,* who find they can only afford smaller quantities of the goods at higher prices. In addition, the wage increases reduce gross investor profits and rates of return, and other things equal, the higher wage costs will only be fully passed on to consumers when some of the firms have left the industry. Thus *part of the gains of union workers retaining their employment do come at the expense of investors,* but the gaining workers will then be a smaller pool, since employees lose their jobs as those firms exit the industry.

Despite the cartelizing powers granted to unions by numerous acts of Congress before World War II, it has become clear since the war that competitive forces not only continue to operate in labor markets, but are increasingly effective in limiting and reducing union power. For one thing, in a contract dispute, firms are allowed by the NLRB to hire replacement workers, who have often been willing to work despite union picketing and intimidation. Often this allows firms to keep operating and avoid having to accept excessive wage rates. In addition, though workers can certify a union through NLRB elections, they can also *decertify* a union through such an election. In the 1980s, as workers in many locals became dissatisfied with national negotiations that took little account of local conditions, unions lost a large majority of decertification elections.

One competitive force that unions have never been able to control is substitution by *consumers* among products or providers that has the effect of causing substitution among union and non-union workers. Such substitution occurs whenever products of unionized firms or industries have close substitutes produced by non-union firms. In the construction industry, to take one obvious example, where some firms are unionized and others are not, if the bricklayers, carpenters and/or other skilled workers in the unionized firms force wage rates up above their skill differential over similar workers in non-union firms, then non-union firms will be able to bid lower than the union firms. They will take more of the contracts, reducing the unionized sector of the industry. This has happened, though the unions attempted violently to stop it in the 1970s.

An increasingly important form of product substitution limiting union power comes from foreign product substitution in an increasingly integrated world economy. When close foreign substitutes exist for domestic products of union labor, and excessive wage increases by those domestic unions force costs and prices up for the domestic products, American consumers simply substitute the foreign goods in their own purchases. The presence of such foreign substitutes makes the demand for the domestic products of union labor, and for the union labor itself, more elastic, so that a given union wage increase causes a larger loss of unionized employment.

An excellent example here concerns the steelworker's unions. In 1962, steelworkers, as highly productive workers in a capital intensive industry, earned approximately 38 percent more on average than other manufacturing workers. The unions, however, kept pressing for large wage increases. The domestic industry resisted, but when strikes occurred, the government intervened repeatedly on behalf of the unions. By 1980 the steelworker's differential over other manufacturing workers was 64 percent. The firms attempted passing these massive cost increases on to steel buyers, such as the auto industry, but buyers simply switched in droves to German and Japanese steel, which was available at lower cost. The result was a massive decline in the domestic steel industry and in steelworker employment.[19] To no small extent, the United Auto Workers are responsible for the similar decline in their own employment since the 1960s. It is no wonder that unions campaign for tariffs and quotas to raise the prices of foreign products, and for Americans to "buy American to keep Americans working," without ever telling consumers that they are the ones to be hurt by the elimination of low cost purchase options.

One last source of competitive substitution should be mentioned, and that is non-labor input substitution. As long as inputs are at least marginally variable in production, they are partly substitutes. When a union forces wage rates up *relative to the price of capital* it motivates employers to substitute capital for labor at the margin, displacing some workers, until changes in the marginal products of labor and capital re-equate the marginal costs of producing with each of these factors. This also makes labor demand curves more elastic over time, and increases the job loss resulting from union cartel actions. Nothing in the panoply of government labor regulation provided by the Norris-La Guardia or Wagner Acts can prevent such adjustments in input proportions as firms try to minimize costs.

It is possible now to explain the effects of unions on the structure and distribution of incomes. Though unions certainly do not benefit the level or rate of growth of earnings of workers as a class, they generally do obtain a positive wage differential over non-union labor through their cartel activities for those of their members who manage to retain their employment. This has two sources, however. The first is the direct wage gain for their remaining employed members. The second is a slight *decline* in the wage rates of *non-union* workers as some of those union members who are *disemployed* by the union wage increases shift to non-union segments of the labor market and compete for jobs, increasing labor supplies relative to demands by those employers. The wage increase in the unionized firms and the decline of wage rates in the non-union firms together generate the union wage differential. Thus the gain of union workers retaining employment comes partly at the expense of workers disemployed by their union's action, partly at the expense of non-union workers, partly at the expense of consumers required to pay higher prices for products, and partly at the expense of investors forced out of business. The differential is estimated, on average, at around 15 percent.[20]

The more intelligent union leaders, once having created such a differential, simply act to maintain it in subsequent contract negotiations. Thereafter, general productivity growth acts to raise the real wages of both union and non-union workers over time, but the illusion is maintained, in the unionized sector, that those gains are coming from the unions. Many union leaderships, however, as already made clear, have been unable to resist the temptation to expand the differential, with all of the consequent effects of strife, conflict, resource misallocation, price increases, increased unemployment, and lost production. This whole process is not only harmful to American society, the rule of law, and the economy at large, but is ultimately self-destructive to the unions themselves. The decline of union membership over time is no mystery.

In summary, what pro-union labor theorists term 'labor's bitter struggle' was an effort on the part of an organized special interest to redistribute income forcibly to themselves. It was a particularly objectionable private cartelization effort because it employed literal violence and physical intimidation, which producer cartels almost never do. When the private labor cartelization efforts failed, the movement turned to politics and tried regulatory cartel formation, since government force is so much more systematic and effective than private force. As usual, the necessary legislation was made palatable to the very consumers and voters who were among those it was to harm through propagation of a historical mythology and a false ideology of social justice and injustice.

Notes

1 See the graph showing the trend in employment shares in Council of Economic Advisers, *The Economic Report of the President, 1991* (U.S. Government Printing Office, 1991): 114.

2 See Gary M. Walton and Hugh Rockoff, *History of the American Economy* (6th ed. Harcourt, Brace, Jovanovich, 1990): 218-223 and 371-375.

3 Michael R. Darby, "Three-and-a-Half Million U.S. Employees Have Been Mislaid: Or, an Explanation of Unemployment, 1934-1941," *Journal of Political Economy* 84 no.1 (1976): 1-17.

4 In a later chapter I will significantly question and amend the argument that the primary cost of organizing a special interest group is the cost of overcoming the free-rider problem. For now it is enough to grasp that some such significant organizing costs exist.

5 William H. Hutt, *The Strike Threat System: the Economic Consequences of Collective Bargaining* (Arlington House, 1973): Chapter 1.

6 Unless the argument here is actually that of Karl Marx, that *all* employer earnings are unjust and constitute exploitation of labor. But that is nonsense, and the unionists themselves understand it. They grasp very well that capital *is* independently productive (as Marx did not), and hence that their work is made more productive and valuable by its presence as a complementary factor of production, or they would not be so anxious to retain, exclusively, their jobs.

7 Three (among many) characteristics shared by nearly all false political ideologies are therefore, first, that they assert the existence of unjust conditions or social harm that cannot be proved, either logically or empirically; second, that they assert the injustice or social harm to be the outcome of a set or subset of *voluntary* transactions; and third, that they advocate the application of force against particular persons to correct the alleged injustice without any prior legal demonstration of guilt on the part of those persons.

8 What is true for the payment of labor also follows for the payment of owners of the other complementary inputs. This is the famous marginal productivity theory of factor price and income share determination, that originated in the late 19th century and has held up so well under rigorous scrutiny and hostile criticism that it has only received slight qualification and modification in the 20th. For the classic treatment, see John Bates Clark, *The Distribution of Wealth: A Theory of Wages, Interest and Profits* (Macmillan Co., 1899). For the modern literature see George Stigler, *Production and Distribution Theories* (Transaction Publishers, 1994).

9 The data and basic arguments employed here were first employed by the author in James Rolph Edwards, "Deflating the Union Mythology," *The Margin* 8 (Fall 1992): 58-59.

10 This data actually *understates* the real income gains of workers from 1866-1890 because the average number of hours worked per week declined in excess of 6 percent over the period.

11 It will be noted that I am here comparing a thirty-year period to the earlier
35 year period. There are various reasons for this. First, the earlier period
began in a recession year (1866) and ended in an expansion year (1900),
and hence there is a very small upward bias in the computed average compound growth rate. For accurate comparison, I wanted the second period to
also begin with a recession year and end with an expansion year. Had I run
the second series forward to 1982, it would have ended in a recession year.
Actually, that would have added two recession years, 1980 and 1982,
which would have brought the number of recession years in that period to
9, making it much more comparable to the earlier period (which had 11) in
that respect. But it would have reduced the average annual growth in real
non-farm income in the second period, and at bottom, I wanted to be as
charitable as possible to the union period.

12 Harvard school advocates of the "new view" of unions argue that some of
the activities of unions raise productivity, but even they admit it is a mixed
bag. See Richard B. Freeman and James L. Medoff, *What Do Unions Do?*
(Basic Books, 1984). For a perspective critical of the new view, see Leo
Troy, C. Timothy Koeler, and Neil Sheflin, "The Three Faces of
Unionism," *Policy Review* 14 (Fall 1980): 95-109, and Morgan O.
Reynolds, *Power and Privilege: Labor Unions in America* (Universe
Books, 1984): Chapter 4.

13 Union workers often complain bitterly about the willingness of firms to
hire lower skilled workers at lower wages. But as I have already argued, a
union would need no strike to obtain a positive productivity differential.
Other things equal, a firm would be indifferent between employing members of two different worker groups having a 20 percent skill differential at
a 20 percent pay differential, since its unit labor costs would be identical in
each case. If the employer has a desire to substitute members of the lower
skilled group for those of a highly skilled union group, it is likely a consequence of the union demanding a pay differential greater than the skill differential.

14 Charles Baird, "Labor law reform: lessons from History," *Cato Journal*
(Spring/Summer 1990): 175-209

15 Sylvester Petro, "Injunctions and Labor Disputes: 1880-1932," *Wake
Forest Law Review* 14 (June 1978): 341-576.

16 See Armand J. Thieblot Jr. and Thomas R. Haggard, *Union Violence: the
Record and the Response by Courts, Legislatures, and the NLRB* (The
Wharton School, University of Pennsylvania, 1983).

17 In this regard, see the 1973 case of *U.S. vs. Enmons,* 410 U.S. 401.

18 It seems puzzling that unions would do this only if one fails to see the
crass self-interest operating at all levels in the process. Claims of worker

solidarity are essentially a hoax. Union contracts have nearly all been deliberately written to institute the rule "last hired, first fired." Workers with seniority dominate the unions, and are perfectly willing to see newer workers laid off if it means higher wage rates for them. If the risks of being disemployed following wage increases were evenly distributed among workers union militancy would be *severely* reduced.

19 See Yale Brozen, *Revitalizing the American Economy* (University of Missouri, Kansas City, 1981): Chapter 7.

20 C. J. Parsley, "Labor Unions and Wages: a Survey," *Journal of Economic Literature* 18 (March 1980): 1-31.

Appendix 6
Table 6-1: Annual Growth of Real Annual Earnings of Non farm Employees, 1866-1900

Year	Real[1] Earnings	%Δ(E/P)	Year	Real[1] Earnings	%Δ(E/P)
1866	$322	-1.83	1884	$478	4.14
1867	338	4.97	1885	492	2.93
1868	367	8.57	1886	499	1.42
1869	380	3.54	1887	509	2.00
1870	375	-1.32	1888	505	-0.79
1871	386	2.93	1889	510	0.99
1872	416	7.77	1890	519	1.76
1873	407	-2.16	1891	525	1.16
1874	403	-0.98	1892	527	0.38
1875	403	0.00	1893	505	-4.17
1876	393	-2.48	1894	484	-4.16
1877	388	-1.27	1895	520	7.44
1878	397	2.32	1896	521	0.19
1879	391	-1.51	1897	529	1.53
1880	395	1.02	1898	527	-0.37
1881	415	5.06	1899	563	6.83
1882	431	3.85	1900	573	1.78
1883	459	6.49			

[1]In constant 1914 dollars, as reported in *U.S. Historical Statistics,* series D 735-738.

Note: The average annual %Δ(E/P) ≈ 1.659, and the average number of recession years per decade over the period was 11/3.5 ≈ 3.14.

See Graph 6.1 on the following page.

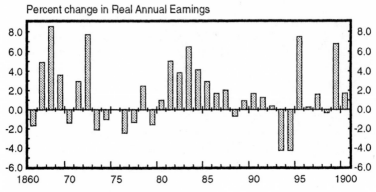

Graph 6.3 Correlates with Table 6.1

Appendix 6
Table 6-2: Annual Growth of Real Annual Earnings
of Non farm Employees, 1948-1977

Year	Real[1] Earnings	%Δ(E/P)	Year	Real[1] Earnings	%Δ(E/P)
1948	$10,205	-0.13	1963	$14,466	1.94
1949	10,533	3.35	1964	14,751	1.97
1950	11,052	4.93	1965	15,172	2.85
1951	11,183	1.19	1966	15,295	0.81
1952	11,432	2.23	1967	15,255	-0.26
1953	11,923	4.29	1968	15,509	1.66
1954	12,016	0.78	1969	15,644	0.87
1955	12,664	5.93	1970	15,491	-0.98
1956	13,038	2.95	1971	15,753	1.69
1957	13,054	0.12	1972	16,412	4.18
1958	13,013	-0.31	1973	16,406	-0.04
1959	13,567	4.26	1974	15,715	-4.21
1960	13,629	0.46	1975	15,242	-3.01
1961	13,810	1.33	1976	15,468	1.48
1962	14,191	2.76	1977	15,649	1.17

[1]In constant 1982 dollars, computed from *The Economic Report of The President*, 1991, table B-44.

Note: Average annual %Δ(E/P) ≈ 1.45 over this period, and the average number of recession years per decade was 7/3 ≈ 2.33.

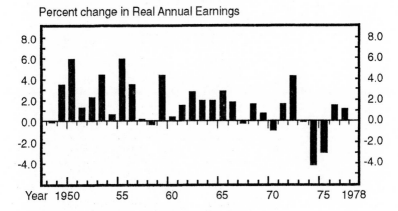

Graph 6.4 Correlates with Table 6.2, opposite page.

Chapter 7

Health and Safety Regulation

In the late 19th and early 20th centuries regulatory laws began to be passed that had the ostensible function of protecting the health and increasing the safety of the public. Some of these, such as the federal meat inspection laws discussed in Chapter 4, were industry specific, and are subject to charges of special interest motives. Indeed, some, such as the state laws requiring restriction of medical practice to graduates of state approved medical schools run by the American Medical Association were clearly cartelization laws.[1] Many health and safety laws, however, such as the Agricultural Appropriation Act of 1928 that created the FDA, covered more than one industry. Under the guiding hands of Presidents Lyndon Johnson and Richard Nixon, this type of legislation expanded rapidly in the late 1960s and early 1970s. This period saw the creation of such regulatory agencies as the Occupational Safety and Health Administration, the Consumer Product Safety Commission, and the National Highway Traffic and Safety Administration.

It is often claimed that such legislation is immune from charges of special interest character since it is not industry specific, and must have been undertaken in the genuine public interest. This argument is overstated, though it has some merit. It does seem true that an anti-market, pro-regulatory ideology has been more the driving force, and organized interests the supporting cast in such legislation. But even assuming that altruistic intents were primary, which is not obvious, the best of intentions will not generate good results if they stem from a bad grasp of reality. That is, even legislation undertaken in the public interest may not serve it.

Theory and Practice of Safety Regulation

Safety regulation aims not at suppressing crimes involving private force and fraud, but at forcibly altering certain resource allocations that have resulted from peaceful, voluntary interactions among suppliers and demanders of goods or services in the market. All such regulation is justified by some theory of 'market failure' or capitalist exploitation, usually both. The solution sought is to substitute the coercive rule of technocrats through bureaucratic regulation to correct such alleged exploitation or market failures. Since the intellectual advocates of such theories see themselves *as* the technocratic experts who are so much wiser than the average person as to be able to perceive and correct the mistakes of the market, and as the ones who will make and enforce the rules, there is arguably a special interest motivation behind the ideological arguments for such legislation.

The starting point of market failure theories is the economic theory of perfectly competitive markets under which correct resource use takes place. That theory assumes that market demanders have perfect information about the product, including its price, where it is available, and any risks associated with its use, while suppliers also have perfect information about production technology, including associated risks. This is simply an heuristic model, however. In the real world, people face chronic uncertainty about many things. Instead of being complete, information is scarce and valuable, and must be produced or acquired through the use of scarce resources (including time) that have other valuable uses. Hence there is an opportunity cost to its acquisition. The optimal amount of information for any person to acquire and/or disseminate is *never* perfect information, but that amount at which the estimated marginal benefit of the last increment acquired just equals its estimated marginal cost.

Just as clearly, product or workplace safety will *never* be perfect. Products (or the workplace) can be engineered for improved safety, but only at a rising marginal cost for each additional unit of risk reduction. Increasing product safety thus increases the cost of the product unless other features, which may be as valuable to consumers, are reduced to offset the higher cost of improved safety. Producers try to find a *combi-*

nation of product features including safety that most satisfies customers, and since customers differ in their risk attitudes, different producers will fill different segments of the market. Product safety will therefore vary across producers, as will other quality dimensions, just as the auto industry offers Cadillacs at one end of the spectrum and Yugos at the other. This process constitutes an efficient matching of scarce resources to the spectrum of public tastes and needs.

Over time, as technology advances, additional reductions in product (or workplace) riskiness take place, just as improvements in other product quality dimensions occur. But at any point in time, with a given level of technology and structure of public tastes, perfect safety is *not* optimal. As long as the market process generates the optimal amount of information given the marginal costs and marginal value of information, and generates the optimal workplace safety at given technologies of production and worker preferences, resources are being allocated correctly *despite* the absence of perfect information and the continued presence of some product and workplace hazards.

Market failure theorists see two problems. First, information generated through the private use of resources is often passed on and confers benefits to others *beyond* those who generated it, or who initially purchased it. These are known as *external* benefits. Assuming external benefits are not considered in private information investment decisions, but only personal ones, the total social benefits of information generated exceed the private benefits. Consequently, market participants will employ fewer resources to generate less information than would be optimal from a social perspective.[2] This is argued to be particularly true of information about the hazards associated with product use or workplace technology. In addition, if risk characteristics of products or production conditions are hard to observe relative to other product characteristics or workplace conditions, it is argued that people may underestimate risks, and hence be subjected to excessive risks without knowing it.[3] Such arguments seem to justify government provision or requirement of additional information (such as product labeling regulations) or regulatory actions to reduce or eliminate allegedly excessive risks.

There are several things to note about this sort of argument. First, informational market failure is just a theory, and is not particularly persuasive as such. People who pass on information thereby demonstrate that it has value to them *for doing so* in *addition* to its direct use value. In one way or another they are compensated. Also, second-hand information is often less valuable than first-hand information. For either or both reasons, the difference between the private and social value of information may be negligible or zero, so that its entire social value may essentially be included in the initial demand. Likewise, difficulty in observing risk characteristics of products or workplace conditions seems as likely to cause *overestimation* of riskiness as underestimation. Most likely, people's estimates of the risks associated with products or job conditions are normally distributed around the correct values.[4]

Second, even if the market failure theory were true, it says only that *more* information, or *some* risk reduction is needed. It does not say how much, or provide *any* method of measuring the magnitude of external informational benefits or required product or workplace risk reduction. *Hence the theory is not only inherently impossible to test, it provides no policy guidance at all for decision makers in a regulatory bureaucracy.* The notion that market participants cannot know or attain the correct resource use, but bureaucrats can, is simply an intellectual conceit. The necessary information is simply not available to regulators, since it consists of personal, subjective preferences for risk and other variables. Lacking the information required for policy guidance, members of such a bureaucracy will be guided more by other incentives, including their own desire to exercise power, and there is no reason to suppose that a correct resource allocation will be achieved.

It is certainly true that corporate malfeasance sometimes occurs, and generates harm to consumers or workers. There are non-regulatory legal remedies such as law suits, however. Also, there are law firms willing to invest resources in pursuing meritorious claims against manufacturers and employers, so that here also no market failure exists. At root it seems to be simply because perfect product and workplace safety is *not* optimal, and hence is *never* achieved, but people do not understand that, that it has been easy for interventionists to point to random workplace accidents and product injuries and convince people of the need for regulation. After all, in the absence of the basic knowledge (which the government *never* supplies to the public[5]) that reducing risks is costly, and that after some point the marginal costs of further risk reduction exceed the marginal benefits, so that the optimal level of risk is *not* zero, who can oppose proposed government efforts to reduce risks?

Food and Drug Regulation

The results of the regulatory philosophy in action many be illustrated by reference to the grandfather of all product safety regulation agencies, the Food and Drug Administration. Though the agency that became the FDA originated in 1928, its powers to prevent the marketing of unapproved drugs and cosmetics were established by the Food, Drug and Cosmetics Act of 1938. Under that authority, only drugs and cosmetics proven 'safe' by FDA standards could be marketed. The Keefauver-Harris Amendment of 1962 added the requirement that such products be proven *effective* (again by FDA determined standards), and in 1976, medical devices were brought under the FDA regulatory authority subject to the same standards for marketing.

It is vital to grasp that producers of drugs, cosmetics and medical devices have always had incentives to test their products for safety and effectiveness before marketing them, and *have always conducted such tests*. The primary incentive is market competition; specifically, threatened loss of customers who will quickly shift from sellers of less safe and effective medical or cosmetic products to sellers of more safe and effective products, *ceteris paribus*. In addition, the manufacturers are subject to suits from persons harmed by their products. The only question is whether such testing generated purely by the incentives of market competition and legal liability, generates *adequate* information and products with the *optimal* (not zero) degree of risk.

On an essentially ideological, unproven and unprovable belief that it hasn't, FDA regulation forces firms to undertake much more stringent, detailed and lengthy testing than they otherwise would. This adds enormously to the cost and price of drugs, cosmetics and medical devices, which in itself makes them unaffordable to some persons, *reducing* the health and safety of those persons. In addition it enormously lengthens the testing and approval process, delaying the marketing of such products. This 'marketing lag' increased significantly after the 1962 amendments, rising from an average of two years to nearly a decade. There is some evidence that other factors may have contributed to this lag, but the FDA was surely responsible for much of it. New drugs approved annually by the FDA fell 60 percent after the amendments.[6]

In part the excess delays generated by FDA testing regulations were and are a consequence of the incentives the agency faces. New drugs, even after testing, may turn out to have harmful side effects undiscovered in the testing process. Possibly the worst example is Thalidomide, a sedative prescribed to pregnant women in Europe in the 1960s, which caused several thousand babies to be born with deformities. Certainly additional testing reduces the probabilities that such harmful products reach the market. On the other hand, testing delays aimed at finding such harmful effects also keep *beneficial* drugs from reaching the market, which *extends the misery or causes the deaths of people with medical conditions that could be cured or alleviated by such drugs.* It is estimated, for one example, that FDA action keeping beta-blockers off the market in the 1970s resulted in the unnecessary deaths of between 10,000 and 45,000 cardiac patients. But nearly by definition, unmarketed drugs are unknown to those who need them, and such deaths result in few complaints and little political pressure for reduction in regulatory delay. The highly visible deaths from bad drugs that do reach the market, in contrast, result in *enormous* pressure for the government to require more testing.[7]

Defenders of the FDA claim the additional testing to be necessary and beneficial on net. Since new drugs reach markets earlier in most other countries, however, their beneficial and detrimental effects can be observed, and the consequences of FDA delays can be estimated. That the FDA has little confidence in its claims to benefit the public through regulation is indicated by its unwillingness to make such cost-benefit comparisons. Private academic researchers, however, have done so. In the most famous such study, Sam Peltzman found that FDA testing regulation was generating social costs that were four times larger than the benefits.[8] Peltzman's study was criticized as having methodological faults.[9] Dale Gieringer, however, found that the FDA marketing delay was taking between 21,000 and 120,000 lives per decade, while saving only 5,000-10,000 lives, which is actually a larger average cost-benefit ratio than Peltzman's 4:1 estimate.[10]

Examples of such deaths from excessive FDA testing requirements, both for drugs and medical devices, abound. A single recent article in the respected magazine *Reason* listed the following: About 7,000 Americans currently die every year because of the failure of the FDA to approve a CPR device called the Ambu CardioPump. About 3,500 kidney Cancer patients died from November 1988 to May 1992 waiting for the FDA to approve the use of the drug Interlukin-2. In 1988, between 7,500 and 15,000 people died waiting for the FDA to approve the use of

Misoprostol. And 22,000 people with blocked coronary arteries died between 1985 and 1988 because of FDA delay in approval of Streptokinase, a drug that, administered intravenously, can open such arteries.[11] The same article in *Reason* had as its primary focus another pathology of such regulatory agencies. The FDA is extremely abusive and authoritarian in its regulatory control of the firms and industries under its jurisdiction, and legal suits to limit its abuses are almost never successful.

Traffic and Automobile Safety Regulation

Almost since the origin of automobiles, their use has been subject to safety regulation. Drivers must obtain a license, passing written and driving tests, and the license must be renewed periodically. On the road one is subject to speed limits and numerous other regulations of driving behavior. The command and control elements are identical to other forms of regulation. Drivers are subjected to continuous or random intermittent inspection of their behavior without warning or warrant. They are forced *ex-ante* to act in ways desired by the regulators. They are often punished for actions in which nobody is hurt, and where they had no intention of causing harm, rather than being punished *ex-post* after proof in a court of law of actions causing harm to or having intent to harm specific persons. The only difference is that accused traffic violators are tried in genuine law courts rather than in the kangaroo courts of a regulatory agency.

All this is such a common experience, and so obviously beneficial, as to cause nearly anyone to reject the very *thought* that a modern, complex society could function without regulation. In this it is easily overlooked that traffic regulation has a special rationale that other forms of regulation do *not* have: the roads are the property of the government.[12] As such, the government has a *property* right to set the rules for those using its property, just as a private owner would have the right to specify the behavior of persons choosing to come on his or her property. But there is clearly an enormous difference in justification between the government telling people what to do on *its* property, and the government telling people what to do with and on *their own* property, which is the case with most other forms of regulation.

An important example of the latter case is automobile safety regulation, which was generated politically by the same economic theory of market failure and ideology of capitalist predation as other forms of safety regulation. In 1967, two agencies were combined by executive order to form the National Highway Traffic Safety Administration. Now it is beyond dispute that safety is a desirable property of automobiles, *but only one of many* properties that consumers desire. Also, at a given technology, engineering for increased safety comes at the expense of either reductions in other qualities or increased cost of the automobile. The auto industry has both market and legal liability incentives to improve the safety of its products (along with other quality characteristics), and did so as technology advanced over time. Thus auto manufacturers added or offered such features as improved brakes, better tires and door locks, shatter-resistant glass, padded dashboards and seat belts, years before federal regulation required them. As a consequence of progressively safer autos, accumulating driver experience, and improved highways, motor vehicle death and injury rates fell over the entire post-war period, though they flattened out after 1960. Since many safety (and other) features were optional, consumers differing in their tastes, incomes and risk preferences, could pick and choose the bundle of safety and other auto product characteristics they preferred. Arguably this allowed efficient matching of scarce resources to consumer tastes.

Explicitly rejecting the idea that consumers should be *allowed* to make such choices for themselves, the NHTSA began mandating the installation and use of seat belts, air bags, collapsible steering columns, padded dashboards, and other safety equipment. Shortly thereafter the automobile death rate resumed its secular decline, and in 1975 the NHTSA attributed a 35 percent reduction in traffic fatalities over the period to its regulations, most particularly the requirement of seat belt installation.[13] Despite the failure of many drivers to even use them, massive propaganda that "seat belts save lives" ensued. Additional NHTSA regulations poured forth, and nowadays most new cars have at least driver side air bags preinstalled. Needless to say, the relative cost of automobiles has been increased enormously by the regulated addition of excessive safety devices, literally pricing some people out of ownership.

Economists not employed by the NHTSA or blinded by leftist ideology were immediately suspicious of NHTSA claims. There are obviously many factors besides safety equipment that affect the automobile death rate. In addition, adding such equipment could well alter people's choices of driving behavior. Here again the seminal study came from the ubiquitous Sam Peltzman.[14] Peltzman employed such variables as consumer incomes, driving speeds, per-capita alcohol consumption, and the age distribution of drivers, in a multiple-regression model to explain the automobile death rates both before and after NHTSA regulation. He found that increased alcohol consumption, faster driving speeds with the powerful cars popular at the time, and a larger proportion of younger drivers resulting from the post-war baby boom, were responsible for the flattening out of the death rate in the early 1960s. In addition, changes in such variables, particularly a reduction in the proportion of younger drivers as the boomers aged, fully explained the resumption of decline in the death rate after 1965. NHTSA mandated safety devices had no significant effect. Even the NHTSA admitted that much of the decline came not from safety equipment, but from rising fuel prices and the 55 MPH speed limit.[15]

Peltzman actually found statistical evidence that the safety regulations made things worse, partly offsetting the beneficial effects of the changes in the other variables. Drivers made to feel safer by the devices drove faster than they otherwise would have, got into more accidents (offsetting the decline in likelihood of death per accident produced by the safety devices), and killed more pedestrians. Similar driver substitutions have been found by subsequent researchers. Despite the pervasive claims that air bags save lives, the facts appear different. True, air bags reduce the probability that an occurring accident will result in death or injury to those they protect, perhaps as much as 25 percent, and it is at this point that advocates of regulation usually stop their analysis. But by reducing perceived risk, air bags alter driver *behavior* in ways that *increase* the number of accidents, offsetting the reduced risks per accident faced by the driver and increasing the risks to others.

In a recent study, George Hoffer and Edward Milner examined fatal driving accidents in Virginia involving cars made after 1989, some of which were air bag equipped and others of which were not. They found that drivers with air bags were *more* likely to be killed than those without air bags. They also found, by examining accidents between cars with an air bag and cars without, that the driver with an air bag was at fault almost three-fourths of the time, but that the other drivers were subjected to the bulk of the injuries and fatalities.[16] Summing up the evidence available on the effects of NHTSA regulation by 1992, Paul MacAvoy, one of the nation's most outstanding regulation economists, wrote the following:

The studies of NHTSA operations over two decades do not indicate that agency operations reduced fatalities from automobile accidents. Equipment regulation has probably not benefited the consumer
by enough to allow costs to be matched against benefits and considered as changes in GNP as in other industries.[17]

Workplace Safety Regulation

State regulation of workplace safety long preceded federal regulation, which seems not to have been guided by that earlier experience so
much as to have occurred despite it. As Albert Nichols and Richard
Zeckhauser wrote in 1975, there was no evidence that *states* with tighter
safety standards or higher workplace regulatory expenditures enjoyed
safer or healthier working conditions than other states.[18] One of the best
studies here was that by Paul Sands in 1968, in part because of the simplicity and directness of his approach, and in part because his results
turned out so differently than he expected.[19]

Construction is a highly risky industry, and in the early 1960s the
state of Michigan, which had very little safety regulation for that industry, was considering enactment of a comprehensive safety code, under
pressure by the construction unions and other groups. Sands decided to
compare conditions and attitudes in the Michigan industry with those in
Ohio, where in contrast strict safety regulations and inspections already
existed. Sands initially anticipated that injury rates would be lower in
Ohio due to the regulation, and that information efforts by the Ohio regulators would result in greater knowledge about and concern with safety in the industry than would be found in Michigan. He also presumed
that the payroll costs of workmen's compensation would be lower in
Ohio since that state excluded private sales of such insurance in favor
of a single state monopoly fund. Sands thought that, given economies
of scale and the absence of profits, taxes and selling costs, the Ohio system should have reduced costs overall. Michigan, in contrast, had many
private firms selling such insurance.

Randomly choosing a sample of 50 contractors consisting of five
firms from each of the five largest cities in the two states, Sands inter-
viewed and examined the records of each one to determine injury rates,
workmen's compensation costs, as well as knowledge of and attitudes
toward safety. What he found was the opposite of what he expected.
First, differences in injury rates in the two states were negligible,
despite the stringent regulation in Ohio. Second, workman's compensa-

tion costs were *higher* for firms under the state-run Ohio system than they were in Michigan. He also found that the firms in Michigan got as much help on safety issues from *private* sources as the Ohio firms did from the regulators (contrary to the claims of the regulators whom he termed the "Ohio propagandists"), and that the Michigan firms actually had a greater understanding of safety and engaged in greater efforts to prevent injuries than did the Ohio firms.

Such evidence as this was apparently either not considered or was unpersuasive to Congress in 1970 when it created the Occupational Safety and Health Administration to regulate workplace safety nationwide. The primary excuse employed was the alleged existence of a health and safety crisis in manufacturing employment. Both the industrial death and injury rates had been falling since the end of World War II. Between 1960 and 1970, however, the rate of industrial accidents had risen nearly 27 percent, though the number of workdays lost annually to injuries and deaths held steady, and deaths per 100,000 workers, kept falling.[20] Much of the rise of the accident rate was due to the same demographic shift that caused auto traffic deaths to stop falling for a time after 1960: the Post-War baby boom. Younger persons enter the labor force shortly after they begin driving, and for the same reasons that they engage in riskier behavior on the road, they are less safe on the job. In both cases the phenomenon was self-reversing as the boomers aged and gained experience, and a smaller population cohort followed them onto the roads and into jobs. It is true that this demographic shift did not entirely account for the rise in the accident rate in the 1960s, but other factors, such as increasingly generous state-run workmen's compensation funds, were also acting at the time to increase the number of on-the-job accidents, both real and reported.

It is important to grasp that the secular trend of improving workplace safety, which long preceded both federal and state regulation, is no accident (no pun intended). Workers value safety, among other job conditions, and many are quite willing to switch to less risky employments and occupations. Consequently, employers in fields that face workers with high risks, must pay *wage premiums* to attract and retain needed workers, in comparison to employers in alternative fields in which the same workers can be employed at lower risk. The same is true for high risk firms in the *same* industry as other firms that face their workers with lower risk. Many empirical studies have demonstrated the existence of such risk premiums.[21] The point is that unsafe working conditions are *costly* to firms, and that a strong competitive incentive exists for firms to substitute safer methods of operation whenever they can find a way to do so at a cost lower than the resulting savings on their risk premium. Some economists estimate the safety enhancing incentive of market risk premia to be much higher than the regulatory incentive.[22]

Additional incentive for safety results from the (legally limited, but still existing) capacity of workers or their families to sue employers when malfeasance on their part results in worker injury. Still, as long as other employment conditions are also important to workers, and safety cannot be raised costlessly, *perfect* job safety will *not* be optimal. Some risks will exist and some accidents will occur. Enemies of freedom will always be able to point even to random accidents (much less a temporary bulge such as occurred in the 1960s) as constituting evidence of systematic capitalist abuse of workers or consumers requiring government regulation. In the case of OSHA, this regulation, like that of the NHTSA, took the form of detailed equipment standards and specifications. Initially, OSHA's task was made easier by simply adopting preexisting federal regulations and voluntary codes written by private industry groups, as well as promulgating its own. The voluntary codes instantly became mandatory, however, and a heavy handed bureaucratic inspection and enforcement apparatus came into play across the land.

Compliance with OSHA regulations was extremely costly. Corporate managers complained bitterly not only of the nearly tyrannical character of OSHA, but of the absorption of funds in compliance that would have otherwise gone for research and development, new capital investment, and job creation. OSHA needed to show results on workplace safety, and fast. The problem was, that demonstrable beneficial results were scanty to nonexistent. The frequency of less serious injuries (not resulting in lost work-days) fell steadily from 1972 to 1975, and OSHA pointed to this with pride, but the pattern of more serious injuries in those years was the same as it had been before OSHA.[23] Robert Smith found evidence that OSHA inspections reduced injury rates in 1973, but had no effect in 1974.[24] DiPietro, however, found no evidence of differences between the accident rates of companies that had been inspected by OSHA and those that had not.[25]

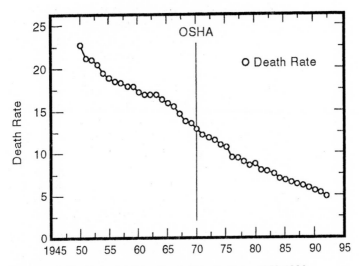

Graph 7.1: The Industrial Accidental Death Rate, 1950-1992

Evidence accumulating since those early studies does not seem to show discernible benefits on workplace safety from OSHA regulation. Graph 7.1 shows the trend in the industrial accident death rate per 100,000 workers since 1950, with a vertical line at 1970 separating the pre-OSHA and post-OSHA periods. No significant effect of OSHA regulation seems visually apparent. Graph 7.2, below, charts the annual percentage rate of rise or decline in the industrial death rate over the whole post-war period, both before and since OSHA. It is negative for nearly all years because the death rate itself has been falling over the whole period. Here some evidence of a regulatory effect seems apparent, since the percentage rate of decline is larger on average post-OSHA, but the improvement in the rate of risk reduction began in 1963, six years *before* OSHA. Other variables must have been at work. Indeed, in a recent study, when the effects of the unemployment rate, occupational composition, and worker's compensation costs were considered along with OSHA, Richard Butler found no statistically significant effect of OSHA regulation.[26] Kniesner and Leeth cite two studies that find some small improvements in safety due to OSHA, though they point out that most studies find no effect.[27] Paul MacAvoy's conclusion on the matter as of 1992 seems correct: There have *not* been significant reductions in workplace accidents due specifically to OSHA regulatory activities.[28]

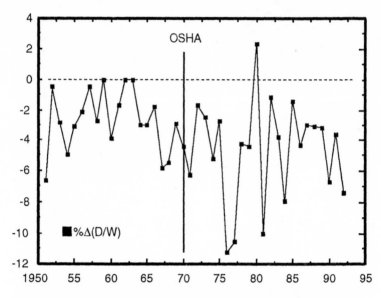

Graph 7.2: Annual Percent Change in Industrial Accident Death Rate

It is important to remember the basic argument of this chapter, however. Even if it *were* to be shown that OSHA (or some other health and safety regulation agency) had reduced risks, and perhaps even saved lives on net through regulation, that would *not* demonstrate that such regulation was socially beneficial. To say that it is costly to reduce risk, and that the marginal costs rise (and marginal benefits fall) for additional increments, is precisely to say that, for some range of risks eliminated, other things are given up that have a higher value to us. Until the market generated level and rate of increase of product and workplace safety (with its associated accidental injury and death frequency) can be *shown* not only to be less than optimal, but the degree of suboptimality *measured,* so that the precise needed correction is known, it can never be shown that regulation produces a superior result.[29]

Notes

1 The facts of this matter have been explained in such detail and clarity by Friedman that I shall not attempt to do so here. See Milton Friedman, *Capitalism and Freedom* (University of Chicago Press, 1962): Chapter IX, particularly 149-160.

2 See Joseph E. Stiglitz, *Economics of the Public Sector* (2d ed. Norton, 1988): 78-79. Stiglitz asserts that information is a public good.

3 Douglas F. Greer, *Business, Government, and Society* (3rd ed., Macmillan, 1993): 416.

4 This is a straightforward application of what is known among macroeconomists as the *Rational Expectations Hypothesis*. It makes clear that the obligation is on those who assert chronic human underestimation or overestimation of variables to demonstrate why people would be subject to such irrationality.

5 Is it then the market, or the *government* that undersupplies information? One should not be surprised. Historically, it has been precisely in those nations where government was most powerful, that information has been most restricted. The literal explosion of knowledge and information available to the ordinary person that has occurred since the industrial revolution and the rise of free market based industrial/technological nations itself contradicts the claim that markets undersupply information. Nor can this be attributed to public education, since both knowledge and literacy were expanding rapidly *before* public education was instituted.

6 Steven Neil Wiggins, "Product Quality Regulation and New Drug Introductions: Some New Evidence from the 1970s," *Review of Economic Statistics* 63 (November 1981): 615-619, and Wiggins, "The Impact of Regulation on Pharmaceutical Research Expenditures: A Dynamic Approach," *Economic Inquiry* 21 (January 1983): 115-128.

7 This is a crucial point, since the interventionist argument is that the incentives for generating information and safety conditions in the market are faulty. Clearly, however, it is the incentives faced by the *regulatory* agencies that are faulty. Such agencies are unlikely to generate socially optimal values of risk and information. George Stigler once characterized the argument that an alleged market failure justifies government intervention by likening it to the producer of a opera who was trying out two vocalists for a part. Hearing the first singer, he immediately awarded the part to the second.

8 Sam Peltzman, *Regulation of Pharmaceutical Innovation: The 1962 Amendments* (American Enterprise Institute, 1974).

9 Richard Nelson and Thomas Spavins, "An Evaluation of Consumer Protection Legislation: The 1962 Amendments, A Comment," *Journal of Political Economy* 83 (1975): 665-661.

10 Dale H. Gieringer, "The Safety and Efficacy of New Drug Approval," *Cato Journal* 5 (Spring/Summer 1985): 177-201.

11 Alexander Volokh, "Clinical Trials: Beating the FDA in Court," *Reason* (May 1995): 22-29. *Reason* has a Libertarian philosophic orientation, but also has a reputation for care and accuracy in its research.

12 Of course they are a monopoly, leaving one very little alternative to using the government roads, and I do *not* say this should be so. In fact, early in our history, roads were often privately created and operated. As public goods, roads are a marginal case. Their use is excludable and depletable, but a highway *system* is a necessity. Suppose the matter were solved by intergovernmental planning of the highway system, after which competitive bids were let for private firms to build, own and operate (on a toll basis) specific highway segments. Even without governmental mandate, the firms would find it necessary to promulgate rules for their use by the public essentially identical in form, if not detail, to current traffic regulations.

13 Paul MacAvoy, *Industry Regulation and the Performance of the American Economy* (W. W. Norton & Co., 1992): 94, hereafter cited as MacAvoy, *Industry Regulation*.

14 Sam Peltzman, "The Effects of Automobile Safety Regulation,"*Journal of Political Economy* 83 (August 1975): 677-725.

15 U.S. National Highway Traffic and Safety Administration, *Motor Vehicle Safety, a Report on Activities Under the National Traffic and Motor Vehicle Safety Act of 1966 and the Motor Vehicle Information and Cost Savings Act of 1972* (U.S. Government Printing Office, 1976): 7, 10-11.

16 George Hoffer, Steven Peterson, and Edward Milner, "Are Drivers of Air-Bag-Equipped Cars More Aggressive? A Test of the Offsetting Behavior Hypothesis," *Journal of Law and Economics* (October 1995): 251-263.

17 Macavoy, *Industry Regulation* : 96.

18 Albert L. Nichols and Richard Zeckhauser, "Government Comes to the Workplace: an Assessment of OSHA," *The Public Interest* (Fall 1977): 39-69, particularly p. 40.

19 Paul Sands, "How Effective is Safety Legislation?" *Journal of Law and Economics* 11 (April 1968): 165-177.

20 Nichols and Zeckhauser, "Government Comes to the Workplace ": 40.

21 See Robert Smith, *The Occupational Safety and Health Act* (American Enterprise Institute, 1976), and Richard Thayler and Sherwin Rosen, "The Value of Saving a Life," in Nester E. Terleckyj (ed.), *Studies in Income and Wealth* Vol. 40 (National Bureau of Economic Research).

22 See Thomas J. Kniesner and John D. Leeth, "Abolishing OSHA," *Regulation* No. 4 (1995).

23 Nichols and Zeckhauser, "Government Comes to the Work Place": 52.

24 Robert Smith, "The Impact of OSHA Inspections on Manufacturing Injury Rates," *Journal of Human Resources* 14 no. 2 (1979): 145-169.

25 Aldona DiPietro, "An analysis of the OSHA Inspection Program in Manufacturing Industries, 1972-1973," Draft Technical Analysis Paper, U.S. Department of Labor (August 1979).

26 Richard Butler, "Safety Through Experience Rating: A Review of the Evidence and Some New Findings," unpublished paper, University of Minnesota, 1994.

27 Thomas J. Kniesner and John D. Leeth, reply to Fred Siskind, *Regulation* No. 1 (1996): 12-14.

28 MacAvoy, *Industry Regulation* : 90

29 This argument focuses on *ex-post* outcomes under alternate legal regimes. In an interesting paper Robert Higgs has made an even stronger argument, by showing that it is not possible for regulators to raise the *ex-ante* well being or happiness of *anybody* by banning a risky product. See Higgs, "Banning a Risky Product Cannot Improve Any Consumer's Welfare (Properly Understood), with Applications to FDA Testing Requirements," *Review of Austrian Economics* 7 No. 2 (1994): 3-20

Appendix 7-1
Accidental Industrial Death Rates, 1950-1992,
and Percentage Change in Death Rates, 1951-1992

Year	Deaths per 100,000 Workers	%Δ(D/W)	Year	Deaths per 100,000 Workers	%Δ(D/W)
1950	22.7		1972	11.9	-7.8
1951	21.2	-6.6	1973	11.6	-2.5
1952	21.1	-.5	1974	11.0	-5.2
1953	20.5	-2.8	1975	10.7	-2.7
1954	19.5	-4.9	1976	9.5	-11.2
1955	18.9	-3.1	1977	9.4	-10.5
1956	18.5	-2.1	1978	9.0	-4.2
1957	18.4	-.5	1979	8.6	-4.4
1958	17.9	-2.7	1980	8.8	2.3
1959	17.9	0.0	1981	8.0	-10.0
1960	17.2	-3.9	1982	7.9	-1.2
1961	16.9	-1.7	1983	7.6	-3.8
1962	16.9	0.0	1984	7.0	-7.9
1963	16.9	0.0	1985	6.9	-1.4
1964	16.4	-3.0	1986	6.6	-4.3
1965	15.9	-3.0	1987	6.4	-3.0
1966	15.6	-1.8	1988	6.2	3.1
1967	14.7	-5.8	1989	6.0	-3.2
1968	13.9	-5.4	1990	5.6	-6.7
1969	13.5	-2.9	1991	5.4	-3.6
1970	12.9	-4.4	1992	5.0	-7.4
1971	12.1	-6.2			

Source: Computed from data in the National Safety Council, *Accident Facts* (1994 edition), p. 37.

Note: The NSC data included work-related auto deaths. From a suspicion that most of these involved simple travel to and from work, I removed those before computing the industrial accident death rates reported above. This should allow closer focus on the deaths in the workplace that OSHA actually regulates.

Chapter 8

Environmental Regulation

By far the most important and rapidly expanding form of modern regulation is environmental regulation. It originated in the turmoil of the 1960s when several loose and separate groups coalesced into the modern environmental movement. The ideology of the movement is, essentially, a pagan pantheistic religion of earth and animal worship that is implicitly misanthropic and explicitly anti-capitalist. Corporations are argued to spew forth massive and increasing quantities of pollutants and wastes that are poisoning the earth, air and water. Scarce mineral and metal resources are allegedly being depleted to feed omnivorous, expanding industry, unfairly depriving future generations and facing our society with inevitable collapse when things run out.[1]

Forests and other natural eco-systems are everywhere being destroyed, and animal species are being driven to extinction by expanding human populations and economies. In addition, it is claimed that we are faced with massive catastrophes from human generated global warming and ozone depletion. The 'moderates' in this movement, if any can be termed such, merely advocate enormous expansions in government control and regulation of industry to reduce pollution, preserve nature and alleviate such threats. The radicals advocate the end of technical/industrial civilization itself.[2] As the power of the movement has grown, one almost feels grateful that the 'moderates' have prevailed.

It seems hard to accuse environmental regulation of having a special interest character, due to the large public acceptance of the environmental ideology in recent decades, and because it seems so obvious that, *if* the regulation has the claimed effects, everyone benefits. As is clear from earlier chapters, however, even the most blatantly redistributive special interest regulation requires successful propagation of a public interest claim, to anesthetize potential opposition. Under the right conditions, propagation of such claims in a wider ideology can generate a mass movement. We have much experience in this century, however, with mass political movements based on anti-capitalist ideologies, joined by many, many millions of *mostly well-meaning people,* that when politically instituted, generated enslavement, misery and death on monumental scales. One is entitled by this history to question the accuracy and validity of the environmental vision, and the effects, effectiveness, and necessity of its policies.

Production and Emissions

Here as in other cases it is important to begin with first principles. The most fundamental principle of all, perhaps, is the conservation law: Neither matter nor energy can ever be created or destroyed; they can only change their forms. Similar in stature is the entropy law: heat tends to distribute itself equally in a closed system, or, put another way, everything decays, breaks down, spreads out, and mixes. The universe, left to itself, moves from states of higher to lower organization; from order to disorder. In human production, the conservation law applies strictly: *we never make something from nothing.* We should probably refer to production processes as transformation processes, since they simply transform material inputs in accordance with technological recipes into usable products or tools.

Notice that this process of applying human intelligence to the satisfaction of human needs and desires is, at least in part, anti-entropic. Usable materials that are dispersed throughout the earth are collected and put together into highly organized and functional forms not previously existing in nature. But entropy reasserts itself. In the production process there is always some inefficiency of materials transformation and energy use, resulting in some entropic loss of both materials and energy. And as time passes, the products wear out, decay, and may be thrown away. Over a long time, such 'trash' decays, breaks down, and its constituent elements spread out again through the earth from which they were initially collected. The point here is fundamental: with qualifications to be discussed momentarily, *human trash and industrial effluents put nothing into the earth that we did not first take from the earth.* That observation itself should significantly modify the notion that wastes from human production and use activities are poisoning the earth on net.

The qualifications have to do with some specific elements of production processes. There seem to be four such: refining, chemical mixing, machining and/or casting, and assembly. The first two seem crucial for ecological issues. Refining is essentially a process of gathering a substance and purifying it by removing all other substances mixed with it, and concentrating the desired material. This normally increases its toxicity, but only in a restricted locale, and only by reducing the amount of the actual or potentially toxic substance in a great many *other* places. Refining does not create, then, but merely redistributes, toxic substances. Any problem of toxic substances due to refining is therefore locational, not systemic, and locational problems can be dealt with.

Chemistry is also important because, theoretically, in mixing substances that have not been mixed in significant amounts in nature, man may create 'new' chemical substances.[3] Regarding the toxicity (or carcinogenic–i.e. cancer generating) properties of new chemicals, three possibilities must be noted: they may be more toxic to humans and/or nature than their constituent components, no different, or *less* toxic than their constituents (the constituents of Sodium Chloride are far more toxic, amount for amount, than is salt). The crucial point here is that in terms of random chance *there appears to be no reason for assuming that any of these outcomes would occur with greater frequency than any other.* Hence human chemical activities in the aggregate likely have no net poisoning (or carcinogenic) effect on humans or the environment.

The same logic applies to airborne emissions. That is, some will impose costs on third parties, such as when an air pollutant aggravates the health conditions of some persons. But other airborne emissions have positive external effects on humans or the environment. Examples of both are easy to come by. Some smog contains nitrous oxide, which is poisonous in significant quantities. But smog also often contains *nitric* oxide, which is now known to be beneficial to lungs, blood pressure, the immune system and the brain.[4] Sulfate and nitrate emissions that were long accused–rather falsely according to the National Acid Precipitation Program (NAPAP) report–of causing acid rain and denuding Canadian forests, are actually soil fertilizers, and were recently credited with aiding European forest growth.[5] And the quantitatively largest single airborne emission of industrial society, CO_2, is highly beneficial to plant growth and health because it is the crucial nutrient that plants use in converting sunlight into plant matter through photosynthesis.[6] So external effects from industrial emissions can be positive or negative, *and I know of no reason, either theoretical or empirical, to presume that they are not normally distributed with a mean of zero.*

This seems likely despite the fact that specific problems of chemical toxicity and air pollution will arise in specific times and places. Effective and proper policies to minimize such events are justified (and are discussed below), but such events will *not* be evidence of general systemic decay justifying massive alterations in Western society and reductions in economic freedom. Indeed, since the random effects of human industrial activities on human health and the environment will be neutral, the net effect will be and *has been* determined by human *intentions*. Since such activities are aimed specifically at improving human health and happiness, ending disease, and alleviating suffering, that effect has been, and will continue to be, enormously positive.

In the short span of time since the industrial revolution began, dozens of infectious diseases that, as environmental hazards, had plagued mankind throughout history, such as diphtheria, tuberculosis, typhoid fever, plague, smallpox, polio and others, have been either totally eliminated or severely controlled, through the development of chemical medicines, vaccines, and other technologies by profit-seeking businessmen operating in free markets.[7] The associated rise in mean life expectancy in Western nations, for example, from 30 years for Americans in 1800 to 50 in 1900 and 75 today, demonstrates conclusively that the activities of industrial society have drastically *reduced*– not increased–the environmental risks (broadly defined) that people face.

Now consider the nature of industrial emissions, wastes or effluents and the effects of economic growth in light of the theory of production developed above. Industrial wastes or emissions result from incomplete transformation of materials into products, and of fuels into energy, in the production process, and sometimes of chemical byproducts. From their beginning, however, a prominent feature of market economies has been ongoing increases in productivity, due to capital accumulation and technological advance, motivated by competitive efforts of businessmen to reduce costs and increase profits. It is this ongoing productivity growth that has, by raising real per capita output, thereby raised the real per capita *incomes* of ordinary persons so enormously over time. An increase in productivity, however, is by definition an increase in output per unit of input per unit of time. *That can only occur through a more complete transformation of inputs into outputs with less waste.* That is, productivity growth is itself a process that *reduces* waste, effluents and emissions per *unit* of output even as it increases total output.

Consider, for example, the sequence of fuels employed over industrial history. The initial primary fuel, wood, was replaced by coal. Later oil came into widespread use, then natural gas and even nuclear power. The ongoing tendency has been progressively to substitute fuels and methods of power generation that are cleaner and more efficient, generating more energy per unit of fuel with less waste. Technologically improved boilers and furnaces that burn *given* fuels more efficiently have the same effect, and are quickly adopted for profit motives when developed. Both of these processes were in operation long before environmental regulation became prominent. Indeed, the fuel substitution process has been *inhibited* by such regulation, most particularly the ignorant obstruction *by environmentalists* of nuclear power, the cleanest, safest, most efficient and non-polluting fuel of all.[8] This has maintained an enormous amount of fossil fuel use and associated pollution that would *otherwise have been eliminated.* The basic point, however, is that this progressive substitution of cleaner and hence cheaper fuels as they were discovered came about naturally due to the inherent incentives–profit motives–faced by businessmen in the competitive market.

Of course productivity growth, from technological advances and increases in the per capita stock of capital, is not the only source of economic growth, defined as a rise in total aggregate output. Increases in the labor force as population grows also add to total output over time. As long as population growth is positive, therefore, the percentage growth in output will exceed the rate of productivity growth, and the percentage decline in emissions *per unit* of output will not entirely offset the effect of increased emissions from growth in total output. Historically, average annual growth in real Gross National Product in the U.S. has run about 3.4 percent, with productivity growth around 2 percent. Thus, mathematically, total emissions should grow by roughly the difference. This is an enormously different picture, however, than that painted by environmental opponents of economic growth, who invariably imply that growth in emissions is equivalent to economic growth.

Even this picture grossly overstates the effect of economic growth in generating pollution, for several reasons. For one, as per capita output and income rises, the *composition* of production shifts progressively from goods to services, and service generation is less polluting.[9] Another important factor concerns population. The initial effect of shifting from a stagnant, preindustrial economy to a growing industrial economy with rising incomes is to reduce both infant and adult mortality rates so that population rises. Later, however, rising real incomes change the economics of child rearing, making it more costly and less attractive, so that birth rates fall and population growth declines. Few of the world's high income nations are now experiencing *any* growth in their indigenous populations. As less developed nations continue developing, the same thing will happen to them. Indeed, though population growth is still rapid in some low and middle income nations, it is falling world wide, and the U.N. now estimates that the world will reach zero population growth sometime between 2045 and 2075.[10]

Another crucial factor is that cleanliness and safety are what economists term 'normal goods'. As productivity and real incomes rise, people demand more of them, and entrepreneurs supply them. This began early. Iron pipe, flush toilets and sewage treatment technologies were products of the industrial revolution. They solved pollution problems that had plagued cities from the beginning, vastly improving sanitation. Indeed, contrary to the environmental ideology, the dirtiest and most polluted cities in the world exist in *preindustrial* economies, where such technologies are not yet available. In such cities raw sewage runs in the streets, and animals and animal feces are everywhere. There are between three and five million deaths world wide per year due to poor sanitation, and virtually all of them occur in underdeveloped nations.[11]

In the primitive societies and economies that so many environmental gurus romanticize, the primary fuels are wood and cow dung, and there is *nothing* healthful about breathing smoke from such fuels. This has been so throughout human history. CNN reported on September 29th, 1996, that examination of the 5000 year old ice man found a few years back near Innsbruck, Austria revealed that, though relatively young, he had diseased lungs much like those of a habitual cigarette smoker, most likely from breathing wood smoke in confined spaces. Modern electrical and natural gas home heating and cooking eliminated wood smoke and coal dust from the home, making them *enormously* cleaner and more healthful. It is now well established that the worst air pollution problem around the world is *indoor* air pollution, and that it is much worse in underdeveloped nations than in developed ones.[12]

The automobile serves as another example. Autos emit carbon monoxide, various fluids, and other substances, but their development replaced a technology that was probably worse. As several analysts of environmental issues have noted, one can only imagine the pollution problem and the associated environmental risks that would exist in modern cities if we were still relying on horses for transportation. An adult horse emits 45 pounds of manure a day, which is a hazard that must be collected and disposed of in any urban setting. Horses also die. In 1900, the city of New York had to remove 20,000 dead horses from its city streets. Such instances of new products and technologies replacing older ones that were *more* polluting and risky are easily multiplied. When the insecticide DDT (about which, more later) came into use at the turn of the century, for example, it replaced and displaced older insecticides using Arsenic, Lead, Mercury, Fluorine and other agents that were much more toxic to humans and animals.

Productivity Growth and Forest Habitat

Suppose the argument of the prior section is correct: technological advance in products and production methods tends to make society *cleaner* and *reduce* the environmental hazards people face. What about wilderness and animal habitat? Does not expanding human population and industry inherently press on and crowd out natural habitat over time? Are not forests being ravaged by agriculture and logging for human consumption, diminished by urbanization, and disappearing everywhere? As it turns out, the answer is *no,* at least not in the 20th century, for reasons stemming from the same principles already discussed. True, for much of human history before the industrial revolution, and some after, improvements in agricultural methods and technology had the effect of increasing agricultural output (and food availability) per person by increasing the amount of land a person could cultivate.[13] The horse and plow had this effect, and even the modern tractor and combine do so. Expanding populations as food availability and nutrition improved, and the associated expansion in cultivated land, resulted in progressive deforestation as land was cleared.

European forests declined continuously through the medieval period, reaching their smallest extent (area and volume) around 1850, *after which a reforestation began that continues to this day.* When colonization of the U.S. began in the 17th century, 40 percent of U.S. land area, or about 1,044 million acres, was forested. Clearing for agriculture reduced this by about 114 million acres, or 11 percent, by 1850. Over the next 60 years U.S. forests declined about another 19-20 percent, mostly due to logging for railroad ties and industrial fuel, then stopped declining. At their lowest, the U.S. still had 70 percent of its original forest area, and *after 1920 both forest area and volume began expanding.* [14] In the post-War period U.S. forest area has been roughly stable, rising slightly in some decades and declining slightly in others, while volume (density) has continued increasing. Indeed, temperate area forests are expanding world-wide.

What was responsible for the recovery of forests in the temperate climes of the world? Was it due to government action? Actually government land reservation was a trivial element. The primary factor was the invention and innovation of a host of agricultural technologies and techniques such as fallowing and herbicides to control weeds, insecticides to control destructive pests, and chemical fertilizers, all of which had the effect of increasing output *per unit of land cultivated.* This is known as *yield takeoff.* Plant breeding began adding its effects in the 1930s, when high yield corn varieties were developed that allowed corn output to rise from an average 25 bushels per acre then to 138 bushels per acre now. Similarly, grain production has risen from 1.1 tons per hectare in 1950 to over 2.8 tons in 1992, or by more than 150 percent. Food production world wide has consequently risen much more rapidly than population in this century, so that food and calorie consumption per person has risen steadily.[15] Indeed, agricultural productivity growth is *not* slowing, and with biotechnology in its infancy, no limits are foreseeable.

Regarding land use, the effect of the yield takeoff was to allow an expanding population to be fed *better* from *smaller amounts of agricultural land.* In the South, Northeast, and Great Lake states of the U.S., millions of acres of marginal farm land were abandoned over time (some as early as 1850) and began immediately to reforest, a process that is complete in one or two decades.[16] The substitution, by industry, for profit motives, of cleaner, more efficient and hence cheaper fuels in place of wood, and the adoption of more efficient boilers and furnaces, as discussed earlier, also reduced pressure on the forests. Another factor was the creation and expansion, for profit motives, of private timber cropping, in which trees are harvested and replanted on a sustained yield basis, such that more board feet are grown each year than are cut, and total timber stocks rise. As a result of these factors (and of industrial CO_2 emissions), *all of which were natural outcomes of market incentives and processes rather than government planning and regulation,* temperate area forests in the world have stabilized and preserved wildlife habitat.

True, the situation is not the same in the less developed tropical regions of the world, where expansion of cultivation is still generating deforestation and threatening some plant, insect and animal species with extinction.[17] One reason for this is that such nations have not yet reached yield takeoff, though they certainly will as their economies continue to develop. Other factors are more important, however. In West Africa, deforestation is one result of chronic tribal warfare and lawlessness. In South America, deforestation is a result of many nations heavily subsidizing agriculture, both through direct cash payments and indirectly, through tax incentives and tariffs on agricultural imports. Such nations are *not* the world's low cost producers of primary agricultural commodities. If such harmful *government* interventions were eliminated, their food imports from the U.S. and Europe would expand, extended cultivation would cease, and tropical deforestation would end. Indeed, the government of Brazil *did* eliminate many such policies after 1989, and deforestation there has diminished severely.

Outdoor Air Pollution and Economic Efficiency

As pointed out above, *indoor* air pollution is a far more serious problem than *outdoor* air pollution.[18] Outdoor pollution gets much more press, however, and is much more closely tied in the mind of the public with the alleged need for regulation. It is also true that, as home and industrial use of wood and coal reached their peak, before economic fuel substitution reduced the problem, there were some severe air pollution episodes. In 1930 atmospheric particulate and Sulfur Dioxide (SO_2) content in the highly industrialized Meuse Valley of Belgium reached levels so high as to raise the mortality rate to more than nine times its normal level for a period. In October of 1948 the industrial town of Donora, Pennsylvania, about 20 miles from Pittsburgh, experienced severe concentrations of SO_2 and particulate matter due in part to a four day weather inversion, in which 18 people died. And for five days in December of 1952 the air was so thick with particulate matter and SO_2 in London, England, that an estimated 4000 extra deaths occurred in a population of 8.5 million.[19] Wide publication of these episodes created a sense of crisis that helped stimulate public support for governmental action

At least since A. C. Pigou, early in this century, economists have analyzed the nature of externalities associated with economic activities and the proper policies for dealing with them.[20] In the standard Pigouvian analysis, significant external costs or benefits create a divergence between the private and social costs of an economic activity, and cause resources to be mis-allocated. The social costs of an economic activity are the sum of the private costs incurred and the external costs unintentionally imposed on third parties, as when production of a useful good generates a noxious air pollutant that irritates the lungs of citizens in the area. The private costs include expenditures for labor, materials and marketing, as well as capital costs, etc. Only if external costs are *zero* are the private and social costs the same.

Likewise, the social benefits of an economic activity are the sum of the private benefits resulting for those directly involved and the external benefits that may be experienced by third parties, as when production of a useful good also generates a beneficial emission like Nitric Oxide, or perhaps large CO_2 emissions that improve crop growth of surrounding farms. Here again, only when external benefits from an economic activity are zero do the private benefits equal the social benefits, so that the distinction is meaningless.

Taking the first case, suppose a production activity generates significant net external costs (i.e. external costs in excess of any external benefits also generated). Under competitive conditions, private decision makers in each firm employ additional units of variable inputs (such as labor) to raise the rate of production per time period (hour, week, year, etc.) as long as private marginal revenue from the sale of the additional output exceeds the private marginal cost incurred. The profit maximizing production rate is found where the two are equal. But each increment added to production per hour adds an increment to emissions, and since the external costs are *not* considered, the private costs are lower than the social costs. Hence firms in the industry will employ too many resources, produce too much output, and generate too much pollution.

In the second case, in which production of a good generates net external benefits, the opposite occurs. Again, producers each draw additional resources and raise their rate of production until profits are maximized (or losses minimized) at that rate at which private marginal cost rises (due to diminishing returns) to equality with private marginal revenue. But the external benefits, accruing as they do to third parties, are not considered by decision makers of the firm, hence marginal revenue is less than the social benefits, and the firms employ too few resources, produce too little output, and generate too *little* of whatever is causing the *beneficial* externality.

As a policy measure to reduce negative externalities, many economists since Pigou have favored the use of emissions taxes. Assuming that the amount that members of the public would be willing to pay on average not to have an increment of a noxious effluent emitted was known, a tax of that amount could be placed on the firms for each such increment emitted. This would raise the private marginal and average costs of the firm to equivalence with the social costs, thus 'internalizing' the external cost. Assuming the industry was competitive and that firms were just making a normal return before the tax was imposed, its imposition would cause financial losses to the industry. Some firms would leave, reducing employment and market supply until unit output price increased enough that remaining firms were once again covering all costs and earning a normal rate of return on capital invested. At that point the industry would employ the *right* amount of capital and labor resources, produce the *right* amount of output per hour (or other time period), and generate the *correct* amount of the effluent.

There are certainly some severe problems associated with application of such a policy. First, even with the best of intentions, in the absence of a market to establish a price per unit of the effluent that firms must pay citizens for their willingness to accept its emission (in the presence of which no effluent tax would be necessary, since the external cost would already be internalized), it is very difficult for government agents to estimate the unit cost of the externality. Indirect sorts of information must be used, such as the frequency and severity of health problems generated, associated medical costs, the value people place on their lives through wages and insurance, the loss (if any) in residential property values due to the emissions, etc.

It may be that through the use of increasingly sophisticated statistical and mathematical methods, reasonably accurate estimates of external production costs can now be made. A more serious problem looms, however: the apparent *lack* of desire on the part of regulators and their congressional supporters to attain an efficient resource use and maximize human well being in the first place. For some decades economists have advocated that both new and existing regulations be required to pass cost-benefit tests to attain or retain legal force, demonstrating that their actual or prospective benefits exceed the costs they generate.[21] Economists have been conducting studies applying such tests for decades. The first startling fact is that regulations almost always fail such tests.[22] Even more startling, however, is that since application of such tests would justify much less regulation than is presently occurring, *the regulatory agencies and their* (mostly Democratic) *Congressional supporters have bitterly and successfully opposed any requirement of such tests.* Indeed, in regulatory enabling laws, Congress has repeatedly *forbidden* their use.[23]

Consider, for example, the NAPAP (National Acid Precipitation Assessment Project) report, the result of a decade long scientific study by a large governmental task force. The scientists found acid rain to be a trivial problem, actually beneficial to forest growth in may instances, contrary to the massive propaganda of the environmental movement and the EPA. In 1990 a law amending the 1970 Clean Air Act, including acid rain reduction provisions forcing emissions control costs on utilities that would add billions of dollars to consumer utility bills, was in Congress. Incredibly, the Democratic majority, having already decided on this legislation, wanted nothing to do with the best scientific evidence on the matter, which the government had spent $500 million and a decade of effort to acquire. The NAPAP report was considered for only one hour in Senate deliberations, and was not even introduced into the House.[24]

Another indication that regulation is *not* employed with intention to achieve human well being and economic efficiency is that, though the effluent tax option was known and available when Congress wrote the original Clean Air Act of 1970, it deliberately chose to employ an inferior command and control regulatory strategy. The act required firms to purchase and install specified forms of emission control equipment, and enacted the associated quasi-totalitarian enforcement process of continuous emission monitoring and random intermittent plant inspection. This totally subordinated the minds, knowledge and intelligence of persons in the industry that *might* have been employed to solve emissions problems to the will and command of the regulators. In contrast, an emission tax *mobilizes* such human resources. Business decision makers have an *ongoing* incentive to reduce pollution because the tax is *avoidable* by doing so. Any time a way can be found to eliminate an increment of pollution at a cost lower than the tax payment that would be saved, it pays to do so. Under specified equipment regulation no such incentive exists. Once the firm is in compliance, no option exists to substitute cheaper and more efficient methods of pollution control.

The existing regulatory approach has been defended as at least having attained its goals, even if it could have been done at lower cost under other methods. But has it? Data for the U.S. going back to the turn of the century pieced together by the EPA itself shows that emissions *per person* for most airborne pollutants either leveled off or began declining between 1920 and 1940, long before any meaningful state or federal regulation existed.[25] Keep in mind that, due to productivity growth, *output* (and hence real income) per person has risen steadily. So for *emissions* per person to fall, emissions per unit of *output* must have fallen a great deal.

Of course, since productivity growth increases total output at the same time as it decreases emissions per unit of output, the question becomes what happens to total emissions. In fact, total emissions of particulate matter have been declining since World War II, long before regulation began. This decline is shown in Graph 8.1 below, which plots EPA data on PM-10 emissions taken from the 1996 *Statistical Abstract of the United States.* This early decline in particulate emissions as a result of *market* forces is particularly important, since according to the EPA itself, suspended particulate emissions account for 90 percent of the increased mortality and morbidity attributable to *all* air pollutants.

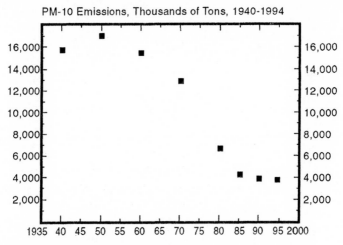

PM-10 Emissions, Thousands of Tons, 1940-1994

Graph 8.1 Particulate Emissions since 1940

Total emissions of most other pollutants only began declining after 1970, however, as shown in Table 8-1 below. Since the Clean Air Act (amendments) and the EPA became law in 1970, it would be natural to believe that this resulted from regulation. Professor Paul MacAvoy of Yale University, however, one of the nation's premier regulation economists, disputes this claim. He points out that the emissions declines of the 1970s bore the same empirical relationship to the growth of industrial production as they did in the 1960s, which would *not* be the case if regulation was effective.[26] In fact, MacAvoy found that, when other factors affecting emissions were included in a multiple regression analysis, Pollution discharge levels turned out to be *positively* related to EPA mandated expenditures on emissions control equipment, *not* negatively related.[27]

Table 8-1

Pollutant	%Change 1948-88	%Change 1970-88	%Change 1980-88
Particulates (PM/TSP)	-70	-63	-19
Sulfur Oxides	18	-27	-12
Nitrogen Oxides	187	7	-5
Reactive Volatile Organic Compounds	22	-26	-12
Carbon Monoxide	-26	-40	-23
Lead	N/A	-96	-89

Source: *National Air Pollution Emission Estimates, 1940-1989,*
Environmental Protection Agency, March, 1990.

The timing of the regulatory legislation with the emissions declines is misleading. Actual regulation was partial and fragmented for some time. The legislation of 1970 required the EPA to set National Ambient Air Quality Standards within a year, and states were to submit State Implementation Plans (SIP) within three years. As already mentioned, the regulation itself took the form of mandated installation by plants (and automobile manufacturers) of specified emissions control equipment. Compliance was not only fragmentary throughout the 1970s, but when MacAvoy examined SO_2 emissions in six industries, he found that there was no difference in emissions by plants in states that were in compliance and those that were *not* in compliance.[28]

The point of reducing total emissions, of course, is to improve air quality, which is usually measured in pollutant content per cubic meter. Atmospheric Total Suspended Particulate concentration has been declining since at least 1955, a few years after particulate emissions began falling. Air quality for most other traditional pollutants, such as SO_2 and Carbon Monoxide improved significantly in the 1960s, *prior* to any systematic state or Federal regulation, with air content levels falling by 20 percent overall. As regulation was instituted in the 1970s air quality continued to improve for most pollutants (Nitrogen oxides were the exception), but as MacAvoy shows, at a *slower* rate than in the 1960s.

What then was responsible for the improvements in total emissions and air quality levels? The primary factors turn out to be precisely those discussed earlier in this chapter. It is worth quoting MacAvoy directly.[29]

> Even though standards have now been enforced for fifteen years, neither the EPA nor the state plans can take the credit for these improvements in nationwide air and water quality. Implementation was too incomplete. At the same time, process improvements from newer technologies, which reduced pollution, were taking place regardless of regulation. Indeed, they were accelerated by the energy price increases of 1974 and again in the 1980s.

The energy price increases MacAvoy here mentions are the oil price increases by OPEC, capitalizing on the supply disruptions of the 1973 Mideast war and the 1979 Iranian revolution. The natural response of businessmen was to accelerate introduction of cleaner burning technologies and fuels in an effort to offset these energy cost increases.

Indur Goklany, Manager of Science and Engineering in the Office of Policy Analysis at the Interior Department, reaches a similar conclusion regarding the improvements in pollutant emissions and air quality in recent decades, though he gives some credit to regulation. To quote Goklany:[30]

> The timing of these reductions indicates that a substantial portion of the initial reductions was undertaken voluntarily. These voluntary actions included switching to cleaner energy sources and new technologies for combustion equipment in all sectors. These were supplemented by regulations imposed by local and state jurisdictions for sulphur-in-fuel, incinerations and industrial sources in urban areas, which in many cases preceded the 1970 Federal Clean Air Act.

Goklany, MacAvoy, and other neutral analysts, peering through the toxic fog of EPA and Environmentalist propaganda, seem to correctly recognize that the emissions and air quality improvements in the last half of the century have largely been the result of *natural* market processes, undertaken for *profit* motives, and *not* of regulation. The primary effect of the environmentalist political pressure and EPA airborne emissions regulation has been to hurt the economy, reducing output and employment below their prior trend values, *without* benefiting air quality to any significant extent.[31] Nor have they preserved life and health–on net–through regulation of chemical emissions, as we shall now see.

The Hazardous Regulation of Chemicals

The birth of the modern environmental movement in America is often traced to the publication in 1962 of Rachael Carson's literary polemic, *Silent Spring*. Carson's book propagated the thesis that nature in its purity was benign and non-carcinogenic to humans, since mankind had adjusted through millennia of evolution to natural chemicals. Modern industry, however, increasingly produces artificial chemicals, and introduces them into the environment through products and wastes. Mankind was *not* adjusted by evolutionary survival to such unnatural chemicals according to Carson, hence they were not just poisoning the earth and endangering wildlife, but generating a plague of cancer among humans in modern industrial nations. She was particularly incensed with pesticides, which are deliberately poisonous to insects, and are deliberately introduced into the environment, and she predicted the decimation of bird populations that feed on insects.

The leftist pseudo-intellectuals who control opinion media and the school system in the U.S. and other Western nations, aware of the near universal human love of animals and nature, immediately recognized this as a powerful anti-capitalist argument that could be used to support extension of the centralized government controls they desired. Almost overnight disparate groups formed around this vision and the modern environmental crusade was born. One of its primary and most effective expressions has been in propagating repeated scares concerning toxic or carcinogenic chemicals, often claimed to be in food, and using the public hysteria generated to support both specific extensions of regulation and general animosity toward business and capitalism.

The powerful character of the argument for regulation here was pointed out in Chapter 3. If a chemical introduced into the environment can be shown by strong evidence to generate a significant *statistical* risk of harm to others, but its effect is diffused among other factors so that its decisive character in causing the harm in *specific* cases could not be proven by rigorous standards of evidence in court, it *seems* difficult to reduce such a threat by other than regulatory methods. Of course to say that an argument is powerful is not to say that it is correct, and this one is internally inconsistent. If an artificial chemical introduced into the environment and assimilated by a person through food or contact with wastes really has a significant toxic or carcinogenic effect in the doses contracted, it *would* be possible to rigorously establish its decisive effect in particular cases. Indeed, in earlier times, the common law dealt quite effectively with cases of pollution.[32] Nevertheless, the powerful, intuitive argument for regulation was quickly applied by the nascent environmental movement to batter down resistance.

It was known among the relevant experts at the time, and is now better known, that nearly every element of Carson's thesis was wrong. In the first place, there are numerous natural toxins and carcinogens, ubiquitous in the environment. Bruce Ames, the famous biologist at U.C. Berkely, has repeatedly pointed out that 99.99 percent of the pesticides in foods that we eat are *natural* chemicals that plants developed over their evolutionary history to protect themselves from insect predators.[33] Half of those chemicals have been shown in high-dose tests to be carcinogenic to rodents. According to Ames and Gold, humans have biological defenses against all such carcinogenic chemicals, which react no differently to natural carcinogens than to artificial ones.[34]

Given that the environmental content of industrial chemicals is trivial against the natural background, and given that artificial chemicals are derived from natural chemical constituents, and are unlikely on *average* to be more toxic or carcinogenic than those constituents, it is unlikely that in the *aggregate* they increase the environmental risks people face. Indeed, there simply is no cancer plague in modern industrial nations. True, a larger fraction of the U.S. population dies of cancer now than in earlier days, but this is a result of increasing human *health*. Modern medicine has reduced or eliminated so many *other* diseases, and modern agriculture, refrigeration and packaging have so improved nutrition, and average life span has so increased as a result, that cancer simply ranks high among a declining list of factors remaining to claim human life. Excluding lung cancer (which is primarily due to smoking), the overall cancer mortality rates in the U.S. actually fell from 1950 to 1990 for all age groups except those 85 and older, according to the National Cancer Institute.[35] Most cancers are due to avoidable behaviors, such as smoking. Very few are due to pollution, chemical or otherwise.[36]

Of course these observations only deflect the general anti-capitalist philosophic thrust of environmentalism, they do *not* deny the argument for regulation of specific chemicals proven to be harmful in doses that people could assimilate from the environment As the environmental movement coalesced in response to Carson's powerful book, its first target was the elimination of chemical pesticides, and in particular, DDT. This episode is illuminating in several respects. The benefits of pesticides in helping raise farm productivity and *preserve* animal habitat have already been discussed. Dr. Alvin Young of the U.S. Department of Agriculture Office of Biotechnology estimates that eliminating pesticide use would reduce U.S. food output by 40 percent. The National Academy of Sciences only predicts a 30 percent fall in food output, with a 70 percent rise in prices.[37]

DDT seemed an unlikely target because it combined deadly effectiveness against disease spreading insects with an unusual safety record for humans. First synthesized in the late 19th century, it was used in World War II to kill body lice that spread typhus. In previous wars, as Ray points out, typhus often killed more soldiers than enemy weapons, but due to the use of DDT in the second World War, *no* American (or allied) soldiers died from that disease. Nor is there evidence that DDT harmed the soldiers.[38] It was also highly effective in controlling the insect vectors of other diseases, including yellow fever, plague, and malaria.

Malaria is a deadly and debilitating disease that is among the world's worst, particularly in tropical regions. It is spread primarily from those infected to those not by Anopheles mosquitoes which bite the former and then the latter, transferring blood. In some African nations, more than half the population has malaria at any time. Before the War approximately 200 million people contracted malaria each year, and about two million died. After the war, a coordinated international spraying program was undertaken in tropical nations to control or eliminate malaria. Since mosquitoes feed at night and rest on vertical surfaces DDT was sprayed *inside, on the walls,* not in the outdoor environment. This program was so effective, that by the time Carson's book was published, many tropical nations were on the verge of eradicating the disease. In India, for example, ten years of spraying reduced malarial infections from 750,000 to 1500.[39]

DDT was used as a general insecticide in other nations, including the U.S., and because of its effectiveness and low cost, was in some cases used to excess. Fish died in some small lakes and streams when DDT spraying killed their insect food. Instruments began to detect DDT in soil and water in minute quantities. As the campaign for banning DDT developed, three main charges were made. The first was that DDT was a *persistent* substance that accumulated in the environment with additional spraying, and since it was stored in body fat would accumulate in higher concentrations up the food chain (bioaccumulation). It was argued to already be responsible for reducing populations of raptors (birds of prey) such as eagles and hawks, some of which were declining in numbers. Second, it was claimed that DDT caused thinning of bird eggshells, reducing hatching rates. Third, it was argued to be both directly toxic and carcinogenic to humans.

It is certainly true that DDT does not break down and dissipate immediately. Its relative stability in sprayed areas, so that it controlled pests for a significant period, was initially thought its advantage. But DDT is *not* as persistent as environmentalists claim. Except in extremely dark, dry soil it loses its toxicity to insects in two weeks or less.[40] In sea water its half-life is only ten days. Biological organisms absorb some DDT, but the *total* amount present in the world's biota is a fraction of 1960's annual production. Woods Hole Oceanographic Institute researchers expecting to find bioaccumulation of DDT in Marine species were disappointed.[41] Neither of the other charges against DDT have been confirmed. By actual count, most bird populations in the U.S. increased during the period of heavy DDT spraying.[42] The robin, which Carson said would become extinct, became the most abundant bird in North America in that very period. The decline in raptor populations was a result of other factors, and had begun long before widespread DDT spraying occurred.

Eggshell thinning has several causes and was never proven to be an effect of DDT. In one study of DDT that seemed to show such thinning, it was found that the researchers had fed the birds inadequate amounts of calcium. Other studies showed no thinning or significant reduction of hatchings. As for toxicity, contrary to Carson, researchers feeding both young and adult birds food containing extremely large amounts of DDT were unable to kill them, and human volunteers fed 35 milligrams per day (in contrast to the .065 mg. daily intake of an ordinary person) for two years showed *no* ill effects, then or since.[43] Nor is DDT carcinogenic. Environmentalists relied on a study in which large DDT consumption in daily amounts 100,000 times greater than could be gained from the environment produced tumors in mice.[44] In 1978 however, after two years of study, the National Cancer Institute announced that it had not found evidence that DDT was carcinogenic.[45]

Beginning in 1969 pressure from the Environmental Defense Fund, the Audubon Society, the Sierra Club and other organizations motivated several states to ban DDT use. When the EPA was created in 1970 these organizations began lobbying for hearings to ban DDT use entirely. The hearings began in 1971. Chemical industry scientists and many independent researchers, aware of the enormous health and other benefits of DDT, and the weakness of the charges against it, opposed the ban. After exhaustively review of the testimony and evidence, the hearing examiner issued a decision in April 1972 allowing DDT use for essential purposes. Two months later, William Ruckelshaus, the Administrator of the EPA, overruled his own examiner and issued a total ban on DDT use.

The most shocking and amazing thing about this decision is not the attitude it reveals concerning the primacy of politics and regulation over scientific evidence, but that its human consequences were known beforehand. As a result of the hysterical fright caused by Carson's book, several tropical nations had already stopped their spraying programs, with deadly results. The nation of Ceylon (now Sri Lanka) had 2.8 million cases of malaria in 1948, before spraying began. By 1963, with heavy spraying, there were only 17. Spraying stopped in 1964, and consequently there were 150 cases that year. By 1969 there were 2.5 million.[46] Seventy percent of the inhabitants of the island nation of Zanzibar, off Africa's east coast, had malaria in 1958. This was reduced to under 5 percent in 1964, when they stopped DDT spraying. By 1984 infections were between 50 and 60 percent of the population again.[47]

This history must have been known to both sides involved in the 1971 hearings. Both the U.N. World Health Organization and the Communicable Disease Center of the U.S. Department of Health and Human Services had issued warnings about the inevitable consequences for people in tropical nations of stopping DDT use. On February 2, 1971, for example, WHO officials announced that more than one *billion* people had been freed from the risk of malaria through DDT spraying over the prior 25 years. The officials asserted this to be an achievement "unparalleled in the annals of public health." They went on to point out that this had made the work forces healthier, breaking the cycle of poverty and disease in those nations, and had opened up vast areas for agricultural production, increasing the output of rice and wheat.[48]

The opponents of DDT, motivated by the misanthropic belief that the world is overpopulated and that humans are a curse, did not care. When Dr. Charles Worster, chief scientist of the Environmental Defense Fund, was asked by a reporter about the effects on human population and health in poor countries of stopping DDT use, Worster specifically stated that there are too many people, and that "this is as good a way of getting rid of them as any."[49] Victor Yannacone, an attorney in the Environmental Defense Fund who had helped found the EDF, is reported to have resigned in disgust over this statement, though it is not clear whether he disagreed with the genocidal policy itself, or simply over its public disclosure.

In any case, supporters of the ban got their way. When the EPA issued the ban, the international effort to end the curse of malaria through DDT spraying stopped. The results are explained by Ray.[50]

> In 1970, of two billion people living in malarial regions, 79 percent were protected, and the expectation was that malaria would be eradicated. Six years after the United States banned DDT, there were 800 million cases of malaria and 8.2 million deaths per year.

But of course, nearly all of these deaths have occurred outside the United States, and the Environmental Defense Fund, Audubon Society, and other environmental groups responsible have breathed not a word to the American public about these effects of the ban, nor has the EPA. Instead, emboldened by their regulatory success with DDT, they have gone on to repeatedly allege other chemical health threats to the public, generate hysteria about them, and obtain bans on the chemicals involved.

It is important here to briefly discuss the scientific methods employed. Since the actual causes of cancer are not known, the effect of specific substances can only be established empirically. One method is through the use of epidemiological studies, such as when a group of persons that have been exposed to a substance are observed and their rates of cancer contraction are compared with a control group not exposed (smokers with non-smokers for example).

Sometimes a substance under question is literally administered to a volunteer group. Since this is often regarded as unethical, and such studies normally take much time, resort is frequently taken to a faster method. A sample group of rodents are repeatedly fed or injected with the *maxim amount of the substance that will not kill them* (the Maximum Tolerated Dose, or MTD), in an effort to see if tumors are generated over time. If it appears at scientific levels of statistical significance, that members of the injected sample of rodents get tumors in rates in excess of those experienced by a control group of the same type of *rodents,* then linear extrapolation is employed to estimate the carcinogenic risk for *humans* at the much smaller amounts of the substance they would contract from the environment.

Every aspect of this procedure is objectionable. In the first place it is biased toward finding carcinogens because the process of continually and repeatedly wounding an animal is itself known to generate tumors with some frequency.[51] Second, classical statistical methods estimate the strength of an X-Y variable relationship in a population by inference from that found in a sample *taken from that population.* It does *not* infer from a sample taken from some *other* population that is merely assumed (without proof) to be similar in some respect. In short, rodents are not human beings, and it has never been shown that the carcinogenic response of humans to various substances is the same as that in rodents. Indeed, toxic or carcinogenic effects of particular substances on particular types of rodents often do not even predict well their effect on other types of *rodents.*

And last, the process of linear extrapolation is hard to defend. It is well known that the relationship of effects to doses in many substances, is nonlinear. Substances that are poisonous in high doses (such as iron and potassium, for example) are often *beneficial* and even *necessary* to the human body in lower doses. In short, the whole MTD procedure for estimating toxic or carcinogenic risks to humans for purposes of chemical regulation is essentially lacking in scientific value. Nevertheless, what valid scientific component it contains has been found excessively binding by the regulatory agencies. The scientific standard for accepting the existence of an X-Y correlation, is that the probability that the sample is showing a false correlation must be 5 percent or less. Since adherence to this professional standard limits the number of chemical substances that they can declare to be toxic or carcinogenic hazards and bring under their regulatory authority, the EPA and other regulatory agencies have openly advocated the subordination of demonstrated correlation to looser standards and criteria.[52]

In any case, lack of valid scientific evidence has often not stopped the EPA or the environmental movement from creating scares and frightening the public into accepting regulatory action. Chemicals such as PCBs (Polychlorinated biphenyls), Alar (a growth regulator sprayed on apple orchards to prevent early ripening and reduce mold toxins), Red Dye number 2, and Dioxin were all banned following panics generated by grossly inflated or flatly false claims made by the regulatory agencies or environmental organizations concerning their toxic or carcinogenic properties.[53] Subsequent research, as a result of which even the regulatory agencies have often severely reduced their estimates of the dangers of such substances, has not been widely propagated by the sycophants of environmentalism in the television networks or academy. They are usually too busy helping propagate the next scare.

The lack of demonstrated detrimental health effects from such substances is literally striking. Nobody has ever become chronically ill or died from dioxin exposure in the U.S. Monsanto Chemical Company workers exposed to high levels of dioxin in 1949 showed no long-term effects. No one was ever shown to have been harmed by exposure to dioxin in Love Canal or Times Beach, Missouri. When the residents of Seveso, Italy were exposed by an explosion to three pounds of dioxin, the worst health effect was the development of Chloracne (skin irritation caused by chlorinated compounds) by some residents. This despite widely published claims by environmentalists Michael Brown and others that three ounces of dioxin distributed among a million people would kill them all.[54]

There is even less evidence that anyone was ever harmed by eating apples treated with Alar. The Natural Resources Defense Council claimed Alar to be carcinogenic on the basis of an MTD test that generated tumors in mice by feeding them so much that a human would have had to eat 28,000 pounds of apples daily for 70 years to obtain proportional amounts. The NRDC never told people, however, that when the mice were fed half that amount–equivalent to a human eating 14,000 pounds of apples daily for 70 years–*no* tumors were generated.[55] 1,300 people were indeed made sick in Kyusho, Japan from eating rice that had somehow been contaminated with a fluid used in air conditioning that contained PCBs. It turned out that the PCBs were not per se the agent that made them sick, however, and cases of accidental food contamination (or of deliberate poisoning) do *not* justify banning all normal use of a chemical substance.

Neither the EPA, the National Cancer institute, nor anyone else has ever been able to identify a *single person* whose cancer resulted from waste site carcinogens. The response to environmentalists who claim that toxic or carcinogenic industrial chemicals leaking into the environment are killing large numbers of people in the U.S. and other Western nations should always be: *name one*. If they could do so, of course, the problem would be solved, since such standards of proof could be used in court to generate sanctions against those emitting the chemicals. There are indeed demonstrable victims here, however, persons who can be literally identified and named. They are those who have lost large fractions of their incomes, and perhaps their entire businesses, or who have otherwise lost employment through the banning of such chemicals as Alar, Dioxin, PCBs, and DDT, and Red Dye #2. They are also the consumers who have been deprived of the beneficial uses of such substances. Almost certainly these losses outweigh any gains to the public from risk reduction through chemical regulation. Any genuine risks or harms generated could have been dealt with through other legal mechanisms–such as tort law–that are far more consistent with the rule of law in a free society.

As the DDT episode demonstrated, those suffering economic and financial losses are not the only victims of the environmental pseudo-science and EPA regulatory depredations. To show that such incidents are ongoing, one more example is needed. One factor many chemicals accused of harming the environment and increasing public health risks have in common is that they are chlorinated compounds. A major source of chlorine in the environment is runoff from municipal water supplies, which are often treated with chlorine to kill bacteria. Nevertheless, the movement has begun to advocate a ban on chlorinated compounds. For years the EPA has seconded such sentiments, and it proposed a rule in 1994 that would eliminate the chlorination process known as pre-disinfection of U.S. water supplies. In the early 1990s, the government of Peru, taking the warnings of environmentalists and our EPA seriously, actually reduced chlorine use in their water treatment. The result was that Cholera got into Peruvian water supplies (possibly from a Chinese merchant ship that emptied its bilges while in harbor). Over a five year period in the ensuing epidemic a million people became sick, and 10,000 died.[56]

For the regulators and the intellectual and organizational leaders of the environmental movement, the fortunate thing here is that, once again, the genocidal effects of their policies have occurred abroad. Their reflexive supporters in the opinion media have, by their silence, been able to keep the public from learning the facts. But that very silence reveals much about the character of those leaders, the regulators, and their intellectual, academic, and media supporters. Unless the public comes to an awareness of the truth, sooner or later we will experience the effects of such policies directly. The real nature of the environmental movement and its ideology will then be understood, but too late.

Notes

1 Predictions of resource depletion by industrial society have been made since they originated with Thomas Malthus in the early 19th century, and they have always been wrong. See Julian Simon and Herman Khan, eds., *The Resourceful Earth: A Response to Global 2000* (Blackwell, 1984), Herbert I. London, *Why Are They Lying to Our Children?* (Stein and Day, 1984), Dwight Lee, "The Perpetual Assault on Progress," Center for the Study of American Business *Contemporary Issues Series* 42 (May 1991), and Steven Moore, "The Coming Age of Abundance," in Ron Baily, ed., *The True State of the Planet* (The Competitive Enterprise Institute, 1995).

2 For a good cross section of the misanthropic and anti-capitalist sentiments and statements in print by intellectual and organizational leaders of the environmental movement, see Dixie Lee Ray, *Trashing the Planet* (Harper Collins, 1990): Chapter 12.

3 Strictly speaking, it may be impossible for humans to create a new chemical substance. Through millions of years of entropic mixing, nature has probably tried every possible chemical combination.

4 As reported by CNN News on the 29th and 30th of December, 1994. CNN News is marginally less assiduous than are CBS, ABC and NBC (who failed to report both this matter and the one about the Innsbruck Ice man discussed below) about filtering the news to exclude information that does not support the environmental ideology.

5 See Pekka E. Kauppi, et al., "Biomass and Carbon Budget of European Forests, 1971 to 1990," *Science* 256 (April 3, 1992): 70-74.

6 Sylvan H. Wittwer, "Flower Power," *Policy Review* (Fall 1992): 4-9.

7 See Steven Gold, "The Rise of Markets and the Fall of Infectious Disease," *The Freeman* (November 1992): 412-415.

8 See the discussion of the Rasmussen report of the Nuclear Regulatory
   Commission in Jack J. Kraushaar and Robert A. Ristinen, *Energy
   Problems of a Technical Society* (John Wiley and Sons, 1988): 135-137.
   See also Herbert Inhaber, "Risks with Energy from Conventional and Non
   conventional Sources," *Science* (February 23, 1979): 718-723.

9 Just from 1959 to 1992, the real value of services generated in the U.S.
   increased from less than 44 to over 50 percent of real Gross Domestic
   Product, a nearly 14 percent increase in share. See the Council of
   Economic Advisers, *Economic Report of the President, 1994,* table B-8, p.
   273.

10 United Nations, *World Population Prospects: The 1994 Revision–Annex
   tables* (United Nations Population Division, Department for Economic and
   Social Information and Policy Analysis, 1994): tables A-1 and A-2.

11 World Health Organization, *Our Planet, Our Health: Report of the WHO
   Commission on Health and the Environment* (Geneva, Switzerland, WHO,
   1992).

12 See K. Smith and Y. Liu, "Indoor Air Pollution in Developing Countries,"
   in J. M. Samet, ed., *Epidemiology of Lung Cancer* (Marcel Dekker,
   1994): 151-184.

13 Another possibility would be to simply plow the same amount of ground,
   and obtain the same amount of food *ceteris paribus,* in less time.
   Normally people will divide the gains between the two, obtaining some
   combination of higher output and reduced work time. Thus the evolution
   of both the 40 hour week and higher per capita food availability and real
   incomes.

14 See Roger A. Sedjo, "Forests: Conflicting Signals," in Bailey, ed., *The
   True State of the Planet* (The Free Press, 1995): 184-185.

15 U.S. Department of Agriculture,*World Agriculture, Trends and Indicators*
   (USDA Economic Research Service, 1994).

16 Sedjo, "Forests: Conflicting Signals," in *The True State of the Planet*.
   Environmentalists have chronically engaged in inflated claims about the
   rate of tropical deforestation. The best data comes from the satellite analysis of Brazilian deforestation over 1978-1988 by David Skole and
   Compton Tucker. See Steven Budiansky, "The Doomsday Myths," *U.S.
   News & World Report* (December 13, 1993): 81-91. Skole and Tucker estimate annual tropical deforestation occurred at about 1/5 the rate commonly cited by environmentalists. In addition, as Budiansky also mentions,
   examinations of the Brazilian *coastal* forests that have been severely

depleted (in contrast to the Amazon basin rain forest, which is still 90 percent intact) not only failed to document *any* species extinction, but actually *found* several species previously thought extinct.

18 The level of competence of regulatory agencies to deal with such issues, even in their supposed area of expertise, may be indicated by the fact that nineteen employees of the EPA are currently suing the agency, claiming they were made sick by indoor air pollution at its Waterside Mall office in Washington D.C. See "Bad Environment,"*The Washington Times National Weekly Edition,* 24 November, 1996.

19 On the Meuse Valley disaster, see F. W. Lipfert, *Air Pollution and Community Health* (Van Nostrand Reinhold, 1994). On the Donora, smog, see Helmuth H. Schrenk, et al., *Air Pollution in Donora, Pennsylvania: Epidemiology of the Unusual Smog Episode of October 1948, Preliminary Report,* PHS Bulletin 306 (Public Health Service, 1949). For the London episode, see R. E. Waller and B. T. Cummings, "Episodes of High Pollution in London, 1952-1966," in Proceedings: Part I. International Clean Air Congress, London, 4-7 October, 1966, International Union of Air Pollution Prevention Association (London: National Society for Clean Air, 1966): 228-231.

20 Arthur C. Pigou, *The Economics of Welfare* (4th Ed. Macmillan, 1932). For a critique of the Pigouvian view and lucid presentation of the more modern Coasian property rights paradigm, see Steven N. S. Cheung, *The Myth of Social Cost* (The Institute of Economic Affairs, 1978). The Pigouvian paradigm still dominates, however, and though I agree more with the Coasian view, I choose to report here the orthodox analysis.

21 Modern economics is historically a child of the *Utilitarian* branch of Classical Liberalism. Bentham may have opposed concepts of natural rights, but he favored limited government. His intent in providing his 'felicific calculus' of pleasure and pain with which legislators were to determine policy in such a way as to attain the "greatest good of the greatest number," was precisely to provide *scientific* criteria for policy that would *remove* the arbitrary power and discretion of legislators. His failure was not just in the inadequacy of his felicific calculus circa 1789, but in presuming that legislators and/or regulators would ever be willing to accept limits imposed by such scientific criteria if they appeared.

22 This is true in detail, and certainly in the aggregate, as even the defenders of regulation now seem to admit. See, for example, Cass Sunstein, "On Costs, Benefits, and Regulatory Success: Reply to Crandall," *Critical Review* 8 (Fall 1994): 629.

23 Robert W. Crandall, "Regulation and the Rights Revolution: Can (Should)

We Rescue the New Deal?" *Critical Review* 7 (Spring-Summer 1993): 200-201.

24 See Joseph L. Bast, Peter J. Hill, and Richard C. Rue, *Eco-Sanity: A Common Sense Guide to Environmentalism* (Madison Books, 1994): 74-81.

25 See Indur Goklany, "Richer is Cleaner: Long-Term Trends in Global Air Quality," in Bailey, ed., *The True State of the Planet* : 360.

26 MacAvoy, *Industry Regulation:* 98.

27 Ibid, 101-102.

28 Ibid, 103.

29 Ibid, 97.

30 Goklany, "Richer is Cleaner," *The True State of the Planet* : 359.

31 In 1996 the EPA released a report claiming huge benefits relative to costs for its airborne emissions regulations. The report was subject to peer review, by a committee of "outside experts" hand picked by the EPA itself. The report found that nearly all of the increased mortality and morbidity it claims to have reduced through regulation was attributable to TSP and lead emissions, with 90 percent due to TSP alone. Yet, despite the fact that TSP emissions from utilities had fallen between 1950 and 1970 (before EPA regulation) at a 6 percent annual rate, and fell even more from 1970 to 1990, the EPA assumed they would have *risen* at a 1 percent annual rate from 1970 to 1990 without EPA regulation. Throughout, the EPA claims of large health benefits relative to costs are dependent on this sort of absurd view of the effectiveness of its regulation and the ineffectiveness of market forces. See Robert W. Crandall, Fredrick H. Rueter, and Wilbur A. Steger, "Clearing the Air: EPA's Self-Assessment of Clean-Air Policy," *Regulation* No. 4 (1996): 35-46.

32 See Roger E. Miners and Bruce Yandle, *The Common Law: How it Protects the Environment,* (Political Economy Research Center, Policy Series Number P.S.-13, May 1998).

33 Bruce N. Ames, Renae Magaw, and Lois Swirsky Gold, "Ranking Possible Carcinogenic Hazards," *Science* 236 (April 17, 1987): 272, 277.

34 Bruce N. Ames and Lois Swirsky Gold, "The Causes and Prevention of Cancer," in Baily, ed., *The True State of the Planet* : 143-145.

35 B. A. Miller, et al., *SEER Cancer Statistics Review: 1973-1990* (National Cancer Institute, NIH publication No. 93-2789, 1993).

36 David A. Dunnette, "Assessing Risks and Preventing Disease from

Environmental Chemicals," *Journal of Community Health* (April 21, 1990): 169-186.

37 See Jerry Taylor, "Pesticides and Food Safety: Separating Fact from Fiction," *The State Factor*, American Legislative Exchange Council (July 1992): 20-21.

38 On this and the ensuing debate and regulatory struggle see Thomas R. Dunlap, *DDT: Scientists, Citizens, and Public Policy* (Princeton University Press, 1981).

39 Elizabeth Whelan, *Toxic Terror* (Jameson Books, 1985): 71.

40 Ray, *Trashing the Planet*: 70.

41 See Robert L. Ackerly, "DDT: A Re-evaluation, Part II," *Chemical Times and Trends* (January, 1982): 48-55, particularly p. 46.

42 J. Gordon Edwards, *Silent Spring–Broken Spring* (National Council for Environmental Balance, 1981).

43 Robert L. Ackerly, "DDT: A Re-evaluation, Part I," *Chemical Times and Trends* (October 1981): 47-53, particularly p. 48. This study cited by Ackerly was conducted by U.S. Public Health Service researcher Dr. Wayland J. Hayes.

44 On this study Whelan cites George Claus and Karen Bolander, *Ecological Sanity* (David McKay, 1977): 346-351.

45 `Technical Report Series No. 131, National Cancer Institute, Bethesda, Maryland, 1978. DDT ingested by humans is emulsified and stored in body fat. Persistent charges that this caused breast cancer in women were recently found to be unsupported. See Nancy Krieger, Mary S. Wolff, et al., "Breast Cancer and Serum Organochlorines: A Prospective Study Among White, Black, and Asian Women," *Journal of the National Cancer Institute* (April 20, 1994).

46 Whelan, *Toxic Terror*: 69. See also Norman Borlaug, "In Defense of DDT and Other Pesticides," *UNESCO Courier* (February, 1972): 4-12, particularly p. 10, and the paper by the National Communicable Disease Center of the Department of Health and Human Services, "Malaria Control and Eradication," (July 25, 1969).

47 See Barry Schlecter, "Malaria on the Rise in Many Third World Areas," Associated Press wire story, 6 May 1985.

48 The statement of WHO officials is quoted exactly in Borlaug, "In Defense of DDT and Other Pesticides": 10.

49 Whelan, *Toxic Terror*: 67 cites remarks by J. Gordon Edwards, presented

to the International Meeting on Pesticides in Pakistan, August 1980.

50 Ray, *Trashing the Planet*: 69.

51 Yet despite this known bias in the methodology, with some frequency scientists find chemicals that are *anticarcinogenic* to rodents. That is, they cause the rodent groups receiving the MTD to experience *lower* rates of tumor generation than the control groups. See Edith Efron, *The Apocalyptics*. Two points are interesting here. First, the existence of such chemicals supports the proposition developed early in this chapter that the externalities associated with industrial products, emissions, and wastes, are likely to be symmetric in the aggregate. Also interesting is the thundering silence on the part of the regulatory agencies, the environmental organizations, and their leftist sycophants in the media and academy about the very existence of industrial chemicals with inadvertent anticarcinogenic properties.

52 The EPA's 1996 guidelines on scientific criteria for determining chemicals to be dangerously toxic or carcinogenic specifically eliminate correlation at scientifically accepted levels as a basic requirements for determining causality. See William Niskanen, "Clinton's Regulatory Record," *Regulation* No. 3 (1996): 28. Another egregious case is that of the International Joint Commission, a regulatory agency that fronts for Greenpeace. The IJC specifically argues for banning discharge of chemicals *even if evidence meeting scientific standards that the chemicals have harmful effects does not currently exist.* See Hill, Bast and Rue, *Eco-Sanity*: 170-175.

53 These episodes of manufactured public panic and regulatory banning have been so well and extensively analyzed and reported by others that, for lack of space, I shall not do so here in any depth. See Ben Bolch and Harold Lyons, *Apocalypse Not: Science, Economics, and Environmentalism* (The Cato Institute, 1993): Chapter 4, Hill, Bast, and Rue, *Eco-Sanity*: 166-170, and Ray, *Trashing the Planet*: Chapter 7.

54 Michael H. Brown, "Love Canal and the Poisoning of America," *Atlantic Monthly* (December 1979): 33-47.

55 Charles Knote, *The Amazing Truth about Pesticides' Safety* (Missouri Pest Control Association, 1989).

56 Michael Fumento, "Dirty Water," *Reason* (May 1996): 52-53.

Chapter 9

The Costs of Regulation

In the pervasive condition of scarcity, in which individual human beings always find their resources inadequate to allow them to attain everything they want, they rationally attempt to *economize*. That is, they assign available resources to their most important ends, leaving the less important desires unsatisfied. These efforts can be enormously aided by cooperation with other persons in a social division of labor, particularly if institutional conditions allow and encourage productive actions and interactions (including market transactions) that maximize resource availability and efficiency of resource use. Under the classical liberal philosophy on which Western civilization was based, this requires government to constrain private predation, protecting persons and their property, so that people are forced to deal with one another in voluntary and hence mutually beneficial ways. Also, government must *itself* be constrained by democratic competition for legislative offices and constitutional limits on its power and scope of activities, so that it may *not* be used as an even more efficient instrument for private predation.

This view, in which the 'negative state' simply establishes conditions of private property, security from predation, limited democracy, and equal treatment under the law, otherwise leaving individuals free to work out their own destinies through personal decisions and voluntary interactions, has been specifically rejected by the apostles of intervention. They have claimed that the outcomes of such voluntary interactions in the market economy are distributionally unjust and allocatively inefficient, and that government intervention and regulation improves things. Economists have become increasingly suspicious of these public interest claims, however, as history and empirical evidence have shown various forms of regulation to simply *be* private predation *through* government, justified (and largely made possible) *by* such public interest claims.

From the utilitarian perspective of pure economic science, however, the issue becomes theoretically simple. Where the advocates of regulation claim social benefits, the question of whether and how much state and federal regulation there should be is one of whether or not the social benefits exceed the costs, where both are implicitly measurable.[1] Evidence on the magnitude of regulatory costs is rapidly accumulating, and the picture emerging is not pretty. The effect of such costs is to reduce output and employment, *ceteris paribus,* by processes described in the next section. Published systematic data on the benefits of regulation is much more scanty. One suspects there are good reasons for this.

Still, it may be possible to determine the net effect. If regulation makes products better or safer this should raise their value to consumers, increasing demand and real GDP, the measure of final output in the economy. Regulatory suppression of private monopoly should have a similar effect. In addition, if regulation improves resource allocation, aggregate output should also be raised through increased productivity. Imposing regulatory costs, however, or regulatory creation of monopoly, tend to reduce economic output. So which effect has dominated? Has output and employment in the economy gained or lost from the expansion of regulation since the late 1960s?

The Nature and Effects of Regulatory Costs

Regulation can be broadly defined into three categories. Social regulation covers health and safety, the environment, employment discrimination, and so on. Economic regulation involves controls over product prices, efforts to suppress or create cartels and monopolies, etc. Last, what Thomas Hopkins terms process regulation includes paperwork and other costs of compliance. All regulation imposes costs of many kinds on the economy. In the first place, governments must employ resources extracted from the private sector through taxation in the very process of imposing and enforcing regulations. These budgetary costs thus absorb resources that private individuals would otherwise use in production and/or consumption. Data on the budgets of federal regulatory agencies is readily available back to 1970, having been collected and published by the Center for the Study of American Business (CSAB) at Washington University in St. Louis.[2]

The non-budgetary regulatory costs experienced by private producers and consumers are much larger than these budgeted expenditures of the Federal agencies, running perhaps as much as $400 to $500 billion per year by 1996, or around $4000 to $5000 *per household* in the U.S in 1995. A large fraction of these are costs of compliance, such as the time, effort and resources absorbed by filling out paperwork associated with taxation and regulation. Indeed, the paperwork and associated accounting and legal fees may cost as much as $200 billion annually by itself. Resources are also absorbed when business is required to purchase and install specified pollution control equipment mandated by the EPA, or safety equipment mandated by OSHA, or undertake extra product testing by the CPSC or the FDA. Costs are also imposed when business is required by regulation to rearrange its production facilities as mandated by OSHA, or by the Americans with Disabilities act, and so on. All such costs result in reduced production and employment and higher prices for consumer goods and services, *ceteris paribus* (other determinants of the supplies of such goods and services held constant). The same occurs when regulation creates monopolies or cartels.

The economic effects of imposing regulation or raising the degree of regulation on the producers in a single industry are illustrated in Graphs 9.1 and 9.2 below. Graph 9.1 shows the short-run marginal cost (the incremental addition to total costs resulting from some incremental addition to total output per time period, mc_1) and average total cost curve (atc_1) of a typical firm in the industry. Graph 9.2 shows the consumer demand curve and the industry supply curve. The supply curve is the horizontal sum of the marginal cost curves of the firms in the industry. Each firm finds its best (i.e. profit maximizing) output as in 9.1 by employing additional labor and other variable inputs and raising its production rate to the point that price equals marginal cost. The market clearing price per unit shown in 9.2 is assumed to be just equal to the minimum average (unit) total cost of production, so that for each firm total revenue equals total costs including the market rate of interest on capital invested. Total output in the industry is Q_1, the sum of the outputs of the individual firms.

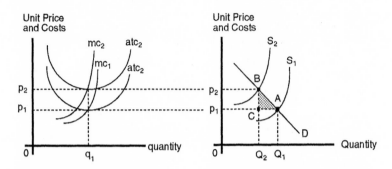

Graph 9.1: Typical firm before and after regulation..

Graph 9.2: Market before and after regulation..

Complying with the new regulations raises the costs of producing each unit of output, as shown by the dashed curves mc_2 and atc_2 in Graph 9.1. At the initial price p_1, each firm is now making an economic loss (a low or negative rate of return on its invested capital) since its total revenue is less than its total costs, even when it reduces its output to the point at which p_1 equals the new marginal cost. Some firms are forced by the losses to leave the industry, and such exit, along with the regulation induced unit cost increases, shifts the industry supply curve left and up to S_2 in Graph 9.2. The resulting excess demand causes price to rise to clear the market at p_2, which is equal to the new minimum unit cost of production. Then the *remaining* firms (let us assume the firm in 9.1 is one such) once again have revenue sufficient to cover all their costs including the normal return on investment.

The social effects of the regulation–at least in terms of costs–can be seen in 9.2. Equilibrium output Q_2 is smaller than before (and so is employment in the industry), and the product price is higher. Consumers can only purchase a smaller quantity at the higher price. Depending on what is termed the 'elasticity of demand' over the range between points A and B, revenue in the industry may have risen, fallen, or remained unchanged. Whichever is the case, however, total costs changed by exactly the same amount. This is a case of pure compliance costs. There is real income that is redistributed from consumers to investors, represented by the rectangle p_1p_2BC in 9.2, but it simply goes to cover the imposed compliance costs, and would generate no rent seeking. The social cost is simply the value of output shown in the shaded 'Harburger' triangle (area CBA) that is not redistributed between consumers and producers or workers and investors, but is simply lost to society.

An opposite pure case would be equivalent to that shown in Graph 1.1 in Chapter 1, in which regulation takes the form of an entry restriction allowing creation of a monopoly or a cartel with no compliance costs. The supply restriction in that case is simply due to the franchised monopoly or cartel restricting output by the optimal amount necessary to maximize profits. Under competitive rent seeking (that is, competitive investment of resources in order to win the grant of monopoly franchise from the politicians) the social losses would, as explained there, consist of the sum of the Harburger triangle, or efficiency losses, and the Tulloch rectangle representing the profits extracted from the consumers for the owners of the firm.

These dollar magnitudes are implicitly measurable (though in practice, only with difficulty), and recent studies of regulated U.S. industries estimate that there are about two or three dollars of transfer costs for each dollar of efficiency costs. A major unsettled question in the measurement of regulatory costs is how much of the transfer costs generate rent-seeking expenditures absorbing resources and creating an actual social loss. But if only half of transfer costs showed up as rent-seeking expenditures, those losses would essentially equal the aggregate economic efficiency losses from regulation.

Before turning to the empirical literature, a few important theoretical qualifications need to be made to the case of pure regulatory compliance costs illustrated in graphs 9.1 and 9.2. First, in its pre-regulation condition, the industry might be generating external costs, such as pollution, and consequently be using *too many* resources initially from a social perspective. In that case, compliance with the regulations might simply internalize the external costs, so that the resulting output and resource reduction is in fact a social improvement in resource use. The actual difficulty of doing that with regulation, and the small probability that regulators really have any such intent, were discussed in Chapter 8, but it remains a theoretical possibility in the relevant cases.

Now suppose the regulations, instead of being environmental, were aimed at forcing the industry to make a safer product. If this worked, *consumers would recognize the improvement, and demand for the product would increase.* If the increase in demand was as large (in its vertical shift at each level of output) as the supply decrease, no firms would leave the industry, and price would simply rise enough to cover the higher costs. That is, the regulatory costs would be self-financing, and indeed, that would constitute an economic criterion for the *proper* type and magnitude of product safety regulation. The contribution of the industry to the value of aggregate output (Gross Domestic Product) would rise without reduction in output or employment. Has this occurred? We will see below.

As a third possibility, suppose the regulation was aimed at increasing worker safety. If it was effective in reducing workplace hazards, workers could not fail to note this, and the wage premiums they demanded to endure the prior unsafe conditions would fall. *Indeed, for the proper degree and type of regulation, wage premiums should fall enough to offset the effect of compliance on costs,* so that production costs of the firms would not rise at all. Again, the world would be made a better place. Has this been the effect of OSHA regulation? Hardly! All evidence is that OSHA induced cost increases and the resulting social losses are enormous, and that, as pointed out in Chapter 7 above, little or no improvement in workplace safety has resulted.

One more caveat. The effects of regulatory mandates and resulting compliance costs shown in graphs 9.1 and 9.2 are what economists call *partial equilibrium* effects. That is, secondary effects on other markets are not considered. But that such effects would be generated is obvious. Firms often sell to and buy from each other, and regulatory cost increases at one level are passed on to another. Also, the changes in consumer real income and the relative price increases generated by imposition of regulatory cost increases in one market affect consumer demand in other markets. Resource allocations are often altered in inefficient ways. Studies that consider such general equilibrium effects usually find significantly larger overall costs to regulation than those that only consider partial equilibrium effects.

The Empirics of Regulatory Costs

Efforts within the economics profession to empirically estimate the aggregate costs of regulation for the U.S. economy are in their infancy, but the data is improving fast. Studies of regulatory costs in particular industries have been made for decades, but regulation is so extensive that the task of estimating such costs for the whole macroeconomy has been daunting. One of the earliest of such macroeconomic estimates was by Weidenbaum and DeFina assessing total regulatory costs for 1976.[3] They estimated that direct compliance and paperwork costs totaled $63 billion that year, which was over 3.5 percent of Gross Domestic Product. A few years later Litan and Nordhaus estimated total regulatory costs for 1977 as falling within a range between $35 and $91 billion.[4] That would imply that such costs ranged from approximately 1.8 to 4.6 percent of GDP. Litan and Nordhaus appear to underestimate total costs, however, since they exclude all of the resulting income transfers.

One of the most detailed studies was published by Hahn and Hird in 1991.[5] Hahn and Hird summarize numerous studies estimating the costs (and where available, the benefits) of various types of regulations, as well as developing their own macroeconomic estimates. They found efficiency costs of about $38 billion in 1988 dollars that had been missed by earlier studies, and estimated that by 1988 total regulatory costs ranged between 2.5 and 3.2 percent of Gross National Product.[6] Like Litan and Nordhaus, however, they excluded transfer costs, assuming away rent-seeking expenditures.

Each of these economists built on earlier work, refining their concepts and measurements of regulatory costs. Probably the most complete, accurate, and useful measures of such costs currently available are by Thomas Hopkins, however, of the Rochester Institute of Technology. Hopkins has developed time series for categories of regulatory costs and total regulatory costs going back to 1977, and has repeatedly updated and refined his estimates.[7] Hopkins' most recent total cost estimates for 1977-1995 (as of this writing), expressed in constant 1995 dollars, are included in the first column in Table 9-1 at the end of this chapter. The second column shows total regulatory costs as a percent of Gross Domestic Product, and the third column expresses the cost data on a per capita basis for the U.S. population. The total cost data series is shown visually in Graph 9.3 below.

The time patterns shown for this series is interesting. The first year of Hopkins' data was 1977, about the time that the deregulation wave swept from the Carter administration through Congress and on into the Reagan Administration. Hopkins has never extended his data further back. I have done so, using an estimated relation between budgeted federal regulatory expenditures and Hopkins' Total regulatory cost estimates after 1977 to infer total costs for the earlier years by adjustment from the known regulatory expenditures for the years

1960-1976. Hopkins' data alone shows a 'U' shaped pattern, erroneously implying that regulatory costs have been essentially flat over time. Adding estimates of costs for the earlier years captures the dramatic rise in those costs through 1977, the leveling off since then, and the overall rising trend.

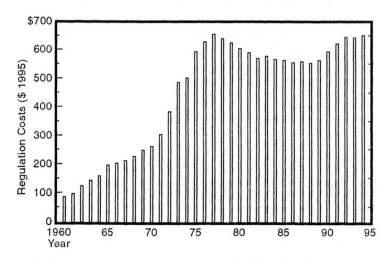

Graph 9.3: Total Private Sector Regulatory Costs in Billions of Constant 1995 Dollars, 1960-1994

By 1995 total regulatory costs had reached $668 billion, or just over 9.2 percent of Gross Domestic Product. Hopkins includes all transfer costs in his time series, however, which amounts to assuming that all such show up as rent-seeking expenditures. This is highly unlikely, so his estimates (and mine) are probably slightly excessive over the whole time series. Due to rising population and economic growth, regulatory costs per-capita and as a fraction of GDP are still below their 1977 peak, though both are rising and are far higher than they were in the 1960s.

Despite the sophistication of these efforts at estimating regulatory costs, there are some startling omissions from all of them. Where is an estimation of the value of the lives of the millions of people in tropical regions who died of malaria after 1972 because the EPA banned the use of DDT and caused the collapse of the international spraying effort? What about the 10,000 Peruvians who died of cholera because our EPA talked their government into reducing chlorine use in their public water supplies? Is the value of those lives included in the aggregate regulation cost estimates? Don't bet on it. And how would one even estimate a dollar value to the freedom lost, and the corruption of the constitutional system resulting from the progressive extension of a debased *form* of law, at the expense of more effective and justifiable legal mechanisms, as unelected Big Brother increasingly watches, commands, and controls through regulation?

The Dynamic Effects of Regulation

The static cost estimates just discussed imply significant reductions in the income and well being of American citizens *ceteris paribus*, but they beg an important question concerning the effects of regulation on the rate of economic growth and hence the level and growth of income over time. In a system of appropriate cultural attitudes and efficient political and economic incentives, such as were created by the Constitution (which was instituted as a *result* of such cultural attitudes), people are motivated to undertake entrepreneurial actions that raise productivity, output and income. Personal saving and investment that raises the stock of capital, tools, and equipment, acts to raise productivity, as does investment in training and education. Likewise, investments in research and development generating improved processes of production also raise productivity, which is generally measured in output per manhour of production.

The market must also be allowed to shift labor and capital resources in accordance with wage differentials and profit and loss signals from lower valued to higher valued uses. In addition, organizational and managerial innovations can raise the efficiency of business operations. When allowed to operate, all of these factors raise productivity and act along with population growth to generate rising output and income at compound rates. The close empirical connection between growth in output per man-hour and rising hourly real income was demonstrated in Chapter 6 above. On an intuitive level, it seems obvious that only as we produce more per time period, can we have more to enjoy and consume per time period.

Empirically, economic growth has averaged near 3.5 percent annually over the last century, and growth in output per man-hour of production has averaged about 2 percent. Approximately one third to one half of this productivity growth has been estimated as due to rising capital per worker. A somewhat smaller fraction is attributable to human capital investment, and the remainder is termed multifactor productivity growth. Multifactor productivity growth is attributed to such things as technological advance, economies of scale, improvements in the allocation of resources, and efficiencies resulting from innovations and improvements in management and business organization.

In the first two decades or so following World War II growth in output per man-hour of production was above average. Around 1970, however, labor productivity growth had begun to fall significantly below average, and has never entirely recovered. This trend is shown in Graph 9.4. For annual observations the graph employs a five-year moving average in order to reduce the effect of cyclic factors, smooth out the series, and make the trend clearer. Thus, the observation for a given year is the average of the productivity growth for that year and the four years previous. The decline in productivity growth in the 1970s and partial recovery in the 1980s is very clear.

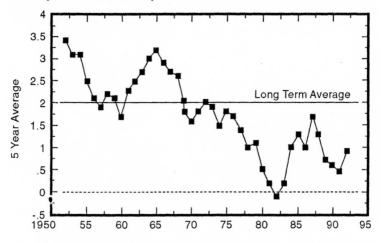

**Graph 9.4: Five Year Moving Average Percent Change in Output
Per Man-Hour of Production, 1952-92**

Economists have termed this "the great productivity slowdown" and have been very concerned to explain it, since it has clearly acted to reduce our overall rate of growth in gross and per capita real output and income. One popular theory has been that the slowdown was the result of the oil shocks of 1973 and 1979, attributable to the Yom Kippur War, the Iranian revolution, and the associated actions of the Organization of Petroleum Exporting Countries–the OPEC Cartel.[8] This may have made the energy intensive portion of the U.S. capital stock unusable, lowering the overall capital stock. It is undeniable that the OPEC actions administered recessionary shocks to the economy of the U.S. and other net oil importing nations, and that U.S. oil and natural gas price controls aggravated the situation. Some economists have doubted, however, that such discrete recessionary shocks would permanently reduce productivity growth, particularly since OPEC control of world oil prices was transitory at best, and oil prices fell in the mid 1980s. In addition, it appears that the productivity slowdown actually began before 1973.

Another explanation some analysts propound is based on the rapid increases in the labor force in the U.S. in recent decades, particularly on the part of women. The contribution of additional labor supply to output, while positive, is subject to diminishing *marginal* returns, and arguably might have also reduced output per man (or person) hour on *average* in this period. Some other economists argue that the productivity slowdown is due to the increasing share of services in aggregate output, on a theory that productivity grows in the goods producing sector, but not in the service sector of the economy.

The time factor here is problematic, since the rise in the service share of output has been ongoing for over a century. In addition, it seems likely that the same factors that raise productivity in the goods sector of the economy would also raise productivity in service generation. Do not computers allow lawyers to search out legal precedents and process paperwork, bills, etc. more rapidly and at lower cost, just as they do for goods manufacturing firms? Doesn't newer and better equipment increase the speed and reduce the costs of fast food preparation, insurance provision, cleaning services, airline travel, etc., just as it does for goods production? Still, both of these factors have found advocates as partial explanations of the decline in productivity growth.

One factor that has clearly changed in precisely the period of the productivity slowdown is the enormous expansion in the size and scope of federal government activity, particularly since the Johnson Administration. This had two primary dimensions. The first was the large-scale increase in income redistributions, known as transfer payments, beginning with the war on poverty. Financing these expenditures required tax increases, expanded federal borrowing, and rapid money stock growth.[9] Federal expenditure, taxation, and deficits all increased as a percent of Gross Domestic Product, and inflation accelerated.

All of these events may have acted to reduce productivity growth. Tax increases in this period extracted productive resources from the economy and directed them into income transfers and consumption. Taxing some individuals at higher rates in order to provide subsidies to others also reduces the incentive of *both* groups to work, save, and invest. Higher business taxes absorb funds otherwise to be used for capital investment, research, and development. In addition, inflation causes business capital consumption when capital depreciation allowances in the tax code are based on the initial prices of the assets. The theoretical case seems strong that the growth of government income redistributions and the associated finance reduced productivity growth.

The second dimension of the growth of government in this period is the expansion of social regulation after 1967, which continued growing during and after the economic deregulation of the late Carter and early Reagan years. Regulation can reduce productivity growth in various ways. First, compliance costs absorb business funds that might otherwise be destined for capital investment or research and development, just as do taxes, thus reducing capital stock growth and perhaps even technical advance. Second, compliance with regulatory mandates for business asset use and employment decisions may interfere with efficient managerial decisions and redirect resources into inefficient configurations and uses, lowering productivity.

Note, however, that the argument made in the section above, on static costs of regulation, also applies here. It is precisely the character of the arguments for regulation to claim that the allocation and use of resources resulting from *voluntary* transactions in the market is *inefficient,* and that regulation will *improve* the efficiency of that allocation. If that is true, then regulation should have a *positive* effect on the level and growth of labor productivity, total output, and real income. A test of the direction of effect of regulation on those variables is then a test of the theory behind regulation, which that theory would fail if the relationship turns out to be either negative or zero.

Many economists have realized that the expansion of regulation since the Johnson Administration may have had damaging effects on the performance of the economy, and have looked for evidence of such effects. Amazingly, good evidence for this belief has been found using some rather crude indexes. In 1992 the economic forecasting firm of

Arthur B. Laffer and V. A. Canto found that over the period from 1946 to 1990 investment activity, as measured by a weighted Standard and Poor's 500 index divided by Gross National Product, was strongly inversely related to the number of pages in the Federal Register, where new regulations and changes in regulations are published each year. That is, the S&P index–GNP ratio fell when the number of Federal Register pages increased over time, and rose in periods when the number of Federal Register pages decreased. The next year the Heritage Foundation published a report showing a very strong inverse relationship between private sector job growth and the number of employees in Federal regulatory agencies.[10]

Several economists have specifically studied the effect of the growth of government regulation in explaining the great productivity slowdown. Edward Denison, one of the most famous theoretical and empirical analysts of economic growth, estimated that regulation reduced productivity growth by a quarter of a percentage point, or about a sixth of the total productivity decline after 1973.[11] This does not sound like much, but one must remember that economic growth compounds, and reductions in economic growth therefore result in compounding *losses* over time. Besides, Denison's estimate appears to be on the low side. Wayne Gray, studying EPA and OSHA regulations in 450 manufacturing industries, found that increasing regulation from the 1960s through 1978 explained over 30 percent of the productivity slowdown.[12] And in a study for the National Bureau of Economic Research by Gray and Ronald Shadbegian in 1993 those analysts estimated that each dollar of regulatory compliance costs reduced multifactor productivity by between three and four dollars.[13]

Another very striking study of the relationship between regulation and productivity growth was conducted recently by Richard K. Vedder in a paper for the CSAB.[14] Vedder developed a multiple regression analysis employing several theorized determinants of the productivity slowdown. For the period 1960-1994, Vedder used five-year moving averages of labor productivity growth as the dependent variable in one set of regressions, simple annual observations of productivity growth in another set, and multifactor productivity in a third set. For a measure of the degree of regulation with which to explain changes in productivity growth, Vedder simply used the annual budgeted expenditures of the federal regulatory agencies expressed as a percent of Gross Domestic

Product. The CSAB has been collecting data on budgeted regulatory expenditures for some years.

To test the effect of government fiscal factors on productivity growth, Vedder used two variables, federal tax revenue as a percent of GDP, and a measure of the federal budget deficit (or surplus) relative to GDP. To test the theory that population growth might be adversely affecting productivity growth through diminishing returns to labor, Vedder included a measure of the annual percentage population growth rate as an independent variable. To see if the OPEC cartel restrictions and Federal energy interventions had an important effect on productivity growth, Vedder employed a measure of fuel prices relative to the general price level. And last, a measure of the value of services as a fraction of GDP was included.

Vedder's regulation variable turned out to be strongly inversely related to productivity growth, as theoretically predicted. This is actually surprising, however, given his use of the simple measure of budgeted regulatory expenditures, since such expenditures are a small fraction of the total costs regulation inflicts on the economy, as shown in the data of Hopkins and others. This would seem to imply that regulatory expenditures are a relatively stable fraction of total regulatory costs.[15] Also high in explanatory power was the tax variable. The relative fuel price also had the correct sign and some explanatory power. None of the rest of the variables, the service share of GDP, the relative deficit, or population growth, added much independently or together to the predictive and explanatory power of the models.

In its best version, however, using all independent variables and employing the 5 year moving average as the dependent variable, Vedder's model explained 90 percent of the changes in business sector productivity growth over the period. He estimated that nearly half of the productivity slowdown was due to regulation alone, and the estimated loss in aggregate output by 1993 was $1.27 trillion. That is to say, had regulation remained at its early 1960s level instead of expanding as it did over the next 30 years, 1993 real GDP would have been $7.614 trillion instead of $6.343 trillion, and the public would now have about 20 percent higher real incomes, gross and per capita, than we do.

Because Vedder did not publish his raw data, I have assembled my own data and conducted an independent test of a simple version of his model. The data and its sources are listed in Table 9-3 in the chapter appendix. Like Vedder I use a five year moving average of productivity growth as the dependent variable to smooth the series and partly abstract from business cycle disturbances. My productivity measure is non-farm productivity growth, however. As independent variables I use regulatory expenditures as a percent of GDP, taxation as a percent of GDP to capture the effect of changes in government size over the period, and a measure of the relative price of energy described in the table. All three variables turn out to have the theoretically predicted signs and are highly statistically significant.

For the interested reader, the statistical results and regression equation are shown in Table 9-4. The measure of Federal regulation has by far the strongest inverse effect on productivity growth of the three variables, and also the highest statistical significance. As a whole, the model explains over 80 percent of the movements in productivity from 1960 to 1995. Graph 9.5 shows the actual path of productivity growth along with the path predicted by the model over the period. The model clearly explains the path of productivity growth well, and its overall errors are small. The cumulative impact of such evidence seems persuasive. Regulation is not the only factor reducing productivity and economic growth since its rapid expansion began in the Johnson administration, but it has clearly had a powerful negative effect on our economic well being, contrary to the claims of its advocates.

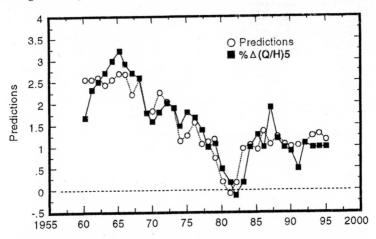

Graph 9.5: Actual and Predicted Percent Changes in Output per Man Hour, 5 Year Moving Averages, 1960-1995

Regulatory Cost Containment Efforts

Almost from the beginning of the modern expansion of the regulatory state in the late 1960s, there were some fears about its potential costs and detrimental effects on output and employment.[16] In 1971 President Nixon created the Quality of Life Review, supervised by the Office of Management and Budget, in an effort to pressure regulatory agencies to consider the effect of the costs imposed by their actions. OMB could not enforce such requirements, however, and most agencies ignored it. During the Ford administration much of the concern about regulation centered on its possible effect in aggravating inflation, which had been accelerating since the mid 1960s. President Ford created the Council on Wage and Price Stability in 1974 and drafted an executive order establishing procedures for inflation impact statements for regulatory proposals. Independent regulatory agencies are not subject to Presidential executive orders, however, and though Ford urged them to reform their regulatory processes to reduce the costs they impose on the economy, only a few, such as the Federal Trade Commission and the Nuclear Regulatory Commission, complied.

As an ex-peanut farmer, President Carter was personally aware of the impact of regulatory costs. Not only did Carter undertake the large scale transportation deregulation discussed in chapter 5, but he made significant efforts to reform the regulatory process to contain costs. In 1978 he established the Regulatory Analysis Review Group (RARG) to review major regulatory proposals. A new executive order required agencies to prepare and publicize regulatory analyses of such proposals. RARG was successful in pressuring some agencies to begin employing economists and analyzing economic impacts of regulations, and even in preventing the promulgation of some highly costly regulations. The effect was limited, however, because the final authority for rule promulgation remained with the agencies.

To his great credit President Carter even tried, though without success, to get Congress to legislatively require agencies to base regulations on cost-benefit analyses. That failure destroys any claim that the very intent of Congress in creating such agencies was to solve social problems or achieve social well being. Mandatory economic cost-benefit tests would make it impossible for members of Congress to use regulation to favor the powerful special interests in exchange for votes, bribes, and political contributions, or to institute ideological views of social justice which, in their nature, cannot pass such tests. So despite the best efforts of Presidents Ford and Carter, regulations, regulatory staffing, and regulatory costs continued expanding. In fact, the number of pages of regulations published in the Federal Register reached levels higher than ever before or since during the Ford and Carter administrations, and regulatory costs reached levels not seen again in over a decade.

President Reagan, for all his free market rhetoric, largely eschewed meaningful efforts at deregulation such as Carter had achieved. Since the main theme of his first term was tax reduction, efforts on the regulatory front simply continued and strengthened the efforts of prior Presidents to reform the regulatory process to contain costs. In his last year in office Carter had created the Office of Information and Regulatory Affairs (OIRA) in the Office of Management and Budget. In 1981 Reagan published an executive order attempting to require cost-benefit tests for major new regulations, subject to review by the OIRA. The President also established a Task Force on Regulatory Relief, chaired by Vice-President Bush, which often acted as a court of appeals dealing with issues on which OIRA and the agencies could not agree. Murray Weidenbaum claims that this reduced the promulgation of new rules. There was also a substantial reduction in the staffing and budgets of regulatory agencies in Reagan's first term. In his second term, however, the regulatory reform effort diminished.

Regulatory reform under the Bush administration had more form than substance. Indeed, his efforts seem little more than cover for a major expansion in regulation reversing the trend of the two prior administrations. President Bush established the Council on Competitiveness in 1989 to replace the Task Force on Regulatory Relief. In 1990 and 1991 Bush signed into law three extremely large and costly regulatory acts: the Clean Air Act amendments, the Civil Rights Act, and Americans with Disabilities Act. In January of 1992, perhaps realizing he had gone too far, particularly during a recession and an election year, Bush placed a three month moratorium on new regulations. This also was appearance more than substance, since many largely unpublicized exceptions were allowed. The result of all this was a renewed rise in regulatory staffing, budgets and costs, offsetting many of the gains made from 1978 through 1988.

The Clinton Administration that took office in 1992 abolished the Council on Competitiveness, but has continued the effort to give the appearance of regulatory cost containment without the substance. In a highly publicized effort, the administration eliminated 10,000 pages of environmental and pharmaceutical regulations, but new regulations were added so fast, through new laws including the Family and Medical Leave Act and the Motor Voter law, among others, as to more than offset such reductions. In 1994, however, the radical Republicans gained control of Congress and serious efforts at regulatory reform seemed imminent. Indeed, they deregulated cable television, and in 1995 a Republican bill requiring agencies to produce a detailed cost-benefit analysis prior to issuance of a new regulation failed by only one vote in the Senate.[17] In addition, Congress passed the Congressional Review Act of 1996 granting itself authority to veto agency regulation within 60 days of promulgation.

Since the public beating of the Republicans by the administration and the television networks over the 1995 federal budget deadlock, the 1996 elections which reduced Republican congressional control, and the humiliation of House Speaker Newt Gingrich over his violation of a House ethics rule, the fire has gone out of the Republican radicals. No serious regulatory (or other) reform appears on the horizon as of this writing. It is possible, however, that events could create conditions under which serious regulatory reform would once again be possible. Since this would likely take the form of a cost-benefit requirement for new regulations, it may be worthwhile to illustrate with a small example some of the requirements for an efficient regulatory policy in cost-benefit terms.

Cost-Benefit Criteria and Efficient Regulation

Table 9-1 below shows four different social problems on which regulations could be written and money spent by the federal government to obtain compliance. The first one, labeled traffic signs, could involve the federal government requiring cities to place stop signs at dangerous intersections in order to save lives, and funding the mandate with federal grants-in-aid. The numbers in that column show the additional lives estimated to be saved by additional $10 million expenditures for that purpose. The numbers decline on the simple supposition that the first $10 million increment will be spent on the most dangerous set of intersections, the second $10 million on the *next* most dangerous set of intersections, and so on, so that progressively *less* dangerous intersections are being treated in sequence. Thus there are diminishing returns, in terms of lives saved, to additional expenditures on traffic signs. The declining numbers of lives saved in each of the other regulatory categories for additional expenditures are based on similar reasoning.

Now suppose the government has appropriated $100 million total for its regulatory agencies to spend on this set of social problems. Assuming the goal is to save the maximum number of lives possible for that total expenditure, and the numbers in each column represent the best, objective scientific estimates, the answer is simple. The agencies should spend each $10 million increment in sequence where it gets the largest number of lives saved, such that for the last $10 million increment spent in each category saves the same number of lives (14). That is, where the *marginal benefit* from the last increment of expenditure on each use is the same. Specifically, $40 million will be spent on traffic signs, $30 million making and enforcing locational smoking prohibitions, $20 million on cleaning up stream pollution, and $10 million on toxic waste dump cleanup. This allocation of funds will save 160 lives, which is the largest possible total for that expenditure. Another way of stating this solution is that the funds must be allocated such that the *marginal cost* per life saved ($714,286 ≈ $10,000,000/14) is the same in each regulatory category.

$10 Million Increments	Traffic Signs	Locational Anti-smoking Prohibitions	Stream Pollution	Toxic Waste Cleanup
1	20	18	16	14
2	18	16	14	12
3	16	14	12	10
4	14	12	10	8
5	12	10	8	6
6	10	8	6	4

Table 9.1: Marginal benefits of Incremental Regulatory Expenditures

To see why this is the correct allocation, suppose the $10 million spent on toxic waste cleanup was added instead to traffic sign regulation. The additional funding there would have a marginal benefit of 12 lives saved, but at the marginal *opportunity* cost of 14 *lost* that *could have been saved* by the cleanup of the worst toxic waste sites. The total number of lives saved would be smaller by two (158), and neither the marginal benefits nor the marginal costs would be equated across regulatory categories. For traffic safety the marginal cost per life saved in dollar terms would be $833,333. Looking at the solution this way correctly emphasizes the trade offs always involved in employing resources one way rather than another.

One obvious question remains unanswered by the exercise thus far: what is the appropriate total regulatory budget for this set of social problems? The $100 million was an arbitrary number. The solution to this issue is also simple, however, at least in principle. Assume not only that the estimates of incremental lives saved in each category are accurate, but that we know the value of a human life. In fact, contrary to the emotional fulminations of the ignorant, reasonable estimates of the value of a life can be made. People place values on their time and lives whenever they decide to work at a certain pay rate, buy insurance, and so on. Present values of lives can be calculated, and most economists estimate them somewhere between $1 million and $4 million. Using the $1 million number for simplicity, the lives saved magnitudes in the table transform neatly into equivalent million dollar marginal benefit magnitudes. The correct total regulatory budget for this set of problems is then obviously $180 million, $60 million of which would be spent on traffic signs, $50 million on reducing smoking hazards, $40 million on stream cleanup and $30 million on toxic wastes. At that budget magnitude and allocation, the marginal benefits in each category would just equal the marginal cost per life saved ($1 million each).

Of course in the real world, for reasons some of which have been discussed in earlier chapters, making the sort of marginal benefit and cost estimates given or implied in the table is often very difficult, and the best estimates available may be highly inaccurate. Indeed, some things may be nearly impossible to measure in terms commensurable with others. What is the value of a snail darter, or a spotted owl? How does one compute the value of benefits from saving such animals, when they are public property, are not subject to market transactions, and hence have no established market values?

On the other hand, this problem might be solved precisely by privatizing the wilderness land and animals themselves, bringing such things *into* the market, where market-based calculations of marginal benefit and cost, profit and loss, can achieve an efficient resource allocation. In and of itself this would quite probably prevent the depletion of such renewable resources as animals and trees, making regulation unnecessary. In many regions of the country, private parks and wild areas, such as the 2.8 million acre North Main Woods, Inc., the Deseret Land & Livestock company in Northern Utah, and the Fossil Rim Wildlife Center in Texas that charge fees for visitors and hunters attracted by the natural amenities, have been very successful in covering their costs while preserving nature.[18]

Another problem in efficient regulation concerns the division of agency responsibility. In the table above, one agency may have responsibility for the traffic safety problem (perhaps the NHTSA), another for smoking regulation (The FDA is currently seeking such authority), and yet another for cleanup of streams and toxic wastes (the EPA). Each agency, with its own budget, under a legal requirement that a regulatory expenditure not have marginal benefits lower than its marginal costs, might make an efficient allocation of its funds. But none will consider the marginal costs and benefit schedules faced by the *other* agencies, so the allocation across all the regulatory uses will almost certainly be inefficient. Only if some sort of final review agency existed, to which all agencies submitted their cost-benefit estimates, and which had authority to allocate funds *across the agencies themselves,* i.e. to determine their budgets, could a remotely correct total regulatory budget and/or allocation of funds across forms of regulation be achieved. Such an agency would have to have close ties to the Office of Management and Budget, which partly explains why Presidents Carter and Reagan structured their regulatory review agencies as they did.

A closely related issue concerns who would perform the cost-benefit estimates. The agencies themselves would have enormous incentives to inflate estimates of the marginal (and total) benefits of regulations under their legal authority, in order to maximize their power, staffs, and budgets. The review agency just discussed would have to have power to check and reject inflated estimates, substituting its own. The history of cost containment efforts shows that this authority would have to be granted by statute. The regulatory agencies and their Congressional, intellectual, and business supporters have in the past strongly resisted any such statute, and will continue to do so.

There can only be one reason for this resistance: honest scientific estimates would discover with great frequency that the marginal costs exceed the marginal benefits for the first increment of expenditure on a huge number of regulations. This would be particularly true if the cost estimates by law included not just regulatory expenditures, as in the numerical example, but the compliance, efficiency and rent-seeking costs generated by each regulation. Very little regulation would be justified, and the power and budgets of the agencies would be severely reduced. Current regulatory absurdities, such as the EPA's hazardous waste disposal ban, which costs an estimated $4.2 billion for each premature death prevented, or the atrazine/alachlor drinking water standard, which costs over $92 billion to avert a single death, would not pass muster.[21] Clearly, the primary goal of the regulators and their political and intellectual supporters has *never* been to achieve the public good, but to attain and employ power over others for their own benefit.

None of this is to say that a strong cost-benefit requirement backed by a powerful review agency is the only necessary regulatory reform. That would involve acceptance of most of the inherently dictatorial and constitutionally abusive characteristics of the regulatory system, even if it severely reduced the power of the regulators, the quantity of regulation, and its social costs. Other reforms, that might essentially eliminate regulation as we know it, replacing it with other legal mechanisms, may be even more crucial, though perhaps less politically feasible at the current time.

Notes

1   Strictly speaking, the problem is one of maximizing the net benefits (benefits in excess of costs), and the condition required is that the marginal benefits (added benefits from additional regulation) equal the marginal costs (the addition to total costs attributable to the additional regulation), where marginal benefits are falling and marginal costs are rising with additional regulation. Much of this is made clear through a numerical example in the last section of this chapter.

2   See Melinda Warren and Barry Jones, *Reinventing the Regulatory System: No Downsizing in Administration Plan* (Center for the Study of American Business Occasional Paper 155, July 1995).

3   Murray Weidenbaum and Robert DeFina, *The Cost of Federal Regulation of Economic Activity* (American Enterprise Institute, May 1978).

4   This data from Litan and Nordhaus is cited in Thomas D. Hopkins, *Cost of Regulation* (Rochester Institute of Technology Working Paper, December 1991). Hahn and Hird (see note 5) cite this paper as R. Litan and W. Nordhaus, *Reforming Federal Regulation* 23 (1983). I have not been able to acquire the paper itself.

5 Robert W. Hahn and John A. Hird, "The Costs and Benefits of Regulation: Review and Synthesis," *Yale Journal on Regulation* 8 (Winter, 1991): 233-278.

6 Gross Domestic Product (GDP) is the total value of all final goods and services (that is, intermediate product transactions between firms are excluded) produced within national borders in the given year. Gross National Product (GNP) is the total value of all final goods and services produced by U.S. firms wherever they are located in the world. For the U.S., the differences between GDP and GNP are relatively small. The U.S. switched in the early 1990s from GNP to GDP as the basic measure of the aggregate economy because most other nations use GDP.

7 See Thomas D. Hopkins, *Regulatory Costs in Profile* (Center for the Study of American Business Policy Study Number 12, August 1996), and the earlier Hopkins paper in note 4.

8 See, for example, John A. Tatom, "Potential Output and the Recent Productivity Decline, Federal Reserve Bank of St. Louis *Review* (January 1982), and Nancy J. Burnett, "Oil Shocks, Productivity, and the Economic Slowdown," *Journal of Energy and Development* (Spring 1991).

9 Two significant facts are, first, that the initial event raising relative government taxation and expenditures in the 1960s was the Vietnam War, and second, that military expenditures as a fraction of both total federal expenditure and GDP began *falling* rapidly and transfer payments as a fraction of both total federal expenditure and GDP began *rising* rapidly several years *before* the end of the war. In essence, the war was used to get the public to accept expanded taxation and spending, then the revenue was shifted into transfer payments.

10 William G. Laffer III, *How Regulation is Destroying Jobs* (Heritage Foundation Background Paper No. 926, February 16, 1993).

11 Edward F. Denison, "The Interruption of Productivity Growth in the United States," *Economic Journal* (March 1983).

12 Wayne Gray, "The Cost of Regulation: OSHA, EPA, and the Productivity Slowdown," *American Economic Review* (December 1987), and "The Impact of OSHA and EPA Regulation on Productivity Growth," *Journal of Regulation and Social Costs* (June 1991).

13 Wayne B. Gray and Ronald J. Shadbegian, *Environmental Regulation and Manufacturing Productivity at the Plant Level* (National Bureau of Economic Research Working Paper number 4321, April 1993).

14 Richard K. Vedder, *Federal Regulation's Impact on the Productivity Slowdown: A Trillion Dollar Drag* (CSAB Policy Study Number 131, July 1996).

15 I used this presumption in calculating the values of total regulatory costs for 1960-1976 in Table 9-3, though I also took account of the variation in the ratio of total regulatory costs to budgeted regulatory expenditures that emerges from the Hopkins data.

16 Much of the discussion in this section relies on Murray Weidenbaum, "Regulatory Process Reform from Ford to Clinton," *Regulation* (Winter 1997): 20-26, and Cesar Conda, *The Regulatory Tide: High and Rising* (Institute for Policy Innovation Issue Brief, September 1994).

17 True to the conservative–rather than libertarian–philosophy of the Republican radicals, however, they simultaneously *added* to regulation of television manufacture (by *mandating* inclusion of 'V' chips), and to regulation of the internet.

18 Lawrence W. Reed, "Privatization: Best Hope for a Vanishing Wilderness," in *Man and Nature* (Foundation for Economic Education, 1993): 153-163.

Appendix

Table 9-2: Measures of Private Sector Costs of Regulation, 1960-1995

Year	Annual Total Regulatory Costs, in Billions of Constant 1995 Dollars	Annual Total Regulatory Costs as a Percent of GDP	Annual Per Capita Total Regulatory Costs in Constant 1995 Dollars
1960	$83	3.4	$458.56
61	96	3.9	521.74
62	122	4.6	652.41
63	142	5.2	751.32
64	158	5.4	822.92
1965	194	6.3	1000.00
66	202	5.8	1025.38
67	211	6.2	1060.30
68	225	6.4	1119.40
69	249	6.8	1226.60
1970	260	7.1	1268.29
71	304	8.1	1461.54
72	382	9.6	1827.75
73	486	11.6	2292.45
74	500	12.0	2336.45

(continued from next page)

(continued from opposite page)

Year	Annual Total Regulatory Costs, in Billions of Constant 1995 Dollars	Annual Total Regulatory Costs as a Percent of GDP	Annual Per Capita Total Regulatory Costs in Constant 1995 Dollars
1975	592	14.2	2753.49
76	627	14.3	2876.15
77	654	14.2	2972.73
78	640	13.2	2869.96
79	623	12.5	2768.89
1980	606	12.2	2657.89
81	590	11.6	2565.22
82	570	11.5	2456.90
83	576	11.1	2462.54
84	567	10.3	2402.54
1985	561	9.8	2357.14
86	555	9.4	2302.90
87	557	9.2	2292.18
88	549	8.7	2240.82
89	561	8.6	2271.26
1990	594	9.0	2376.00
91	621	9.5	2454.55
92	642	9.6	2517.65
93	642	9.3	2488.37
94	649	9.1	2489.83
1995	668	9.9	2539.60

Data Sources: Total regulatory costs for 1977-94, Thomas Hopkins; total costs for 1960-1976, author's estimates from Hopkins data and federal regulatory expenditures. Regulatory costs as a percent of GDP and per capita are from author's calculations, using GDP and population data from the *Business Conditions Digest* (April 1997), and the *Economic Report of the President, 1997*.

Table 9-3: Regression Data for Productivity Growth, 1960-1995

Year	Federal Regulatory Expenditures as a Percent of GDP	Relative Price of Fuels	Federal Tax Revenue as a Percent of GDP	5 Year moving Average Percent Change in Output per Hour
1960	.09	.60	18.0	1.7
61	.10	.59	17.8	2.3
62	.10	.59	17.4	2.5
63	.11	.57	17.7	2.7
64	.11	.55	17.4	3.8
1965	.11	.55	16.6	3.2
66	.11	.55	17.0	2.9
67	.12	.54	18.3	2.7
68	.12	.52	17.2	2.6
69	.12	.50	19.5	1.8
1970	.14	.50	19.1	1.6
71	.16	.52	17.1	1.8
72	.18	.51	17.2	2.8
73	.20	.55	17.1	1.9
74	.20	.78	18.0	1.5
1975	.22	.84	17.6	1.8
76	.21	.86	16.9	1.7
77	.22	.92	18.0	1.4
78	.22	.91	17.9	1.0
79	.22	1.07	18.6	1.1
1980	.23	1.37	19.1	.5
81	.22	1.52	19.8	.2
82	.21	1.42	19.6	-.1
83	.20	1.31	17.6	.2
84	.20	1.25	17.6	1.0
1985	.20	1.16	18.2	1.3
86	.19	.87	18.0	1.0
87	.20	.84	18.8	1.9
88	.20	.77	18.5	1.2
89	.20	.81	18.9	1.0
1990	.21	.88	18.6	.9
91	.22	.83	18.4	.5
92	.23	.80	18.1	1.1
93	.23	.78	17.6	1.0
94	.2	.74	18.1	1.0
1995	.21	.72	18.6	1.0

Data Sources: Reguatory expenditures are from the CSAB. All other data is taken from or calculated from data in the Economic Report of the President, 1994 and 1997. The relative price of fuels, for example, is calculated as the ratio of the index of the price of fuels and power in table B-66 to the GDP deflator value for the same year in table B-3.

Table 9-4: Regression Results for Productivity Growth Determinants

Variable or Statistic	Coefficient or Constant Value	Standard Error	t-Value	p-Value	Partial F
Intercept	9.308				
Reg Exp%GDP	-8.296	1.791	4.633	.0001	21.468
Taxes%GDP	-.305	.092	3.319	.0023	11.014
Fuel/P	-.991	.317	3.128	.0037	9.781
R		.901			
R^2		.812			
Adjusted R^2	.795				
DF	32.0				
F-test	42.107				

Chapter 10

The Ideological Transformation

The Civil War–or the war of Southern secession–seems to be the great divide, both institutionally and ideologically, in U.S. History. Before the war–and for some time after–classical liberal individualism dominated as a political philosophy. Politics was *primarily* focused on the provision of genuine public goods, most particularly protection of the security and property of persons. Distributive politics, both in its direct and regulatory forms, was minimized by any objective comparison with modern times. Sometime around the turn of the century, with the rise of the progressive ideology that eventually became modern welfare liberalism, the dominant political and social philosophy had changed, and with it, interventionist interest group politics increasingly became the primary form of political expression.

The exact timing of decline of the classical liberal philosophy and political practice is less important than understanding why and how it came to be. What is the nature of ideology, and what is the relationship between ideologies and interest groups? Why was the ideological struggle of the period essentially lost by the classical liberal defenders of limited government? Answers to such questions are important in a period in which the social and economic failures of interventionist policies in America and other modern states are so massively manifest as they are today.

Ideology, Morality, and Interests

A political ideology is often defined quite simply as a widely held perspective on who should rule, what policies should be followed, and what political institutions are appropriate. By such definition, an ideology seems to be distinguished from a political philosophy primarily by being less formal and rigorous. This distinction may be important, however. Political and social issues are extremely complex and difficult. Working out a coherent and complete understanding and perspective on such matters requires a large amount of time and mental effort that few people can *rationally* afford. Many people in search of such a political perspective find it easier to adopt one that is relatively simplified and prepackaged, that is, an ideology, as a simple method of economizing on the mental efforts involved.[1]

The suppliers of such simplified and prepackaged political belief sets are often organized special interest groups or unorganized groups of people with recognized common occupations or interests who wish to gain at the expense of others. One vital member of this class consists of those who wish to exercise coercive power over others, either because that is what they *enjoy* or from egotistical belief that others are too stupid or immoral to be left free, and who work to remove legal and institutional restrictions on the exercise of such power. Other suppliers may wish to defend freedom or otherwise obtain the abstract public good. In any case, ideologies are propagated in order to obtain adherents and converts, or neutralize opposition, as part of a competitive effort to influence or control political institutions and policies.

Just as people may employ varying degrees of research and mental efforts in obtaining political perspectives (and hence be ideological to varying degrees), they may vary in the honesty they employ. As beings with both conceptual faculties and moral senses, people may reason and act on reason and plain morality, or they may act as they wish, contrary to reason and ethics, and rationalize doing so. In their selection from among available ideologies, or their efforts to create and propagate such ideologies, many people–though not all–choose that which best rationalizes or tends to further their personal, short term self-interest. *In nearly all cases this involves persuading either others or oneself or both, that a political policy or action that will benefit one personally at the expense of others is actually in the interests of the community at large.*

This observation (hardly original but too seldom stated) appears contrary to some current beliefs in the economics profession. Many economists now speak as if acting on ideology or out of self-interest are mutually exclusive forms of action. Thus an observation that certain politicians on a particular issue voted in a way their constituents might *not* have preferred is interpreted as acting on ideology, rather than self-interest. That is, acting on ideology and principle are equated, and contrasted with acting from self-interest. Now certainly politicians sometimes act on principle, and an ideology may indeed motivate such action. But ideology is an even more inherent element in matters of distributional politics, where the gains of some persons generated by political action cause matching (and usually *larger*) losses by others. Those acting to attain such gains or grant such transfers must both assuage their consciences and anesthetize political opposition.

Thus, corporate leaders in an industry who wish to have a government subsidy or a tariff on products of their foreign competition in order to put more money in their own pockets must generate and propagate arguments claiming that the *general* public well being will be enhanced by such policies. These ideological arguments must deny, or (more effectively) exclude from mention or public *awareness* any reduction in the real incomes of consumers who must pay higher prices for the products as a result of the tariff, or of taxpayers from whom the subsidy is ultimately extracted. And thus union leaders and members who wish to force their own earnings up through coercive cartel action, in the process excluding competing workers from improved job opportunities and hurting consumers, must rationalize that this is in the ultimate good of 'society'. Since capital owners are also to be hurt, it must be rationalized that this is only correction of prior exploitation by capital. Such claims must be widely propagated to obtain public support and suppress opposition.

Examples are as infinite as the number of ways political action can be used to benefit particular parties at the expense of others. Such efforts must be organized, and here is another subtle misconception. Modern public choice theorists have cogently explained the frequency with which organized special interests dominate the policy process in democratic nations at the expense of the general public in terms of differential costs and benefits of political action. The gains from government regulatory grants of monopoly privilege or targeted income transfers are concentrated. The potential recipients are few, and each may make large gains, hence their costs of organizing politically are relatively low and the potential benefits high. The members of the general public who are to be harmed by such policies face the opposite situation. The costs are diffused among consumers and taxpayers so that the losses to each are small, and the costs of informing themselves and organizing politically for their own protection are high.[2]

An element of this argument is that both groups face a *free rider* problem. That is, any private resources employed by persons to either obtain or oppose a special government privilege or targeted income transfer will benefit other members of the same class of persons who have not contributed any of their own time or resources to the effort. Hence many people feel an incentive to avoid contributing, and simply free ride on the contributions of others. This is a form of external benefit argument, and its logic here is simply that due to free riding there should be *fewer* resources devoted to political organization than would be socially optimal. This is very hard to credit in the late 1990s with the Democratic party fund raising scandals and the repeated observation on all sides that there is too *much* money in politics! Also note that the very symmetry of the free rider problem means that it cannot be an important explanation of special interest political dominance. It applies equally to the special interests and those members of the general public who might wish to oppose special interest depredations.

Public choice theorists appear unaware that there is a far more important barrier or cost to political organization than free riding which, if it can be overcome or reduced, clearly shifts power toward the special interests. This is the *personal moral inhibition against using government coercion to steal from others for one's personal benefit, or to force them to act or not act in ways one feels they should or should not, contrary to their freely chosen and mutually voluntary actions and interactions.* It is precisely in reducing this inhibition, by rationalizing that prior income distributions were unjust, or resource distributions inefficient, or that one is being oppressed by others (usually businessmen), or that some good will be achieved by coercively altering the behavior of others, that propagation of statist and collectivist ideology is crucial.

Not only does adoption and propagation of such an ideology reduce the pangs of conscience of those seeking such legislation, but it intimidates and suppresses opposition from those they wish to exploit, to the extent that such persons cannot refute the claims of social justice or general social benefit propagated in the ideology.

Indeed, as more and more individuals accept the justice of coerced governmental privileges and income transfers and join their own groups, accepting and propagating their own claims for special privileges and income transfers, or for the right to force their own moral views on others, the whole distinction between the special interests and the general public diminishes. Distributional politics and interventionist ideology become nearly universal. Social, moral and economic decay, resentment, hostility and psychological angst spread, as nearly everyone tries to use government to steal from or control everyone else, while decrying the political thefts and oppressions of others. Freedom, tolerance, civility and *civilization* diminish.

19th Century Crises and Ideological Struggle

In a very important work, Robert Higgs argues that government growth in America has been related to episodic crises.[3] Specifically, the power, size and scope of government has grown in periods of crisis, when emergency powers or extensions of authority are demanded, or new and broadened policies are presumed necessary to deal with the emergency conditions. Traditional policies and institutions are easily argued to be inadequate in such situations. A reaction reducing such powers usually sets in once the emergency is over, but the size, power and scope of government never declines back to is pre-emergency level, so that government power and authority ratchets up over time. Higgs specifically focuses on the two World Wars in this century and the Great Depression of the 1930s as critical crisis episodes in the Growth of American Government into the modern leviathan it now constitutes.

One must add to this list the Civil War itself, which was almost certainly the original and quintessential episode of this type, and was the first in the series. One of the most terrible features of the war was that neither side was clearly the side of virtue. True, the Northern states had abandoned slavery, and continued enslavement of blacks in the South was an evil thing. It is a northern conceit, however, and a distortion of history, to assert that slavery was the only important issue. Indeed, freeing the slaves was *not* a Northern goal intended by President Lincoln for more than a year into the war.

To the South, the sovereignty of states and the unfair distributional impact of Northern tariffs were crucial sources of disaffection just as important as Northern anti-slavery sentiment and legislation.

Southerners fought for the right to separate themselves from the union and form their own government, *a basic principle of U.S. political philosophy asserted in the Declaration of Independence*. The North, which interpreted any attempted secession as rebellion, in contrast, fought a war of invasion, conquest and occupation of the South. In the pursuit of the war, General Sheridan, under the direct orders of General (and later President) Grant, deliberately and systematically destroyed private property and terrorized civilians in his march through the Shenandoah Valley.

The social, economic and political depredations imposed by the U.S. government on its own people were nearly as bad. Lincoln instituted the first military draft in U.S. history (though many Southern states had drafted civilian whites into slave patrols in an effort to prop up slavery before the war[4]), a gross violation of basic individual rights lacking any constitutional authority. Thousands of suspected Southern sympathizers were imprisoned at Lincoln's order for long periods of time without rights of *Habeas Corpus*. The first income tax was instituted, the federal budget expanded enormously, and wartime mobilization regimented much of society. Few firms or industries were nationalized outright, but corruption spread as firms competed for exclusive government contracts.

All of these events, actions and policies, as applications of coercion against American citizens, required ideological justification on the part of leaders, and by the general citizenry who tolerated it. People must live with their consciences, and make accommodations with and modifications to their prior beliefs to accept the legitimacy of such actions. As remarked in Chapter 1, the Civil War seemed to shock the political ideology of a significant fraction of the public in an interventionist direction. In succeeding decades people in many sectors of society began to organize and agitate for government relief, aid, regulation, privilege or subsidy, always under a public interest cover. Mercantilist rent-seeking returned with a democratic ideological rationale. The principles of the limited 'negative state' began to be called into question, and an overt ideological struggle between defenders of the classical liberal view and advocates of interventionist government began, the outcome of which hung in the balance for the remainder of the Century.

It is difficult to overstress the radical character of the emerging interventionist ideology. The traditional view asserted that the permissible uses of government force focused on the preservation of individual rights, civil order, and personal security from coercion and theft by others. The new view said government force must be applied in redress of injustices and inefficiencies claimed (but never proven or *capable* of being proven) to inhere in or result from the system of private asset ownership and voluntary market transactions. Its advocates implied (and sometimes openly argued) that government officials exercising such expanded redistributive and regulatory power could be trusted to do so accurately and altruistically, never acting from motives of self-interest, much less a simple *desire* to exercise power. As such this view ignored much of the experience of human history, and constituted an attack both on constitutional limits on government and on capitalism itself.

The effect of rapid industrialization and growth in the size of many firms in stimulating this sentiment in certain circles was discussed in Chapter 4 and need not be repeated here. One aspect of railroad history of the period not discussed there, however, that seems important to the present discussion, was the federal subsidization of the building of the transcontinentals through land grants and low interest government loans for each section of track laid. The program began in 1862, after Southern Democrats had left Congress, with passage of the Pacific Railroad Act. The legally designated favored recipients were the Union Pacific, which was to build west from Omaha, and the Central Pacific, which would move east from Sacramento until they met. Eventually, 44 million acres of land and $61 million in loans were given to four favored transcontinentals.[5]

The whole program was corrupt and plagued by scandal throughout. The roads were not built for their economic value and future profitability, but for the subsidies. Since the land grants and loans were tied to the amount of track laid, it was laid hastily by both railroads, with poor route planning and grading. So much built in haste had to be rebuilt that it was five years after the driving of the Golden Spike at Promentory Point, Utah in 1869 before the Union Pacific was actually complete. Much of the track was laid through unsettled territory occupied by hostile Indians, resulting in frictions, raids, and many deaths on both sides. More deaths resulted when both lines entered Utah and the primarily Irish workers of the UP violently attacked the mostly Chinese workers of the CP, causing a series of retaliations. At the end, despite the massive subsidies, the UP defaulted on its loans. The public was infuriated by the corruption. Stung, the Federal government stopped making land grants after 1871.

Oddly, historians who generally allege and disparage massive political depredations by railroads and other corporations of the day usually praise the federal transcontinental subsidization. This simply reveals the interventionist ideology of those historians, however. The lack of necessity of such subsidies is clear from the building of the Great Northern Route, by James J. Hill, from St. Paul to Seattle in the 1890s without *any* land grants or federal aid. The only thing Hill needed was *permission*, in the form of a right of way through four Indian reservations. He built slowly and carefully, personally subsidizing settlement along the route to build business. Consequently, Hill's route was profitable even without a subsidy. Almost certainly such a route would have been built much earlier, if entrepreneurs like Hill had not had to compete with corrupt, subsidized firms like the Union Pacific and Central Pacific.

Certainly, as nearly all historians of the period have noted, this corruption and similar examples of wealthy businessmen engaging in political rent-seeking inflamed anti-business sentiment among the public. Who would not be incensed by the Credit Mobilier, created and run by UP officials to sell iron and other supplies to the UP at exorbitant prices, distributing millions of dollars of stock to Congressmen and even the Vice-President of the U.S. in exchange for federal subsidies? But the precise nature of the political corruption needs to be understood. Every act of political rent-seeking involves *two* sets of parties, including one or more private citizens and one or more politicians. It is not clear *a priori* which initiates the transaction.

It is too easily asserted, as above, that the sequence of ideological change is: businessmen corrupt the political process, public finds out, and interventionist, anti-business sentiment is stimulated. Legions of historians, including even Kolko, have purveyed this half-truth. In the present case, elements in the federal government had been discussing subsidizing the building of a transcontinental railroad since the 1840s, in essence dangling a line baited with potential rewards for the highest bidders. Indeed, Congress spent $150,000 surveying possible routes in the 1850s.[6] The wonder is that it took the likes of Jay Gould, Leland Stanford and Henry Villard as long as it did to take the offer of the federal politicians. Much of the point of the constitution was for government to provide equal protection, *not* special privilege under the law. No businessman (or other citizen) will bribe a politician who lacks either legal authority or willingness to grant a special favor. *The initial corruption, both moral and constitutional, and the initial ideological change in an interventionist direction, had already taken place the moment the mental decision to offer federal subsidies to builders of transcontinentals was made by government authorities.*

Likewise, that the interpretation conveyed to the public by journalists and intellectuals was that the businessmen were the primary parties responsible for the political corruption, and that the logical solution was more government controls on *business,* rather than stronger constitutional limits on the authority of *politicians,* is itself simply an indication that the ideology of the literati had *already* changed in an interventionist direction. It is just as accurate to say that a corruption of the political process was corrupting business than that big business was corrupting the political process, but very few of the journalists and intellectuals of the day, or historians since, have grasped this truth.[7] Once again it seems likely that the moral and ideological corruption began in elite circles, political and intellectual, and was spread to the public by various methods and processes.

Another case is illustrative here. Midwestern farmers were highly incensed by the depredations attributed to railroads and other business firms by left-leaning journalists, since farmer's own profits depended directly on railroad rates, bank interest rates, grain elevator prices, and so on. The resulting radical, agrarian ferment and political agitation had its initial successes in the midwestern state Granger laws of the early 1870s regulating the rates charged by railroads and grain elevators, fixing them at low levels. But the 1.5 million member Grange movement (Patrons of Husbandry) that lobbied for these laws, was deliberately organized by officials in the U.S. Department of Agriculture and other agencies.[8]

Such efforts were not entirely successful, particularly at first. The majority of the public, including most farmers, remained firm in their libertarian perspective. They were suspicious of radical calls for expanding government. They believed in private property and saw no great unfairness in the outcomes of voluntary exchange in the market. Indeed, it was very clear to most that the living standards of ordinary persons–including those complaining the most–were rising at a pace seldom seen in human history, precisely as a result of the growth of railroads and other technical and industrial developments in the free market. By the early 1880s, as a result of business lobbying and the recognition by the general public that the Grange laws constituted gross violations of rights of property and voluntary contract, most of the laws were repealed or amended into insignificance (*despite* the sanction of *Munn vs. Illinois*).

A similar story concerns the provision of charitable relief in the period.[9] From the beginning of the Republic, its largely Christian population had created voluntary organizations to aid the unemployed, destitute, and needy. As the population and economy grew and began to urbanize, increasing the need, such organizations proliferated. As private organizations with mostly religious orientations and limited funds, they were very careful to distinguish, in their aid, between the deserving poor or unfortunate on the one hand, and those who did not wish to work on the other. The provision of aid was often tied to work, and the agencies often simply acted as intermediaries connecting those providing the donations with those needing help, so that the former could work directly with the latter. Aid was normally provided in kind–food, shelter and so on–and seldom as cash, which could easily be spent on alcohol or drugs. Aid was also usually provided in the context and requirement of efforts on the part of the needy to alter the destructive and immoral behaviors and attitudes that were so often responsible for their condition.

After the Civil War, as the nation secularized and socialist perspectives spread among the literati, criticism of the methods of private charities appeared. The private charities recognized from harsh experience that unconditional aid led to dependence and *increasing*, not decreasing, poverty. The secular radicals such as journalist Horace Greeley rejected this belief, and agitation began for unconditional governmental cash aid, known then as outdoor relief. By the late 1860s many larger cities began providing such relief. It soon became a disaster, generating all of the increased poverty, dependency, family breakdown and other social pathologies that have resulted from the War on Poverty a century later, in our own time. Even Greeley admitted it was a failure.[10]

The private charities and their supporters organized and counterattacked both intellectually and politically, and most of the public agreed with them. By the early 1880s outdoor relief had been voted out of existence in Brooklyn, Baltimore, Kansas City, New York, Philadelphia, San Francisco, St. Louis and Washington D.C. Other cities had severely modified and scaled back their programs. The private charities expanded their efforts and took up the slack. Observers of the day concluded that government relief was not necessary or helpful.[11] To this day no systematic evidence has ever shown that the private charitable efforts of the day were inadequate. America's first experiment with the welfare state was dead, and the classical liberal belief in limited government and voluntary exchange, including voluntary *charity,* had triumphed.

One of the most contentious issues separating the radicals and the older libertarians concerned the deflation of the day and the monetary system. The U.S. had long had a bimetallic monetary standard based on conversion of the dollar into either gold or silver at defined rates. To help finance the Civil War Lincoln had suspended redemption and issued large amounts of inconvertible greenback dollars, generating rapid increases in the price level.[12] Restoration of convertibility to prevent peacetime monetary manipulation by government was an article of faith with classical liberals, and most federal officials felt compelled, politically or by moral obligation to do so, at the prewar parity. This required removal of the greenbacks from circulation, or at least little issuance of new currency while the economy and the gold stock grew, with resulting deflation. Milton Friedman and Anna Schwartz estimate that prices fell at a 3.5 percent annual rate from 1867 to 1879.[13]

In 1865 Congress passed the National Bank Act creating a system of federally chartered banks authorized to issue U.S. bank notes. Protection from competition was insured by taxing the bank notes issued by state chartered banks out of existence. In preparation for restoration of convertibility, the government decided to eliminate the problems of a bimetallic system and create a gold standard. Accordingly, the Grant Administration demonetized silver, eliminating free coinage of the metal in 1873, an event which became known in radical circles as "the crime of '73". With the loss of federal demand, the relative price of silver fell. Agrarian radicals, who felt themselves injured by deflation as crop prices fell along with other prices, joined silver mining interests to agitate for the restoration of silver coinage at a high price. Other agrarian radicals formed the Greenback Party to press for renewed issuance of greenbacks and inflation. Frightened, Congress caved in in 1878 and passed the Bland-Allison act authorizing purchase and coinage of up to $4 million worth of silver per month.

In 1879 convertibility of the dollar into gold was restored, and more than a decade of rapid economic expansion ensued. Most other nations also adopted the gold standard, and international trade expanded rapidly. All this vindicated the advocates of sound money. Unfortunately, the Bland-Allison act cracked the foundations of the american monetary system. The additional spending caused by silver coinage generated chronic deficits in the Balance of Payments with foreign nations. As Americans imported more foreign goods, financial assets and capital than they sold abroad, foreigners accumulated dollars which they tendered for gold. The U.S. gold stock declined as the purchase and monetization of silver by the government in essence caused the export of gold. The price level did not rise–indeed it continued falling at an average 1 percent annual rate until 1897–nor were crop prices, in particular, helped.[14]

In desperation the agrarian agitators demanded even more silver purchases, and in 1890 Congress passed the Sherman Silver Purchase Act, in which the silver was paid for with silver certificate currency. This naturally caused an even greater gold outflow. Democrat Grover Cleveland, a true liberal of the old school, was elected President in 1893, just as these unfortunate federal monetary manipulations were about to reach their tragic conclusion. Cleveland got Congress to repeal the Sherman Act, but it was too late. The national gold stock was almost too low to maintain convertibility, certainly if any rush to tender currency ensued, and the public was aware of this. The credit expansion associated with the silver purchases resulted in a great many bad loans, and the banking system was shaky. Banks began to go under, and the populace rushed to redeem their currency. The money stock and credit availability declined and business collapsed in 1893, just after Cleveland took office. Prices fell, raising *real* wage rates and the unit labor costs for firms, to unemployable levels. Layoffs began, and unemployment reached as high as 18 percent of the labor force in 1894.

Through a series of federal bond sales arranged with Wall Street, Cleveland was able to purchase enough gold to save the gold standard and stop the monetary collapse. The economy began to recover in 1895, but relapsed in 1896. Bands of unemployed men marched on Washington demanding federal relief. Cleveland knew that such federal relief was unconstitutional, and, unlike Franklin Roosevelt 40 years later, he also knew that the increased taxes or borrowing required to finance such relief would have simply made things worse.[15] Most of the public and politicians agreed, but populist pressures increased. Labor organizing accelerated and the unions demanded legislative relief from the antitrust acts, along with other legislation exempting them from legal standards applying to other persons. Union radicals acted violently in pursuit of their goals. Violent strikes had already occurred at Andrew Carnegie's Homestead, Pennsylvania steel plant and at the silver mines in Coeur d'Alene, Idaho, in 1892. As employers began reducing wage rates in an effort to compensate for lower product prices during the depression, a huge wave of strikes began around the nation. The worst, a massive railroad strike beginning in Pullman, Illinois, led by the Socialist Eugene Debs, turned violent and destructive. It was only ended when Cleveland sent federal troops to Chicago. Again, the public supported Cleveland.

As Higgs argues, the staunchness and success of the Cleveland administration in resisting populist pressures was probably the last real victory of classical liberalism. Cleveland recognized that the special interest demands for redistribution and interventionist legislation in the 1890s were feeding off the harmful effects of prior concessions to such demands. Other politicians saw which way the ideological and political winds were blowing, however. The populist party, which in 1892 had a virtually socialist platform (calling, for example, for nationalization of the railroads, telephones and telegraphs) and had lost the election badly, merged with sympathetic factions of the Democratic party. As a result, Cleveland's own party repudiated him, nominating William Jennings Bryan on a promise to end the gold standard and support pro-union legislation.

Classical liberalism was not yet dead. A pale imitation of it would see rebirth in the administrations of Harding and Coolidge in the 1920s, and most ordinary citizens would adhere to limited government views into the 1930s. But by 1900 *both* the Republican and Democratic party leaderships were dominated by progressives, and among opinion makers and the political class the prevailing ideology had clearly changed. Transportation regulation had already begun. The next two decades saw the Meat Inspection Act, the beginnings of state regulation of electric utilities, the formation of the AMA medical cartel by the states, the Clayton Act and other federal laws granting unions special privileges, the Federal Reserve Act cartelizing control of the money supply, and so on. Mercantilist, special interest rent-seeking proliferated under the *public interest* cover of progressive *reform* ideology.

If some progressives were sincere in their belief that such laws were *limiting* political corruption and special interest depredations, they were also extremely naive. So were members of the public who, beguiled by public interest arguments, thought that progressive legislation supposedly generated by populist pressures really represented an extension of democracy and democratic control. They failed to perceive the *anti-democratic* and elitist effect of Congress creating executive branch regulatory agencies and franchising legislative powers to *unelected* members of those agencies. They did not see that such agencies immediately became powerful interest groups in their own right, insulated from democratic control and with their own agendas. Others understood exactly what was happening to the constitutional system and the rule of law, and approved.

Public Education and the Ideological Transformation

One crucial and successful strategy employed in the ideological struggle of the 19th century that deserves particular stress is the effort, beginning early in that century and extending over much of it, to institute public education. Almost every nation in the world now has a government owned and subsidized education system, and people everywhere are taught *in the public schools* that this is absolutely necessary, because a system of private, competitively provided education would leave significant numbers of students unable to obtain education. Yet many 19th century observers, such as Alexis de Tocqueville, noted that literacy rates were high and education levels were rapidly rising in America *before* public education was widespread.[16] A dogmatic assertion that public education was necessary to cure defects in a private education system and was instituted for altruistic purposes should be subjected to logical and historical examination rather than accepted uncritically.

E. G. West and others have examined the history of the development of public education in several of the early states instituting such systems. West focused on New York State.[17] He was particularly concerned to explain the historical development of three characteristics of modern public education, that of being universal, free (that is, subsidized at full cost so that the marginal cost to parents is zero), and compulsory. Around 1810 New York authorized five commissioners to prepare a report on whether the establishment of subsidized state 'common' schools was needed. The 1811 report of the commissioners stated that education was *already* widespread, to the point that it was inadequately provided only in the rural areas of the state.

West correctly notes that the facts presented justified only a marginal state intervention, at most. That is, if education was inadequately provided only in rural areas, a state subsidy was justified only in such areas.[18] In addition, though West did not say so, no justification for state ownership or operation of schools was provided, since offer of a subsidy would have encouraged the provision of additional private schools where needed. Instead, however, the commissioners advocated uniform government provision of common schools throughout the state. In response, the legislature acted the next year, 1812, to appropriate and distribute funds among school districts created by three authorized commissioners, in proportion to the number of students in each. An 1814 amendment required each town to raise and contribute tax revenue equal to its distributive share of the school funds. The per student subsidy did *not* cover the full cost per student, however, and the remainder was presented to the parents as a 'rate bill' (fee).

In the original law, the subsidy was not restricted to state operated schools. Religious charity schools were also eligible, and many new ones were created, which competed successfully for students with the state run schools. In an early indication of their monopolistic orientation and dislike of private competition, the state school teachers quickly and successfully lobbied the legislature for a change in the law directing the subsidy solely to secular schools. This makes the substitution of public provision in place of private provision, as a motive at least on a par with increasing the availability of education overall, apparent at an early point.

It is certainly true that attendance increased over time, though West does not give us population growth numbers for comparison. According to West the annual reports of the superintendents after 1812 show steady growth of districts organized, and the 1821 report shows 342,000 students between ages five and sixteen being taught out of a total state population of 380,000 such children. That is 90 percent, and therefore, as West remarks, *by this time schooling was already essentially universal even though it was neither free* (except to the very poor, who were exempted from the rate bills) *nor compulsory.*

The period from 1840 to 1850 in New York is known as the period of the 'Free School' campaign for elimination of the rate bills. The agitation began in the teachers institutes around 1843. The teachers argued that education should be universal as a matter of right, that a free school system would, by providing moral education, prevent crime, and that it would overcome poverty. Like any good propagandists, the teachers apparently played on public ignorance, in this cast of the facts that education was already essentially universal, and already available to the poor. Never did they attempt to *demonstrate* that educational availability was inadequate, or that private education was inferior to the common schools.

In 1849 the New York Legislature responded to the interest group pressure of the teachers by abolishing the rate bills and covering the full cost of public education. Public pressure, however, in the form of parental protest, resulted in repeal of the 1849 Act in 1851, and restoration of the rate bills. Many–perhaps most–parents actually *preferred* the rate bills to full cost subsidization because it allowed them options. As long as the rate bills covered a significant portion of their children's education, that outlay could be recovered and applied at a private school if they found the state schools unsatisfactory. Indeed, between 1832 and 1847 private school attendance in New York increased by 74 percent while public school attendance increased by less than 51 percent. Thus, the real reason the public school teachers agitated for 'free' public schools was to reduce or eliminate the competition from private schools, and thereby accumulate monopoly power to educate and indoctrinate children.

As it turned out, the teachers actually won despite the 1851 repeal of the 1849 Act. The rate bills were restored at so low a level by the 1851 law that very little of the cost of a student's education could be saved by a parent and applied to a private school by pulling a student out of a common school, and the growth of private schooling was effectively checked. In 1867 organized public school teacher and administrator groups got the legislature to finally abolish the rate bills. The last steps for the teacher and administrator lobbies were to get the legislature to institute compulsory attendance laws, creating an educational monopoly that did not even allow its customers the option of not purchasing its product, and to require students to attend within their districts, so that not even public schools were in competition with each other.

Crucial lessons emerge from this history. First, assuming the facts claimed by the Commissioners in 1811 were correct, no rationale existed from the first for more than a rural area educational subsidy. Even at that time, the nearly universal desire of parents to see their children educated was resulting in adequate provision in urban areas, by the Commissioner's own report. And given what we now know about the course of real income and transportation costs over the 19th century, justification for even a rural area subsidy would have rapidly diminished. Just as clearly, however, even a partial subsidy intended as temporary could have been dangerous, since it would have created a lobby of public school teachers and administrators with a strong incentive to expand and crowd out private education.

Second, none of the characteristic features of public education, as we know it, beyond a minimal subsidy, originated in New York State to solve a perceived problem of inadequate amount or quality of private education. Uniform provision of common schools including the urban areas, was instituted even though it was clearly unnecessary from the first. Both 'free' education and compulsory attendance were instituted *after* education was *already* essentially universal, as part of a war on private schools by a public education establishment intent on attaining a governmentally enforced monopoly. The logic of these events as strategic political actions given the end desired by public school employees provides strong indication that the same forces operated to generate the same institutional elements in the other states.[19]

Not long ago Leonard Peikoff, the Objectivist philosopher and associate of Ayn Rand, wrote the following:

> The process of spreading a philosophy by means of free discussion among thinking adults is long and complex. From Plato to the present, it has been the dream of social planners to circumvent this process and, instead, to inject a controversial ideology directly into the plastic, unformed minds of children–by means of seizing a country's educational system and turning it into a vehicle for indoctrination. In this way one may capture an entire generation without intellectual resistance, in a single *coup d'ecole*.
>
> Rarely, if ever, has a free nation capitulated to this kind of demand as rapidly, as extensively, as abjectly, as America did...[20]

In the chapter from which this quote is taken Peikoff demonstrates, as have many others, the statist philosophic orientations and propagandistic *intentions* of the major intellectuals who have most influenced the content and teaching methods of American public education. From Horace Mann (who was influential in originating the system) to John Dewey and William James, these intellectuals have made clear their collectivist perspectives and rejection of classical liberal individualism. In several papers economist John Lott has shown theoretically and empirically that public education everywhere emerged from a specific intent by government officials and collectivist intellectuals to indoctrinate the young with statist perspectives as a means of reducing voter resistance to political income transfers (and, one should add, to regulation).[21]

It should be stressed that neither a systematic federal program of indoctrination (though this is coming in the form of heavily biased national standards for history, environmental education and political science) nor an overt screening of prospective teachers for collectivist views has been necessary to insure this result. Precisely as a public institution, public education attracts few aspiring teachers of anti-statist inclination. Nearly everyone it employs feels motivated to justify its existence as a socialized institution, and philosophic consistency does not allow education to be treated as a special case. Generations of American children have been taught in the government schools that all social and economic problems arise in a private sector ruled by greed and corruption, and that government intervention and regulation is both necessary and benevolently intended to solve them. Subtle social pressures are naturally brought to bear on any public teachers with limited government perspectives, filtering most of them out of the system.

Empirical evidence supports these suspicions. Comparisons of ideological attitudes across occupations show public school teachers and professors to be further and more consistently left-wing than any other occupational group in the U.S.[22] Among other ways, this shows up in a strong left-statist bias in textual materials. Such bias in the content of environmental education has been massively documented by Herbert London.[23] Thomas DiLorenzo, who has shown systematic bias in high school civics materials, points out that every state requires at least one high school course in Civics or American Government, and that course materials are screened and censored. He then cogently asks how likely it is that an agent of the state will approve of a text that is critical of that government.[24]

As the history of New York revealed by West makes clear, the struggle to institute 'free' public education did not proceed without resistance. This was true everywhere. Three factors account for the eventual victory of its advocates, *which perhaps more than any other event sealed the fate of the classical liberal ideology in America.* The first was the superior strength and organizational advantage of the public teacher's lobby in contrast with that of their fragmented private school opponents The second was that the classical liberal intellectuals themselves were divided over the issue. Even some influential libertarians, like Thomas Jefferson himself, supported public education, perhaps from a naive belief that the republican principles they espoused would dominate.

Other libertarian intellectuals, private school teachers, and many members of the public actively resisted government education. Indeed, public resistance was so strong that many states might never have adopted 'free' public schools capable of crowding out private education had not the federal government entered the struggle. The government, for example, began imposing requirements on territories for public education systems as a condition for attaining statehood. The Mormon prophet, Brigham Young, strongly opposed public education, for example, and Mormon Utah only accepted it as required to become a state in 1896. The federal intervention began, however, when the radical Republican Congress, after the defeat of the South, created a department of education and directed the military authorities occupying the southern states to impose public education systems. Here again, the fatal effect of the Civil War on the very principles and ideology for which the founding fathers fought is apparent.

Notes

1 See James Rolph Edwards, "Ideology, Economics and Knowledge," *Reason Papers* 7 (Spring 1981): 53-71. The Nobel prizewinning economist Herbert Simon has called for development of a theory of constrained (i.e. limited) rationality. To my knowledge, however, Simon himself never did so. In a series of three published papers, however, of which this was the third, I developed just such an economic theory of knowledge. This way of looking at ideology is one implication of that theory.

2 For a lucid, elementary exposition of this public choice argument see James Gwartney and Richard Stroup, *Microeconomics: Private and Public Choice* (8th edition Harcourt-Brace, 1997): 103 and 301-302.

3 Robert Higgs, *Crisis and Leviathan: Critical Episodes in the Growth of American Government* (Oxford University Press, 1987).

4 Mark Thornton, "Slavery, Profitability, and the Market Process," *Review of Austrian Economics* 7 No. 2 (1994): 21-47.

5 Folsom, *The Myth of the Robber Barons:* 20

6 *Op Cit.:* 18.

7 Even Higgs not only reports charges that large firms corrupted the democratic political process, but seems to allege it himself. See Higgs, *Crisis*

and Leviathan: 80 and 111. Yet in another place (p. 115) Higgs argues that most of the political activities of big businessmen were essentially defensive.

8 The principals were Oliver Hudson Kelley, William Saunders and Aaron B. Gosh of the Agriculture Department, John R. Thompson and John Trimble of the Treasury Department, William Ireland of the Postal Department, and one or two others. See Edward Wiest, *Agricultural Organization in the United States* (Arno Press, 1975, reprint of the original 1923 edition): 372-378. To be fair, many Grange activities were and are oriented toward farmer self-help through *market* activities, such as setting up cooperatives. But Grange organizations all over the midwest quickly became hotbeds of radical agrarian political organization and agitation, and the Grange gave rise by example to other, even more overtly political groups such as the Farmer's Alliance.

9 For the complete story see Marvin Olasky, *The Tragedy of American Compassion* (Regnery Publishing Inc., 1992).

10 Horace Greeley, *Recollections of a Busy Life* (J. B. Ford, 1869): 193-199.

11 Seth Low, "Out-Door Relief in the United States," *Annual Conference of Charities, 1881* (George Ellis, 1881): 144-154.

12 A similar event occurred during the revolutionary war. The continental Congress had no ability to tax, and attempted to finance the war through issues of continental dollars, which were widely accepted but rapidly lost purchasing power through repeated issues. Indeed, prices rose so rapidly, and the value of the continental dollar fell so low, that for nearly a century after, when people wished to assert that something was essentially worthless, they would say that it was "not worth a continental."

13 Friedman and Schwartz, *A Monetary History of the United States,* p. 33.

14 In the 18th century, David Hume explained the monetary theory of the balance of payments under the fixed exchange rates of a gold standard in two versions. The first argued that a change in the money stock in one nation altered its price level away from Purchasing Power Parity (the condition in which, translating through the exchange rate, the value of money is the same in each nation) with its trading partners. This generated a gold flow (in or out) through the balance of payments, until the price level was restored to its PPP level and the natural distribution of specie prevailed. Hume then explained more subtly that the gold flows really acted to *prevent* money stock disturbances from causing divergence of the price levels and *maintain* PPP. 19th century classical economists such as Adam Smith and David Ricardo understood both versions. Oddly, modern american economists understood only the first until about 1970, when the mod-

ern Monetary Approach was developed and Hume's second version was rediscovered. An accurate understanding of *either* version would have prevented the insanity of the government silver purchases in the late 19th century, however.

15 Roosevelt doubled the income tax in 1933, and raised it again in 1936. Both acts were clearly contractionary, and combined with the other recessionary shocks administered by the Roosevelt Administration, added to the length of the Great Depression. Note also that Cleveland *maintained* the gold standard, where Roosevelt *ended* it. The stark difference in the policies of these two administrations explains why the depression of the 1890s, though deep, only lasted a few years, in contrast with that of the 1930s. Note also that both depressions began with a monetary contraction resulting from federal monetary manipulations.

16 Alexis de Tocqueville, *Democracy in America* (any edition).

17 E. G. West, "The Political Economy of American Public School Legislation," *Journal of Law and Economics* 10 (1967): 101-128.

18 West was here actually being overly kind to the argument of the commissioners. In saying that education was inadequately provided in rural areas, the commissioners can only have meant that children in those areas attended school in smaller proportions and perhaps for fewer years on average than did children in urban areas. But by how much? With lower family incomes, lesser technical occupations and higher costs of obtaining education (particularly transport costs) in rural areas, *some lower level of educational investment would be optimal and efficient, and would not necessarily constitute under investment.*

19 See, for example, Albert Fishlow, "The American Common School Revival: Fact or Fancy," in Henry Rosovsky, ed., *Industrialization in Two Systems: Essays in Honor of Alexander Gershenkron* (John Wiley and Sons, 1966). In this study of the common school movement in early New England, Fishlow found that its primary effect was to shift students away from private schools to the public schools without adding significantly to the percentage of students being educated.

20 Leonard Peikoff, *The Ominous Parallels: The End of Freedom in America* (Stein and Day, Publishers, 1982): 133.

21 John R. Lott, Jr., "Why is Education Publicly Provided? A Critical Survey," *Cato Journal* 7 (Fall 1987): 475-501, particularly p. 492.

22 Everett Carl Ladd, Jr., and Seymore Martin Lipsett, *The Divided Academy: Professors and Politics* (McGraw-Hill, 1975): 115-118.

Economics is the one social science that retains a strong classical liberal perspective.

23 Herbert I. London, *Why are They Lying to our Children?* (Stein and Day, 1984). The economics content of various proposed national standards was recently analyzed by two economists from Vanderbilt University, who noted many systematic biases. They were careful never to use such terms as 'interventionist', 'leftist', 'statist' or 'collectivist' in characterizing these biases, but their nature was clear. See Stephen Buckles and Michael Watts, "An Appraisal of Economics Content in the History, Social Studies, Civics, and Geography National Standards," *American Economic Review* 87 (May 1997): 254-259.

24 Thomas J. DiLorenzo, "The Civics Lie," *The Free Market* 10 (August 1992): 6 and 8.

Chapter 11

The Road Away From Serfdom

Vladimir Ilyich Lenin called his great work "What is to be Done?"
True to the title, his book effectively transformed Marxism from a deter-
ministic theory of history to a theory of revolutionary action. Absent
Lenin's theoretical work and personal leadership in the revolutionary
movement he and others modeled on that theory, Marxism might have
remained an obscure 19th century philosophy with little following or
force in the world. It is sad that Lenin was a communist, and not a libertarian. Modern libertarians, wishing to see a new *American* revolution
must ask and answer Lenin's question for themselves, however. The
work will fall into two categories. The first involves preparing the intellectual groundwork and base of public support for legal and constitutional reform. The second involves the conception and organization of
specific reform programs.

As it turns out, much of what is to be done is already *being* done,
but the issue hangs very much in the balance, and much remains to do
if a definite turn toward restoration of the free society and the rule of
law is to occur. The expansion of regulation has been a crucial expression of the institutional and legal decay our nation has experienced
over the last hundred years. Hopefully, what has been said in the previous chapters will make at least the basic goals of regulatory reform
fairly clear.

The Resurgence of Classical Liberalism

In the 1930s and '40s classical liberalism almost ceased to exist as a living belief. It is true that the deep libertarian sentiment of the American public also caused heavy modification of the advancing collectivist doctrines. Unlike Europe, socialism was never able to obtain many open adherents in this country. Socialist sentiment was deflected into interventionist expressions and covert strategies of incremental nationalization through expanding regulation that *seemed* to maintain private ownership. Of all the subtle strategies employed by the collectivist enemies of classical liberalism, however, the most subtle and effective was to steal its very name. The very intellectuals extending programs of interventionist regulatory command and control by *unelected* technocratic *elitists* loudly proclaimed themselves as advocates of *democracy* and called *themselves* liberals.

In fairness, this use of the term was not *entirely* strategic and dishonest. Modern liberalism is an almost totally secular and humanistic intellectual enterprise that rejects religion as superstitious, and rejects the personal sexual morality and social mores associated with it. As such modern liberals are 'liberal' in terms of their view of permissible sexual behavior, family structures, and so on. They wish to see people 'freed' of what they regard as antiquated inhibitions and repressive social pressures, and in this *libertine* sense regard themselves as advocating freedom.

Though classical liberalism was a purely political philosophy, most of its adherents recognized that a condition of limited government and civilized social interaction only came about and could only be maintained if people were personally restrained in their behavior by strong internal morality and social pressures. They knew that self-discipline, by allowing the individual to increase his or her skills, knowledge, and ability to function, *opens* options rather than closing them, while random, stimulus-response behavior (including sexual behavior) does the opposite. True, a key element of their philosophy was not just tolerance but militant *defense* of the rights of different individuals to have and act on their own values, but they were libertarians, *not* libertines.

By the 1940s the dominance of interventionist liberal intellectuals in the grade schools, institutions of higher learning, and the news media was such that the identification of the term liberal with their ideology of *unlimited* government and sexual expression–both of which are enslaving–stuck. The belief in government constitutionally limited to preserving natural rights of property, self-determination and free association had literally lost its name, and an idea without a name cannot even be *thought*. Unavoidable teachings of the beliefs of the founders in courses in government and civics in the K-12 schools were dealt with through distortion, oversimplification, denigration, and caricature.

People with residual sentiment in favor of limited government and traditional morality, subconsciously aware that something important was being lost, struggled to find a new name and reformulate their belief. Their enemies were even able to provide the name and much of the belief. Modern liberals incessantly denigrated those holding the older political and social beliefs as *conservatives,* meaning, those too reactionary and resistant to change to accept the new and progressive political and social ideas. Eventually, many people accepted this designation of their belief, often, unfortunately, along with elements borrowed from classic british conservativism. Thus the modern american conservative movement, partly libertarian and individualist in its economic dimensions while collectivist and interventionist in its *social* dimensions, was born.

A very few intellectuals and academics in this period retained or rediscovered the vision of original liberalism. Isabel Paterson and Rose Wilder Lane published successful books to willing audiences hungry for an integrated view of the free society and the history of freedom.[1] Such works may only have reached a few hundred thousand people, but it was enough to keep the vision from dying. Not long after, the Russian immigrant playwright Ayn Rand, influenced by Paterson and fascinated by formal philosophy, began publishing popular philosophic novels based on a heroic view of creative individuals oppressed by envious and vindictive mediocrities using the power of the state.[2] Rand's powerful mind and vision attracted a personal following in the 1950s and 1960s that provided her a forum and audience for publications analyzing current social and political events and ideas from her unique libertarian perspective.[3]

An important aspect of Rand's influence was that, as a novelist and playwright with a powerful and systematic philosophic view she was able to attract intelligent laymen and professional persons into a philosophic movement *outside* the academic setting. Academic philosophers of the day were hostile to any rationalist classical liberal view. Even though her dominating character, rigid atheism and intolerance of dissent fragmented the movement rather early, several of her followers such as George Reisman, Leonard Peikoff, and Nathaniel Branden, have gone on to become influential authors and social analysts in their own right. Amazingly, one of her early followers, Alan Greenspan, is now chairman of the Federal Reserve Board. Also, thousands of intelligent lay persons who read her novels gained a vision of and commitment to reason, individualism, and the free society.

More important than these events was the survival, in the 1930s and 1940s, of two groups of economists with classical liberal perspectives. Of all the social sciences, economics, with its conscious individualist methodology, its focus on individual human choice and action as the source of economic phenomena, and origin as a formal discipline in 18th and 19th century France and Britain, is the most inherently classical liberal in its perspective. In 1936, however, in the depths of the Great Depression, the british economist John Maynard Keynes revolutionized economics with his macroeconomic analysis focusing on aggregative variables essentially devoid of theoretical roots in individual human choice and action.[4]

Keynes' model was depression economics, claiming to explain enduring depression and unemployment as due to inadequate private demand, and by denying aggregate equilibrating properties to the market system. He argued that government action in the form of alterations in the federal budget could alter aggregate demand and stabilize the economy. Younger economists such as Paul Samuelson were seduced *en mass* by this perspective. The textbooks were rewritten, separating economic analysis into a schizophrenic division between microeconomics, dealing with choice and interaction by individual decision making units up to the market level, and macroeconomics, dealing with the Keynesian model of the operation of the whole system. The neoclassical perspective in british and american economics was marginalized into microeconomics, and assumed to be irrelevant to issues of aggregate output and employment.

On the continent the neoclassical tradition in economics had already been marginalized. The Austrian School of Economics, begun in the 1880s by Karl Menger, was one of the original sources of modern marginal utility theory and analysis. Of all schools of modern economic thought, it was the most self-consciously individualist, free market oriented, and classical liberal in its perspective. austrian economists were discriminated against, however, and frequently denied academic posts by the collectivist German Historical school that dominated the universities. The Austrian school really consisted only of a few great economists, each the personal student of an earlier member of the school. Menger's great students were Friedrich Wieser and Eugene Bohm-Bawerk. Bohm-Bawerk's great student was Ludwig von Mises, and von Mises' great student was Friedrich A. Hayek.

As a brilliant theoretician and chief economist of the Austrian Chamber of Commerce in the 1920s, von Mises was beginning to widen the influence of the school through a private seminar he held in his chamber offices that was attended by classical liberals from all over the continent. Many of these individuals, such as Hayek, Gottfried Haberler, and Fritz Machlup, became important 20th century economists. But this was the inter war period, and violent revolutionary fascist and communist totalitarian movements were contending for control in Germany and Austria. Both hated classical liberalism. Hitler's Nazi gang began to win, and the Austrian School economists had to flee the continent.[5]

Under the spreading influence of Keynes, american academy was not much less hostile to the Austrians. Von Mises was finally able to find a post with New York University, where much of his salary was paid by a private foundation. He again began attracting a large group of students, and was able to complete and publish many vital works, including his monumental book *Human Action*. Though never really accepted by the American economics profession, his books extended his influence. In 1950 Leonard E. Read, a friend of von Mises, created the Foundation for Economic Education at Irvington-on-Hudson in upstate New York. The Foundation began publishing *The Freeman*, which has been an important journal explicating the economic and political principles of a free society to a general audience of intelligent laymen ever since then.

Friedrich Hayek spent some time in Britain, at the London School of Economics in the 1920s and 1930s, where he had a profound influence until the Keynesian perspective became too pervasive. Eventually he moved to the U.S. and obtained a position in the Social Science department at the University of Chicago, where he was also able to continue publishing numerous influential books on economics. Indeed, Hayek was far more successful than von Mises at getting top professional economics journals to publish his articles. Though he left writing on economics and turned to social theory due to the oppressive dominance of Keynesianism for some time, he eventually returned to economic theory, and in 1974 was awarded the Nobel Prize in economics for his contributions.[6] This was a crucial event marking a return to academic acceptability of classical liberal perspectives, even though, symptomatically, Hayek had to share the prize with the swedish socialist Gunnar Myrdal.

Perhaps the most important of von Mises' american students for the future of the Austrian School was Murray Rothbard, who, for a short time, was also associated with Ayn Rand's circle. Rothbard became von Mises' most faithful and forceful exponent, publishing many influential books and possibly thousands of articles.[7] Most important, Rothbard not only accumulated many students of his own, but was able to organize them into a school of thought that now has groups of economists generating their own graduate students at four major academic centers–New York University, Auburn University in Alabama, the University of Nevada at Las Vegas, and George Mason University. Another student of von Mises, Israel Kirzner at New York University, has also been important in creating this expanding school of free market economists. Von Mises, Hayek and Rothbard have all passed away now, but the new Austrian School is thriving, and spreading its influence through seminars, journals, and institutes associated with its academic centers. So far, however, the new Austrians have not greatly impressed the economics profession at large.

The second group of economists who retained their classical liberal perspective through the period of pervasive Keynesian orthodoxy in the economics profession taught at the University of Chicago. Emerging from this school in the 1940s was a brilliant young economist named Milton Friedman who had enormous theoretical insight combined with superb analytical and empirical skills. Using mathematical and statistical tools *accepted by the profession* with nearly unmatched skill, Friedman over several decades made undeniably original and vital contributions extending knowledge in numerous branches of economics. These contributions altered the perspective of the profession. Perhaps most particularly, he and associates he trained and/or attracted provided improved theoretical and empirical grounding for the quantity theory of money, casting doubt in the process on key claims of Keynesian economics. In this process the publication of his and Anna Jacobson Schwartz' *A Monetary History of the United States* in 1963 and of Friedman's Presidential address to the American Economic Association in 1967, were crucial.[8]

As a brilliant analyst and staunch classical liberal, Friedman was not only able to influence generations of his own students, but to alter the opinions of and attract followers from among *established* economists, something the Austrian School has yet to accomplish on a significant scale. Under Friedman's influence the University of Chicago not only generated a legion of Nobel Prize winning economists (including Friedman himself, in 1976) and influential researchers, but several new schools of thought both microeconomic and macroeconomic. Such new analytical and empirical research programs as the economic theory of regulation, public choice theory, law and economics, and rational expectations theory were all influenced directly or indirectly by Friedman's thought. By as early as 1970 it is fair to say that the Chicago school had shattered the interventionist Keynesian orthodoxy and reestablished the legitimacy of free market and limited government perspectives within the economics profession.

To a lesser extent, a similar revival of classical liberal thinking has occurred in the philosophy profession. It is difficult to know whether the influence of Rand from outside the profession had anything to do with this. The seminal event was publication of Robert Nozick's *Anarchy, State and Utopia* in 1974, but other philosophers such as Jan Narvison, Anthony de Jasey and Tibor Machan have written notable works in the classical liberal perspective. After a long hiatus, classical liberal political theory is once again a hot topic within the profession. Classical liberal philosophers seem to be academically dispersed and isolated however. I am unaware of any cluster of classical liberal political philosophers constituting a self-identified school at a specific academic center.

One thing to note about this strong revival of classical liberal thinking is that it is centered in segments of the intellectual (and particularly academic) class, notably in economics and philosophy. This has spilled over through the creation of several libertarian policy institutes, such as the Cato Institute, and several libertarian news and analysis magazines, into a wider libertarian intellectual movement. Some influence has spread from there to segments of the political classes, particularly some conservative Republican party leaders, who like to claim Friedman and Hayek as their own, even though both have patiently explained that they are *not* conservatives, but liberals in the original sense. But the new classical liberal perspective has yet to reach the popular consciousness where it could result in a mass political movement. The nearest thing to such a movement is the Libertarian Party, created around 1970. The LP is organized in all 50 states and has fielded Presidential candidates in every election for over two decades, but has yet to achieve significant national vote totals.

It should be stressed that events have been as important in the revival of the classical liberal perspective over the last several decades as have the efforts of libertarian writers, academics and organizers. First, the progressive extension of liberal interventionist, regulatory and redistributive policies in this period has been associated with inflation, social decay, and the decline in the growth of productivity and real income, as discussed in Chapter 9. As time has passed it has been increasingly difficult to avoid seeing the connections between those interventionist policies and their socioeconomic consequences. To do so, of course, is precisely to begin thinking in a classical liberal way. In some cases, as with the transportation deregulation of the late 1970s and President Reagan's tax reductions, extending awareness of the harmful effects of such policies and their associated finance has already resulted in beneficial political and economic reforms.

Positive historical examples and events have been as important in teaching libertarian lessons as have negative events in recent decades. Germany and Japan, as defeated nations in World War II, abolished most of their wartime government controls, and recovered rapidly to become not only politically free nations but economic powerhouses. America also eliminated its wartime government controls and prospered, but Britain, another victor nation, retained its controls for some time and stagnated. Also, most economists have recognized that the single most important factor in the rapid post-war recovery of the world economy was the progressive reduction in tariffs and other trade barriers through multilateral negotiations.

In a related set of events, american development economists, heavily influenced by Keynes and Marx, advised third world nations for decades to centralize their economies in order to force capital accumulation and economic growth. This was the same advice given to the leaders of such nations by *Soviet* advisers, and every nation that followed it stagnated. Several nations such as Taiwan, Hong Kong, Chile and South Korea either avoided such advice or learned from their mistakes, however, and have grown so rapidly over time as to lose their underdeveloped status. Every prospering third-world nation has done so by adopting significant elements of the rule of law, limited government and market economies.[9] The demonstration effect on other underdeveloped nations around the world has been immense. Thailand, Indonesia and other nations are now on the same path to freedom and prosperity despite their recent problems. Even China and Vietnam, still nominally communist, are freeing their economies, allowing markets to operate with enormously less government intervention, and by doing so, prospering.

That developed nations can also benefit by liberalizing their economies–in the classical sense–has also become clear from recent events. Decades of experience with nationalized industries in Britain and Europe had clearly demonstrated their inefficiency in comparison with private industries by the 1980s.[10] Under Margaret Thatcher, Britain began a program of serious denationalization, which spread rapidly to many other nations, all of which experienced significant economic benefits. The most striking example is New Zealand. Under a heavy burden of state owned enterprises, price controls, trade barriers, special privileges for unions, a pervasive welfare state and an enormous public debt, New Zealand stagnated. It had accelerating inflation and the lowest rate of productivity growth of any developed nation from 1960 to 1984.

In 1984, under the influence of Chicago School economists, the Labor Party government abolished the price controls and began reducing trade barriers and privatizing nationalized industries. It also restructured its central bank to reduce money stock growth. Disinflation generated unemployment and caused a change in government in 1990. The Labor Party lost and a reformist National government took power. The conservatives, however, *extended* the reforms, deregulating the labor market to make it legal for nonunion workers to bargain separately from unionized workers, thus ending union monopoly power. They also cut government spending, including welfare benefits. The economy soon began improving. The unemployment rate fell, and the budget went into surplus in 1993. Since then real GDP growth has averaged 4 percent per year.[11]

A similar picture emerges from the collapse of the Soviet empire after 1989. Those former satellite states that have gone the furthest in privatizing property, limiting government intervention and freeing the market, such as Hungary, Poland, Latvia and the Czech Republic, have experienced the greatest degrees of economic growth and prosperity.[12] Everywhere in the world, classical liberal political institutions and thought are expanding, government control and intervention is declining, property is being privatized, and voluntary trade in free markets is being extended. Oddly, in the United States, which has moved in the other direction for so long, the issue still seems in doubt.

Evolutionary and Revolutionary Regulatory Reform

America does not have a great many government owned and operated industries needing desperately to be privatized–only its public education system comes to mind–but it is past time to eliminate, or at least severely reduce, its vast, intrusive, costly and destructive system of regulation. There are two basic reform strategies. The first is revolutionary reform, in which massive institutional transformation over a relatively short period aims at realizing an idealized state. The second is evolutionary, or incremental reform, instituted in small gradual legal steps over a long period in the direction of the idealized state. Advocates of both of these reform strategies often denigrate the other. Incrementalists argue, from a pragmatic perspective, that radical ideologues fail to understand and deal with practical political realities, and alienate potential moderate allies. Radical advocates of revolutionary reform, on the other hand, accuse incrementalists, often correctly, of repeatedly compromising principle.

In fact, evolutionary and revolutionary reform programs are not mutually exclusive alternatives, but complementary tactical components of a broader libertarian reform strategy. For one thing, an incremental approach that is not guided by a clear theoretical and ideological vision of the end state desired, will get lost along the way. Incrementalists lacking a clear ideological vision and commitment will never accomplish much. Having such a vision, and this is the second point, *libertarians should not be afraid to institute it rapidly when political conditions allow.* Until such conditions appear, an incremental approach should be followed.

Political failure of an incremental reform program, in the form of large scale institutionalization of expanded regulation and/or redistribution, will generate economic and social costs that sooner or later create conditions allowing revolutionary reform, or at least renewed incremental reform. Higgs' observation that American government has grown in periods of crisis needs generalization. Periods of crisis provide opportunities for *change,* but the nature of the crisis and the state of knowledge and ideology at the time determine the direction of that change, as Higgs himself partly understood.[13] When government intervention is recognized as the cause of the crisis by key political leaders and much of the public, opportunity for deregulation and extension of freedom occurs. Mancur Olson and others have recognized this.[14]

Both ancient and modern experience demonstrate this point. The economic stagnation generated by systematic rent-seeking and regulation in the original mercantile states, and the eventual competitive rent dissipation, combined with the teachings of the classical liberals about how limited democratic governments and free markets *could* operate, spelled the death of mercantilism. The rise of constitutional government and market economies in Britain and the U.S. followed. The classical liberal reform experience of New Zealand, just discussed, is an example of reform occurring massively in a historically short period. And the central lesson of the former Soviet satellite states since 1989 is precisely that when the opportunity for libertarian reform rises, it is best instituted as suddenly and completely as possible, before the special interests and other opponents have a chance to organize or reorganize.[15]

Crises and opportunities for sudden reform may be localized, in particular markets or economic sectors rather than system wide. Competitive rent dissipation and/or other factors may make single or multiple industry reform suddenly possible, as with the transportation deregulation of the late 1970s and early 1980s. Crises and opportunities for sudden reform may also be international. The post-War Bretton Woods conference created an international system of currency exchange rates fixed by central bank intervention. Expansionary Federal Reserve monetary policy in the 1960s, to finance rising income transfers and regulation as the welfare state expanded, generated large and growing U.S. balance of payments deficits.

For more than a decade Milton Friedman had advocated floating (market determined) exchange rates, though few other economists, intellectuals or politicians agreed with him, or thought such a reform possible.[16] Yet, as the balance of payments crisis intensified, foreign nations traded dollars they had accumulated, in for gold, and the U.S. gold stock dissipated, minds suddenly changed. President Nixon closed the gold window in 1972 and the fixed exchange rate system collapsed, to be replaced by floating rates. The balance of payments crisis immediately disappeared as central banks stopped systematically intervening in the foreign exchange markets to maintain fixed exchange rates.

The ultimate libertarian goal for regulatory reform in the U.S. must be to abolish regulation as a form of law. Regulation is an *inherently* medieval and dictatorial form of law, incompatible with personal freedom and limited, constitutional government. We have traveled a long way down the regulatory road to serfdom in the last century, and we must make a 'U' turn and travel back the direction we have already traveled once, following the constitutional signposts along the way. The competitive market must be restored as the primary social mechanism for disciplining self-interested behavior. For those not successfully disciplined by market incentives, supplemental mechanisms of criminal, civil and tort law can be applied.

To apply market solutions to legitimate externality problems a conscious activist program of establishing and clarifying private property rights should be undertaken. Most externality problems are common property problems. Establishing clear property rights allows market transactions to eliminate many externalities. Two examples may suffice. In the absence of a patent law establishing ownership of an inventor's output, anyone observing a beneficial invention may copy and sell it. Any private investments in research and development of beneficial products or processes of production thus generate external benefits for free riders.

Free riding reduces the possible returns to those making risky investments in research and development of beneficial products or processes of production. The amount of resources people will employ in such risky research will therefore be much less than is socially optimal. Establishing private ownership allows the inventor sole authority to exploit the invention (or the right to franchise production and sale for royalties) for a legally defined period of time. Most of the externality is removed, and the amount of resources employed in research and development will be closer to the social optimum. That England had the first patent law is a major reason it had the industrial revolution first.

As a second example, consider the different treatment of buffalo and cattle in the late 19th century as the Great Plains were settled. buffalo and cattle are very similar, large free-roaming herd animals in their natural states. Both are valuable for their meat and hides. As the Midwest and West were settled, cattle ranches were set up, large herds of cattle were bred and raised, and a thriving market in cattle products developed. A market also existed in buffalo products, but the herds did not thrive. Instead, buffalo were shot as rapidly as possible and the herds depleted, almost to the point of extinction.

Why were these animals treated so differently? The simple answer is that nobody owned the buffalo. Nobody had incentives to invest private resources in maintaining or expanding the herds or improving the quality of the animals, because, absent private ownership, anyone could shoot and sell them. Any private resources so invested would have conferred external benefits on free riders. Cattle, in contrast, belonged by law, to particular farmers and ranchers. They were (and are) literally part of the capital stock of such businessmen, and treated as such. Capital wears out with productive use, but is amortized and replaced as necessary to stay in business. Likewise, a rancher raises cattle to sell for meat, and must harvest them for income. The rancher replaces them by breeding and raising new ones, however, so that the herd is maintained and even grows over time. Precisely because they were valuable–and privately owned–cattle never faced extinction.[17]

Here again it is apparent that with clearly established property rights, externalities can be reduced or eliminated, and competitive market processes can operate to establish correct employment of scarce and valuable resources. This implies obvious market solutions to many problems of overuse and depletion of valuable, renewable resources, such as elephants, whales, and even wilderness areas. That wilderness areas can be operated successfully as private businesses, charging fees for visit and use sufficient to cover costs of operation and maintenance of the wild characteristics and amenities that are the attraction and source of revenue, has already been proven. Such private preserves exist in many parts of the nation, competing successfully with government preserves and parks. Examples include the North Main Woods, a 2.8 million acre private wilderness, the Deseret Land & Livestock company in northern Utah, and the Fossil Rim Wildlife Center in Texas, among others.

Not every externality problem can be solved by establishment of property rights, however. A second mechanism, tort law, will need to be employed to allow people to sue and obtain damages for nuisance, negligence, etc. Such awards internalize external costs, and accumulated court decisions themselves essentially establish property rights and legal rules guiding efficient forms of behavior and market transactions. It is true that tort law has its own problems. Jury awards have been excessive in recent decades. An activist, incrementalist program of extending tort law in substitution of regulatory solutions will have to be combined with tort reform. But at least tort law is compatible with constitutional maintenance of natural individual rights and civilized standards of due process. Regulatory law is *not*.

In preparation for the substitution of other social control mechanisms, incremental steps may be taken to transform regulatory law so that it gradually loses its distinct regulatory characteristics. This could begin with a statutory revision of the Administrative Procedures Act to force administrative courts to adhere to the 4th amendment limits on searches of private businesses for obtaining evidence of violations of regulations. This statutory revision should also force the regulatory courts to employ standards of evidence and a presumption of innocence the same as those employed in criminal and civil courts for violations having similar potential penalties. In addition, the power of appointment of regulatory law judges must be removed from the agencies themselves, and the authority of the agency heads to overrule the judges must also be eliminated.

Similarly, incremental reform should aim at removing regulatory authority from the agencies. Republican Party reformers are already attempting to establish Congressional authority to review agency regulations before they take effect. Statutory reform should actually aim at making this *mandatory,* so that the agencies are no longer insulated from democratic control, and elected representatives can no longer claim to their constituents that they are not responsible for what the agencies do. These changes would go a long way toward restoring due process, bringing the agencies under the law and restoring the separation of powers, rather than maintaining them as laws unto themselves exercising legislative, executive and judicial powers.

As an alternate approach to reinvesting Congress with responsibility for regulations, the possibility was discussed in Chapter 9 of requiring agencies to justify new regulations by demonstrating that benefits exceed their costs, and of establishing a regulatory review agency with ties to the Office of Management and Budget. As pointed out there, several Presidents have attempted this, with little success because the agencies retained ultimate authority. Congress must require such tests, and not only establish such an agency, but either make its decisions final or vest the ultimate decisions in a special regulatory court.

As hinted in Chapter 9, such an agency must also have an important function in establishing the budgets of the regulatory agencies, so that overall rationality and efficiency in the allocation of funds can be attained across agencies. This strategy would complement the reform of the Administrative Procedures Act discussed above. It would bring strict, binding scientific standards into the making of regulations (which would itself enormously reduce their number and severity), and establish a separation of regulatory powers with checks and balances within the executive branch itself. By removing the arbitrary use of regulatory power, such reforms would eventually remove opposition by those within the agencies to the abolition of regulation itself, and the substitution of other forms of law and social control mechanisms.

One of the most important regulatory reforms of all will be to make the 5th amendment takings clause effective and binding on the agencies. The general applicability and character of the clause has been demonstrated by Epstein. It says what it says and its meaning is clear. Where the courts have deliberately narrowly construed that applicability to allow the advance of the regulatory welfare state, its general applicability must be restored by statute. The government must be required to compensate people for regulatory takings, in accordance with the reduced value of the assets regulated. Additionally, *the law should require that such compensation come from the budgets of the agencies promulgating the regulations that initiated the takings.* Nothing else would so focus the minds of the regulators on the costs of their actions.

We can expect the road away from serfdom to be rough and uphill all the way. Legions of left-wing intellectuals, regulatory bureaucrats and liberal academics will try to dissuade us from taking that route in an effort to preserve their power to dominate and compel others through regulation. Interest groups that have accumulated money and power from regulatory grants of privilege, or who wish to force their personal moral values or behavioral preferences on others, will join the chorus. However unlikely it may presently seem that we can go that way, it is a road that has been traveled before, and can be traveled again. It is the road to civilization, and whether we go by foot, step by step, or by car with the pedal to the metal, we should never turn back toward serfdom again.

Notes

1 Isabel Patterson, *The God of the Machine* (G. P. Putnam's Sons, 1943), and Rose Wilder Lane, *The Discovery of Freedom* (Arno Press, 1943).

2 Her most influential novels were *The Fountainhead* (Bobbs-Merrill, 1943) and *Atlas Shrugged* (Signet Books, 1957).

3 For an excellent view of her perspectives and those of the supporters she attracted on government, natural rights, economics, and economic history, see Ayn Rand, ed., *Capitalism: The Unknown Ideal* (New American Library, 1967), which reprints articles from her magazine, *The Objectivist*.

4 John Maynard Keynes, *The General Theory of Employment, Interest, and Money* (Harcourt, Brace, 1936).

5 Von Mises wrote his own partial autobiography covering this period. See Ludwig von Mises, *Notes and Recollections* (South Holland, 1978).

6 Heyek's work has been cited in earlier chapters. His recognized contributions in capital theory, monetary theory and policy, information theory, and the theory of competition and the market process are simply too numerous to mention. On top of that, his contributions to social and political theory, such as *The Constitution of Liberty* (University of Chicago Press, 1960), are just as important.

7 Murray N. Rothbard, *Man, Economy, and State* (Nash Publishing Co., 1962) is the most comprehensive and complete introduction to Rothbard's work.

8 Milton Friedman, "The Role of Monetary Policy," *American Economic Review* 53 (March 1968): 1-17. In this paper Friedman made implicit predictions about the course of interest rates and unemployment over the next several years given the trend of monetary policy that both contradicted the claims of the Keynesian model and turned out to be correct. This astonished the profession and gave impetus to several lines of non-Keynesian macromonetary research.

9 There are analysts such as Lester Thurow, *The Zero-Sum Society* (Penguin Books, 1981) who attribute the success of such nations to government industrial policies. Too many successful developing nations (such as Hong Kong) never had such a policy, however, and it is doubtful that those that did were helped by them. To the contrary, systematic evidence (rather than anecdotal examples of the type Thurow employs) confirms a strong positive empirical relationship between the degree of economic freedom and the rate of economic growth across nations. See Steven T. Easton and Michael A. Walker, "Income, Growth, and Economic Freedom," *American Economic Review* 87 (May 1997): 328-332.

10 See Thomas E. Borcherding, et al., "Comparing the Efficiency of Private and Public Production: The Evidence from Five Countries," *Zeitschrift für Nationalökonomie* 42, Suppl. 2 (1982): 127-156.

11 See Lewis Evans, et al., "Economic Reform in New Zealand 1984-1995:The Pursuit of Efficiency," *Journal of Economic Literature* 34

(December 1996): 1856-1902, and Gregory B. Christainsen, "How New Zealand Dismantled the State and Regained its Fiscal Health: Economic and Political Factors," *Journal of Private Enterprise* 12 (Fall 1996): 40-46.

12 Hungary, Poland and the Czech Republic have done so well that virtually as this is being written they are being allowed to join NATO (an event I do not necessarily endorse, but which indicates the Euro/American view of their progress).

13 Higgs puts it this way after pointing out the actions of Cleveland in defense of the (classical) liberal order during the crisis of the 1890s: "Hence my present purpose: to argue that crisis alone need not spawn Bigger Government. It does so only under favorable ideological conditions, and such conditions did not exist in the 1890s..." Higgs, *Crisis and Leviathan:* 78. This is not quite the same, however, as recognizing that under the right ideological conditions, crisis could even result in smaller government and increased freedom.

14 See Mancur Olson, *The Rise and Decline of Nations* (Yale University Press, 1982).

15 Vaclav Klaus, *Renaissance: The Rebirth of Liberty in the Heart of Europe* (Cato Institute, 1997), makes this point forcefully and repeatedly. Klaus is Prime Minister of the Czech Republic.

16 See, for example, Milton Friedman and Robert V. Roosa, *The Balance of Payments: Free vs. Fixed Exchange Rates* (American Enterprise Institute for Public Policy, 1967).

17 A crucial question here seems to be, why Congress did not simply establish private ownership over buffalo. Surely this easy solution was known to be available. There are probably two reasons they did not do so. First, it was thought desirable (partly for racist and nationalist reasons) to subdue the Indians and dispossess them of many of their lands, which required depleting one of their major food sources. Second, the cattle industry, already established as a powerful lobby, may have brought political pressure to prevent a competing buffalo industry from being established.

Index

A

Administrative law courts, 34-40, 228.
Administrative Procedures Act, 228.
Agricultural Adjustment Act, 13, 65.
Alar, 33, 157.
Aldrich, Nelson, 54, 55.
American Medical Association, 117.
Andrew, A. Piat, 54.
Audubon Society, 154, 155.
Austrian School of Economics, 66 n. 1, 218-220.

B

Balance of Payments crisis, 225.
Bank of England, 8.
Black, Hugo, 81.
Bland-Allison Act, 203.
Bryan, William Jennings, 205.
Bush, George, 181.

C

Cancer and Carcinogens, 137, 150-152, 154, 156, 158.
Carnegie, Andrew, 59, 204.
Cartels, 55, 58, 60-61, 65, 69 n. 37, 77-78, 82-83, 86, 95, 117, 169;
      instability of, 5, 64, 83, 88, 98, 108-109;
      labor, see labor unions.
Carson, Rachel, 150-151.
Carter, Jimmy, 84, 88, 176, 180, 181, 185.
Chicago school of economics, 66 n. 1, 220-221, 223.
Chlorinated compounds, 158.

About the Author

James Rolph Edwards' first college degree was a Bachelor of Arts in political science from BYU. After a stint in the U.S. Army and several years working in the private sector, he entered graduate school in economics at the University of Utah in 1976. He obtained his Doctorate of Philosophy in 1983, graduating at nor near the top of his class.Dr. Edwards had published four articles in three different journals on topics as diverse as monetary theory and the economics of knowledge before even graduating, pehaps a record for that graduate school. Oddly, he did not emerge with the radical left-wing views held by so many of its faculty. Dr. Edwards is currently Associate Professor of Economics at Montana State University-Northern. He has published two previous books (including a textbook on macroeconomics and his Ph.D. dissertation on the proper place of Ludwig von Mises in the history of monetary thought) along with numerous journal articles.